IMAGES
of America

EARLY BESSEMER

On the Cover: The March 17, 1894, *Bessemer Weekly* reported that A.S. Leader moved his Marvel City Saloon into the Voelkel building on Carolina Avenue. The saloon sat directly opposite the original Alabama Great Southern rail depot, welcoming thirsty travelers. Leader later owned a dry goods store in Bessemer, and was active in the development of the neighboring town of Brighton. Leader's Brighton home has been featured on HGTV's *If These Walls Could Talk* program. (Bessemer Hall of History Museum collection.)

IMAGES
of America

EARLY BESSEMER

Jason Burnett on behalf of the
Bessemer Hall of History Museum

ARCADIA
PUBLISHING

ISBN 978-0-7385-8803-2

Published by Arcadia Publishing
Charleston, South Carolina

Printed in the United States of America

Library of Congress Control Number: 2011927200

For all general information, please contact Arcadia Publishing:
Telephone 843-853-2070
Fax 843-853-0044
E-mail sales@arcadiapublishing.com
For customer service and orders:
Toll-Free 1-888-313-2665

Visit us on the Internet at www.arcadiapublishing.com

To all of the people of Bessemer whose photographs were lost or never taken. To Mom, my family's historian. And to Glenn, my favorite photographer.

CONTENTS

Acknowledgments

I am grateful that my grandmother Bessie Howell O'Neal often told me about riding into Bessemer on a horse-drawn cart when she was about five years old. She and her grandmother would arrive before dawn on Saturday mornings, and from the top of Nineteenth Street look down at the streetlights. She thought it was the most beautiful place in the world. The sense of wonder that she shared fueled my love of early Bessemer's history.

Special appreciation goes to the Bessemer Hall of History Museum book committee for all of their support—Sara Beasley, Robert Beaty, William Eiland, Dr. Richard Neely, Louise Ayer Tommie, Karen Utz, and museum curator Christopher Eiland.

Don Veasey and Jim Baggett at the Birmingham Public Library Department of Archives and Manuscripts found treasures that helped make the story more complete.

Marjorie White's book, *The Birmingham District: An Industrial History and Guide*, provided wonderful details about Bessemer's early mines and mining communities.

The Bessemer Historical Homeowner's Association has shared their hospitality and knowledge with me for nearly 10 years. They also provided my first contact with Arcadia Publishing. Many, many thanks to Brinkley at Arcadia for her guidance.

The Bessemer Hall of History Museum wishes to thank all of the families and individuals who contribute to the museum. This book is possible because of the wonderful photographic collection and archives that you help build and support.

Unless otherwise noted, images are from the Bessemer Hall of History Museum collection.

Introduction

Over the course of the city's phenomenal first 50 years, Bessemer, Alabama, more than lived up to the promise of its nickname of the "Marvel City."

Bessemer is located just north of the center of Alabama, in the foothills of the Appalachian Mountain Range. The city covers more than 45 square miles and is about 13 miles west of downtown Birmingham and 40 miles northeast of Tuscaloosa.

Iron and steel magnate Henry Fairchild DeBardeleben founded the city in 1887. Of course, the history of the Bessemer area did not begin with Henry DeBardeleben. As early as 1,000 years ago, a site just west of downtown was home to prehistoric Late Woodland and Mississippian settlements. In the early 1800s, before Alabama's statehood was granted, families were settling in the same area. It grew into a trading center, and until the completion of the Alabama Great Southern Railroad in 1871, Old Jonesboro was the second-largest town in the county behind Elyton.

Before Bessemer, Henry DeBardeleben made his fortune in 1870s Birmingham, working with his father-in-law, Daniel Pratt. DeBardeleben married Pratt's daughter, Ellen, and succeeded Pratt as owner of nearby coalfields and mines, the Oxmoor furnaces, and much of Red Mountain's iron deposits.

Even with this success, DeBardeleben longed to build a new city from the ground up, a steel center that would attract manufacturers and people from all over the United States. With the assistance of David Roberts, he secured investors from South Carolina, New Orleans, Natchez, and London. They formed the Bessemer Land & Improvement Company in 1886, bought 4,000 acres of land, and marked off blocks for the town along the Alabama Great Southern railway. George H. Stevenson planned and surveyed the grid of streets. Within five months, the property, for which the original investors had paid an average of $15 an acre, was selling at $18,000 an acre.

While the Town Company worked to attract new industries to the area, DeBardeleben built five blast furnaces for his coal and iron company, and the city's initial investors developed real estate downtown. All of these new companies attracted workers and families from across the country. On June 25, 1887, the *Bessemer* reported that 569 rail tickets to Bessemer were sold on one day the previous week. In its first year, the town had more than 1,000 residents.

Bessemer held its first election of city officials in September 1887. The citizens selected R.M. McAdory as the first mayor with the following aldermen: T.Y. Huffman, J.A. Hall, W.D. Mills, J.B. Cosby, and L.H. King. The same week, the mayor and new council hired a police force and appropriated money for a jail building. A town charter based on neighbor Birmingham's was drawn up, laws were written, and a beautiful city hall was commissioned in 1889.

Industries and the population grew so rapidly that Bessemer was referred to as the "Marvel City." Within three years of its founding, Bessemer was the eighth-largest city in Alabama. While the city and industries continued to grow, DeBardeleben's interest turned elsewhere. In 1892, he and Roberts sold their furnaces and mining companies to the Tennessee Coal Iron & Railroad Company (TCI). The sale made TCI the South's largest operator of furnaces and mines, holding the Bessemer furnaces, the Oxmoor furnaces, Red Mountain from Grace's Gap to Muscoda, and coal mines at Helena, Blue Creek, Blocton, and other nearby communities. TCI purchased the rolling mills in 1898. A May 1901 special illustrated edition of the *Bessemer Weekly* reported that TCI employed 1,500 men at the furnaces, coke ovens, and rolling mills. US Pipe had another 600 workers. Under TCI management, the ore mines around Bessemer became the most productive in the nation.

As the populace grew, so did commerce. By 1900, there were more than 200 licensed businesses in the city, including 46 groceries, 29 general merchandise stores, 15 attorneys, 15 saloons, 10 confection and fruit shops, eight cobblers, seven furniture stores, and three newspapers.

These businesses along with manufacturing brought in so many people that by the 1920s Bessemer was the fourth-largest city in Alabama.

Ample jobs, a warm climate, and convenient transportation made the city an attractive place to live. Recreation for Bessemer's residents was considered from the city's beginning. George Stevenson included green spaces and parks in his original survey. Bessemer's location also offered easy access to lakes and springs for recreation. As the community prospered, churches sprung up, new schools were erected, and residents built homes ranging from simple cottages to Victorian mansions.

For the city's first 100 years, steel, mining, and the railroad remained the area's largest employers. And while iron is no longer at the heart of Bessemer's economy, much of DeBardeleben's legacy is still visible. US Pipe still operates its foundry that was started here in 1889, and in 2009, opened a $45 million expansion. Railroads and transportation are still central to the Bessemer area economy. CSX operates a railroad container hub on the site of the former Pullman-Standard boxcar plant, and Norfolk-Southern has announced a $316 million rail hub just west of downtown. DeBardeleben would recognize many of the town's landmarks, too. The Berney Bank, Cornice Works, Simmons, and other early buildings line downtown streets. Henry Sweet's home stands tall on the corner of Arlington Avenue and Nineteenth Street. And the Bright Star still serves delicious meals every day.

One

Before Bessemer

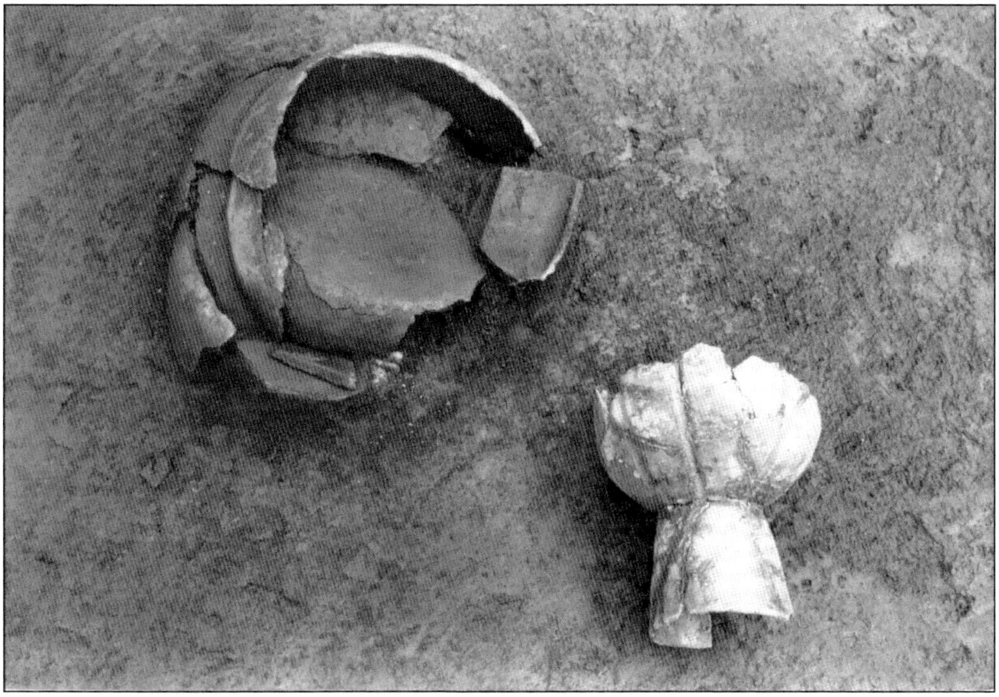

The earliest known settlers of the Bessemer area were part of the Late Woodland culture (500 AD–1000 AD) and Mississippian cultures (800 AD–1500 AD). The Bessemer site, made up of three mounds and the remains of a village, is located in a bend of Valley Creek near Old Jonesboro. It was excavated in 1890 and again from 1934–1941. Artifacts from the site include stone tools, freshwater shells, charcoal, and potsherds, like those pictured above.

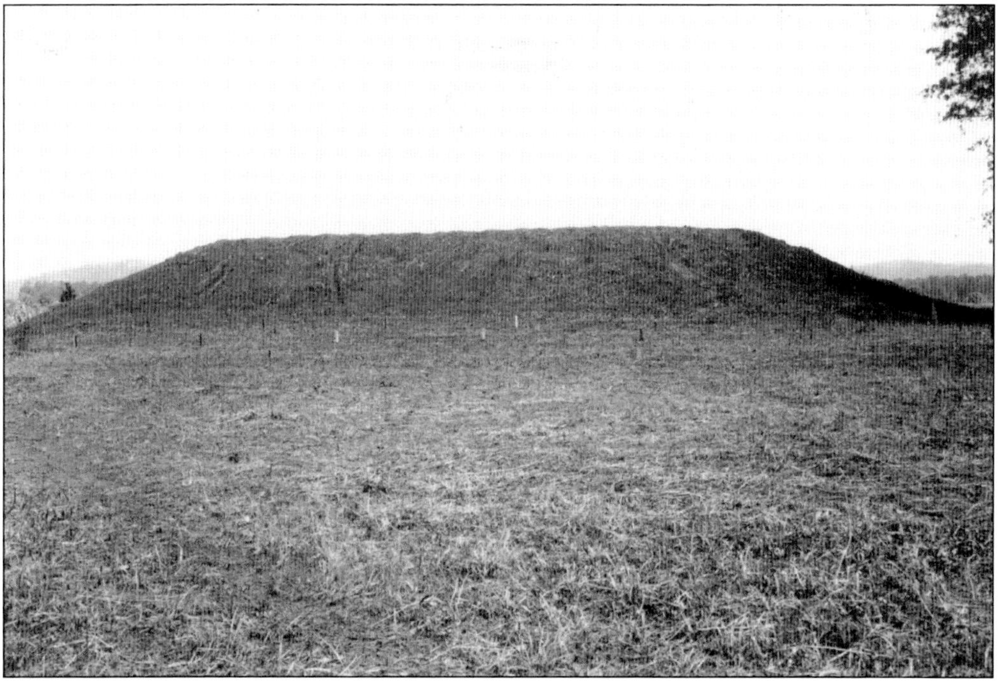

This view of one of the mounds at the Bessemer site was photographed before the 1934 excavation by a University of Michigan field school in conjunction with Birmingham Southern College.

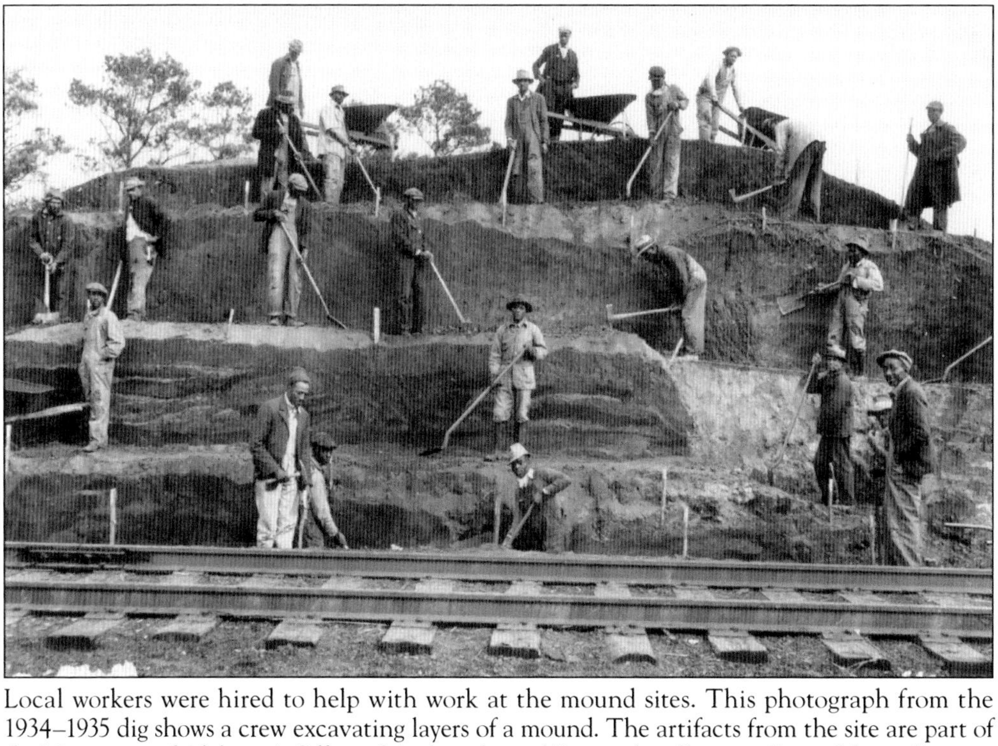

Local workers were hired to help with work at the mound sites. This photograph from the 1934–1935 dig shows a crew excavating layers of a mound. The artifacts from the site are part of the University of Alabama's Office of Archaeological Research collection. Part of this collection can be seen at the Bessemer Hall of History Museum.

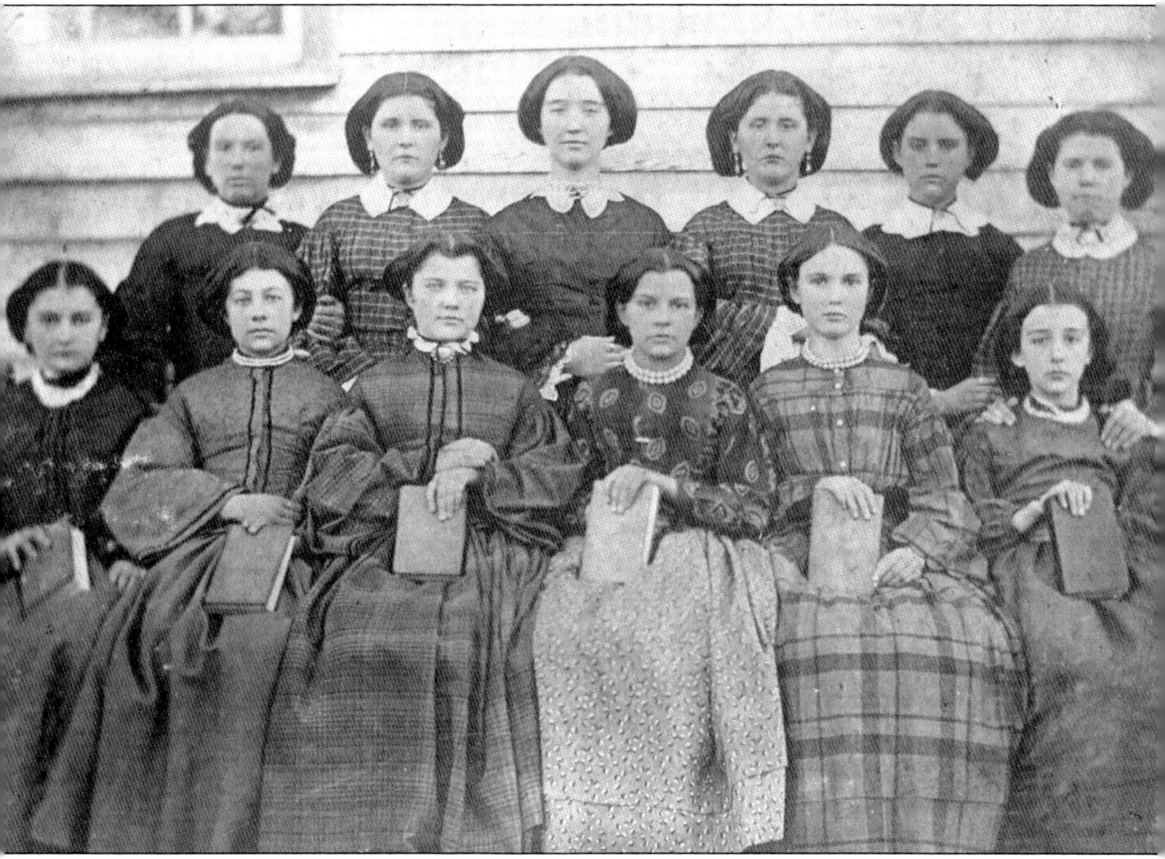

Salem Hill Academy, located at old Jonesboro, was one of the finest private schools in Alabama prior to the Civil War. Wilson's Raiders destroyed the school, along with most of the buildings in old Jonesboro, in 1865. This 1857 class photograph includes, from left to right, (first row) unidentified, Eliza Owen, Fannie Tarrant, Lucy Tarrant, unidentified, and Ollie Sadler; (second row) Miss Hall, unidentified, Eliza Saddler, unidentified, Carrie McAdory, and unidentified.

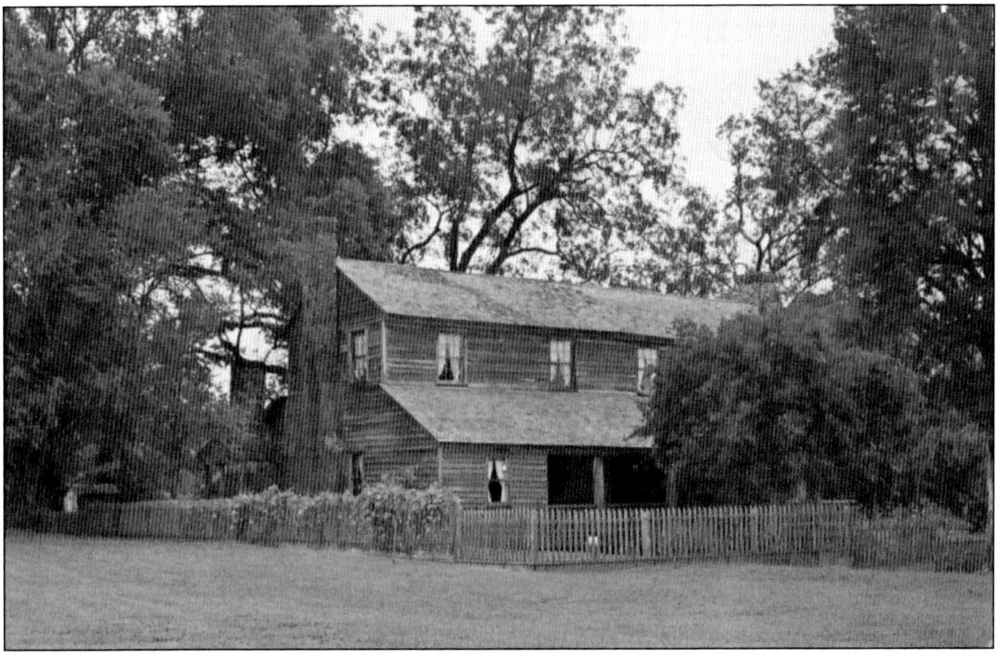

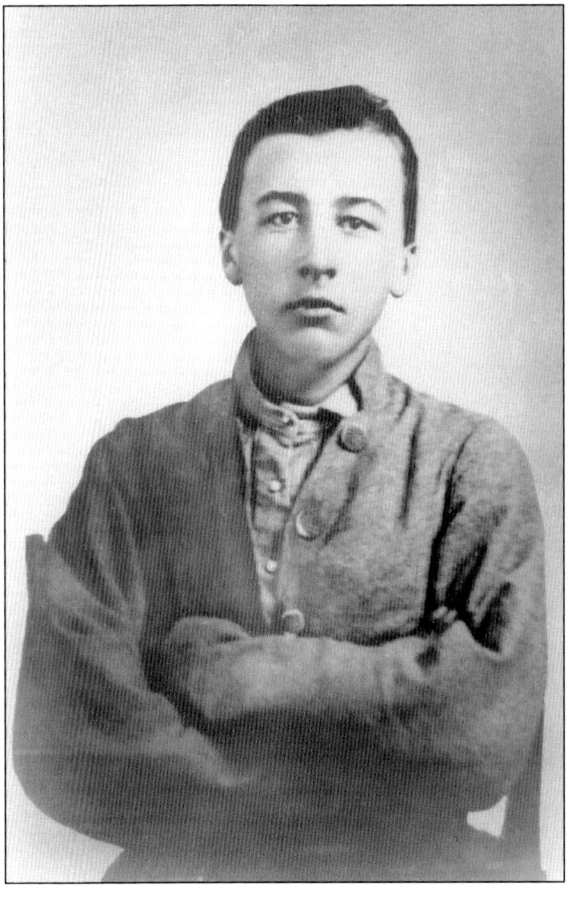

The Sadlers were one of the first families to settle in the Bessemer area. The original section of the Sadler House was built around 1820 by John Loveless. Loveless's widow sold the home to Isaac Wellington Sadler, who expanded it in the early 1830s. By 1865, Sadler's plantation included more than 2,800 acres. The house now belongs to the West Jefferson County Historical Society, and the grounds are open to the public.

David A. Sadler was the son of Isaac and Martha Prude Sadler of Pleasant Hill. David died while fighting as a Confederate soldier near Dalton, Georgia, in 1863. He was 17 years old.

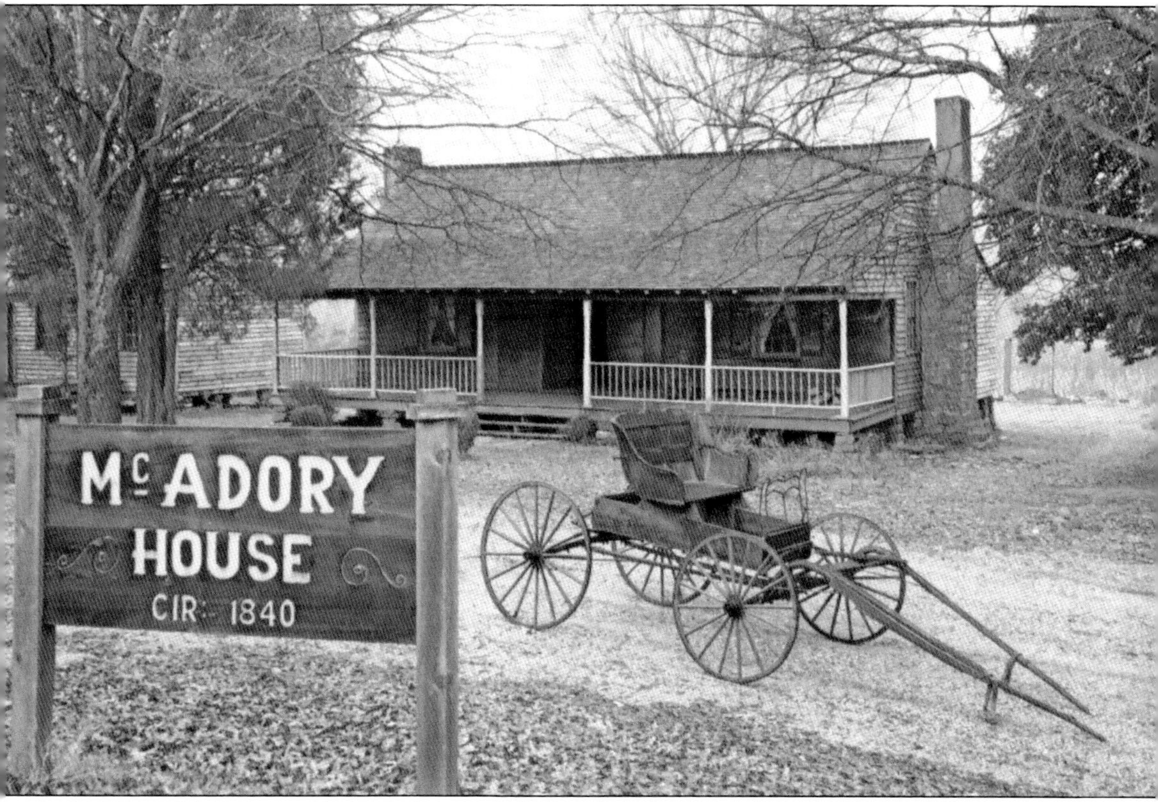

Another of the area's earliest settlers was Thomas McAdory Jr. McAdory's plantation included about 2,000 acres, and the plantation house was built about 1840. McAdory descendants who were born in the house include Isaac Wellington McAdory, an early educator and Jefferson County's first superintendent of education; Robert McAdory, Bessemer's first mayor; and Dr. Thomas Owen, the founder and first director of the Alabama Department of Archives and History.

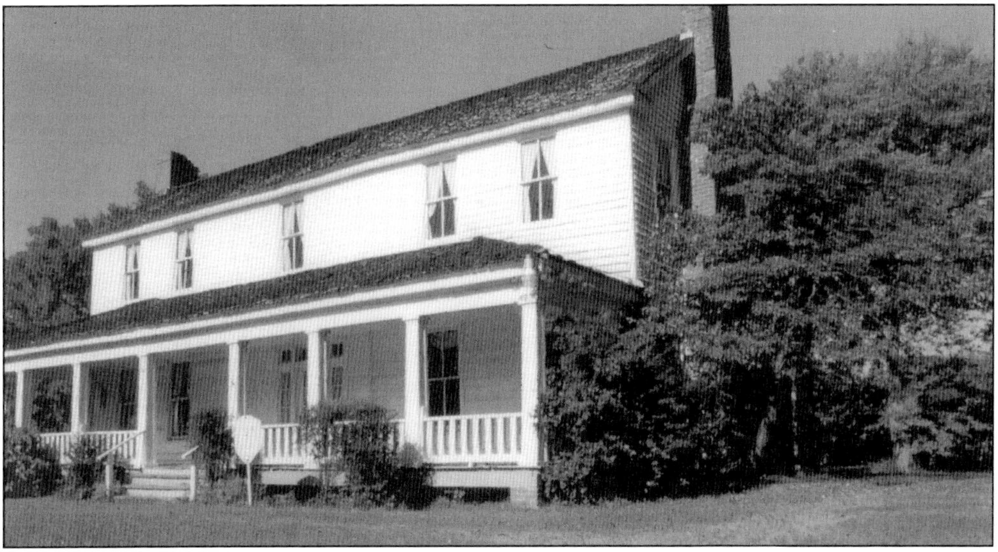

Thomas Hennington Owen was an early settler and industrialist. Owen farmed, and in partnership with Thomas Lightfoot Williams, he operated a foundry near Tannehill Furnace during the Civil War. He and his wife, Malissa Rose Sadler, were among the founders of Pleasant Hill Methodist Church. The Owen Plantation Home was constructed from 1833 to 1838. It now belongs to the West Jefferson County Historical Society and was added to the National Register of Historic Places in 1976.

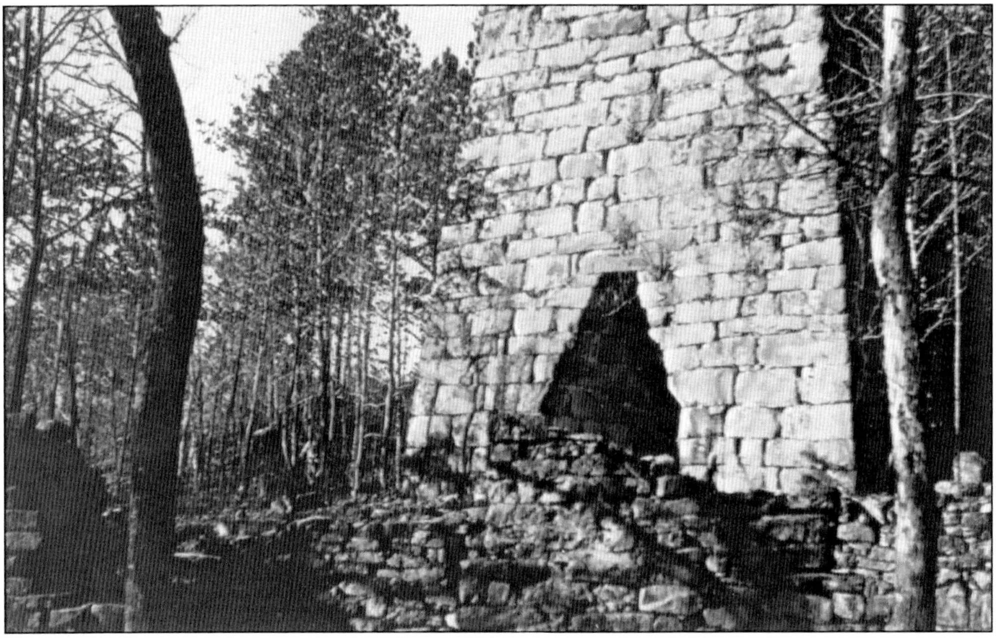

There was an ironworks near Tannehill as early as 1829, but Moses Stroup erected the first blast furnace on the site in the 1850s. William Sanders built two additional furnaces in 1863, to supply iron to the Confederate arsenal at Selma. Tannehill was the only three-furnace works in Alabama, and one of the largest producers of iron for the Confederacy. The furnaces were destroyed by Federal troops in 1865. The rebuilt furnaces, along with camping, hiking trails, and an Iron and Steel Museum, are now part of Tannehill Ironworks Historical State Park in McCalla.

Two

INDUSTRIES

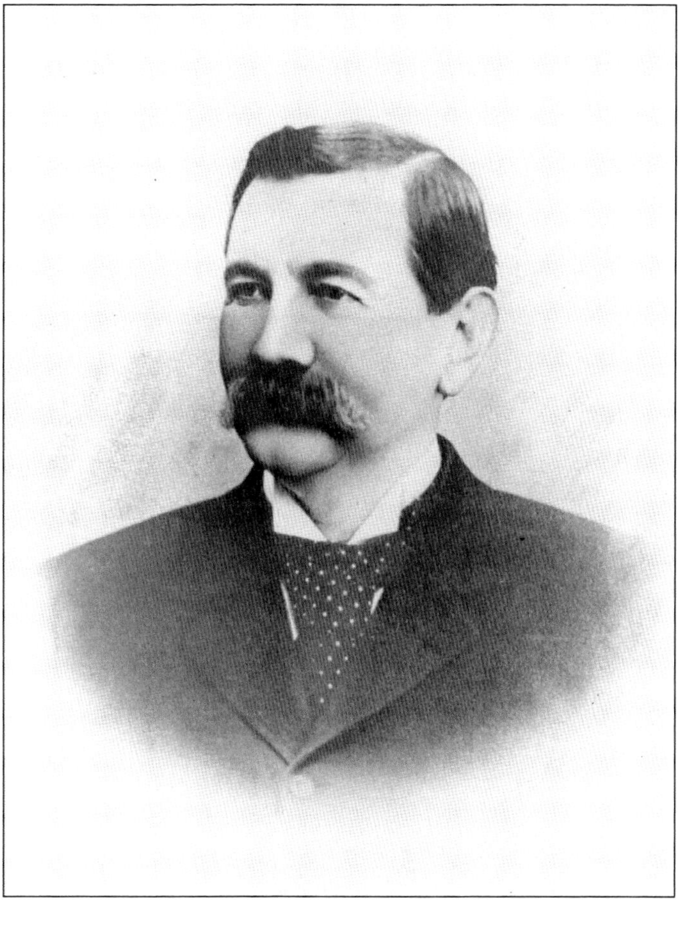

Bessemer would not exist without industrialist Henry Fairchild DeBardeleben. DeBardeleben dreamed of creating a steel center that would attract companies and people from all over the United States. He recognized the local natural resources, the area's promise as a center of transportation, and that the correct mix of these elements could create a manufacturing powerhouse and enormous prosperity.

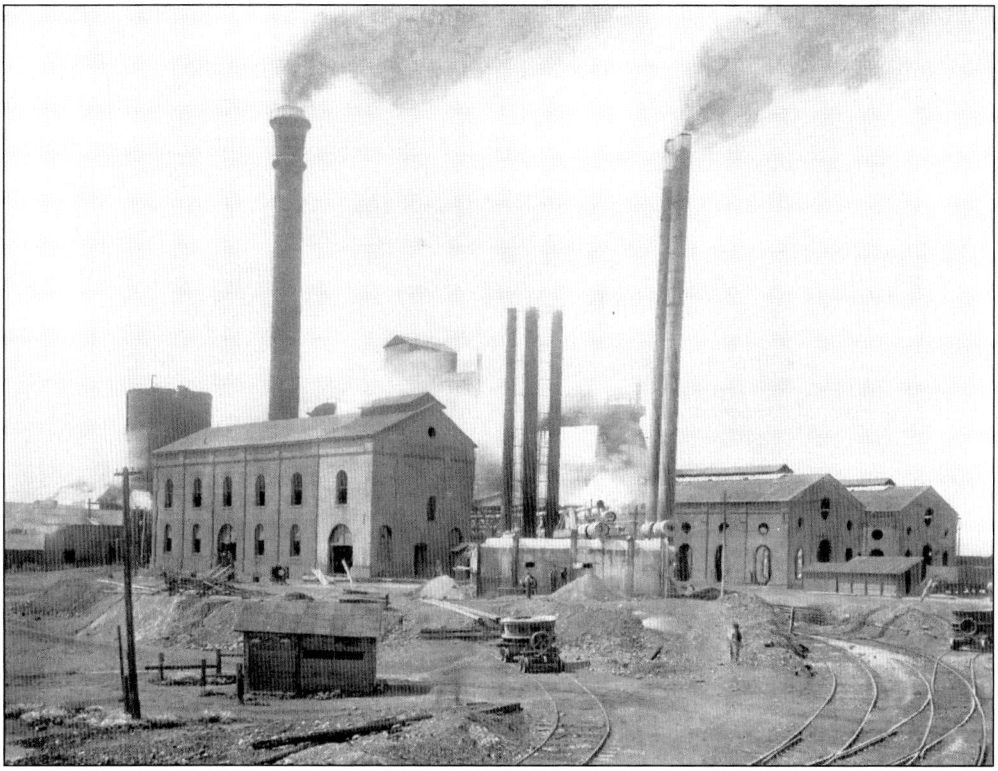

DeBardeleben Coal and Iron Company located its first two furnaces in the city along Second Avenue at Twenty-fourth and Twenty-fifth Streets. He nicknamed furnaces No. 1 and No. 2 "King David" and "Queen Anne" after company vice president David Roberts's children. In June 1888, furnace No. 1 was blown in. Production began at furnace No. 2 the following April. By 1900, each had a capacity of 175 tons daily.

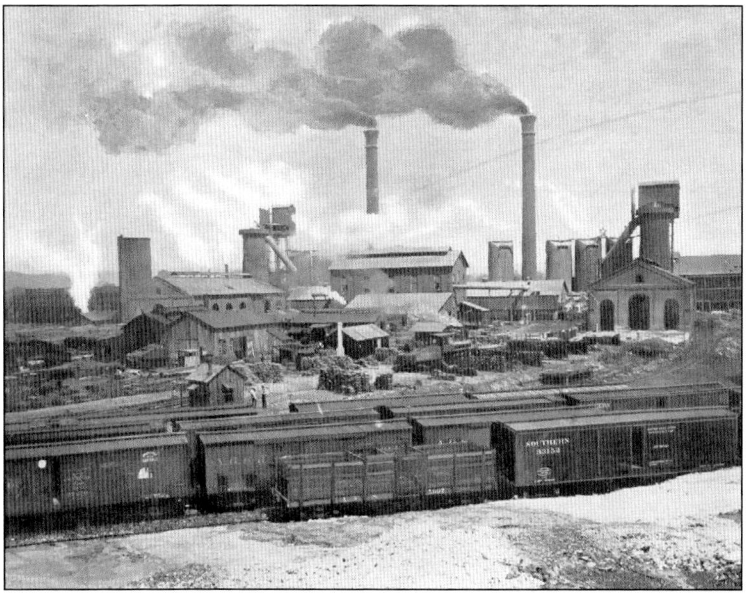

As soon as furnace No. 1 was running, DeBardeleben created Bessemer Iron & Steel Company to build two more furnaces at the Robertstown site. Robertstown was at Twelfth Avenue near 23rd Street. Furnaces No. 3 and No. 4, nicknamed "King John" and "King Henry" after chief mining engineer Llewelyn Johns and himself, were active by 1890.

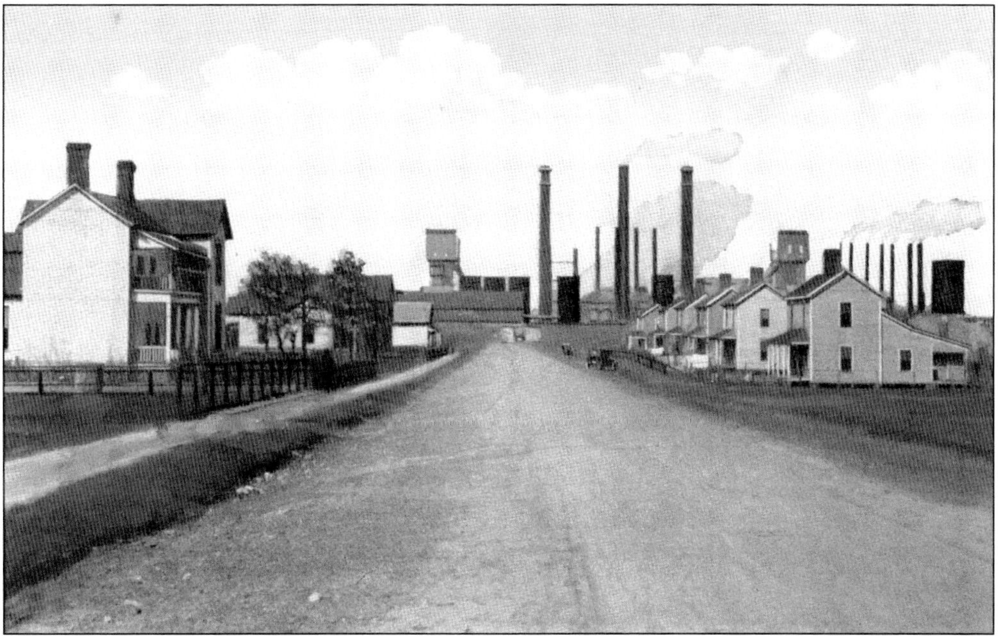

This early postcard view shows company homes along Twelfth Avenue with the Robertstown furnaces (No. 3 and No. 4) in the background.

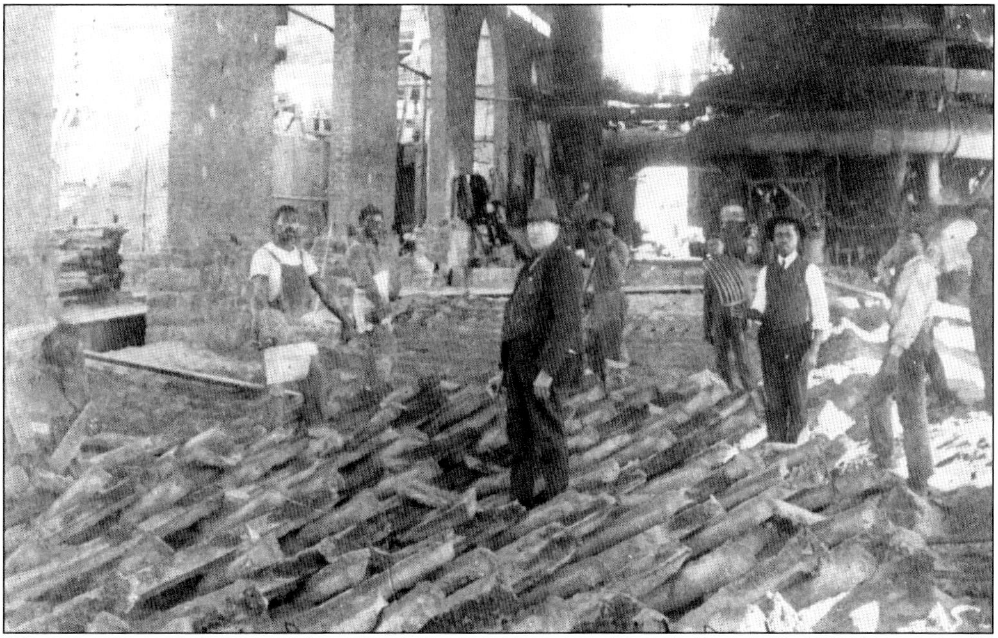

Workers remove pig iron ingots from sand molds at furnace No. 4. Pig iron takes its name from the ingot molding process. The melted iron was poured into a central channel in the sand. The iron flowed down this runner and into ingots at right angles to the channel. The final form made early iron workers think of piglets suckling, so they called the ingots "pigs" and the runner a "sow."

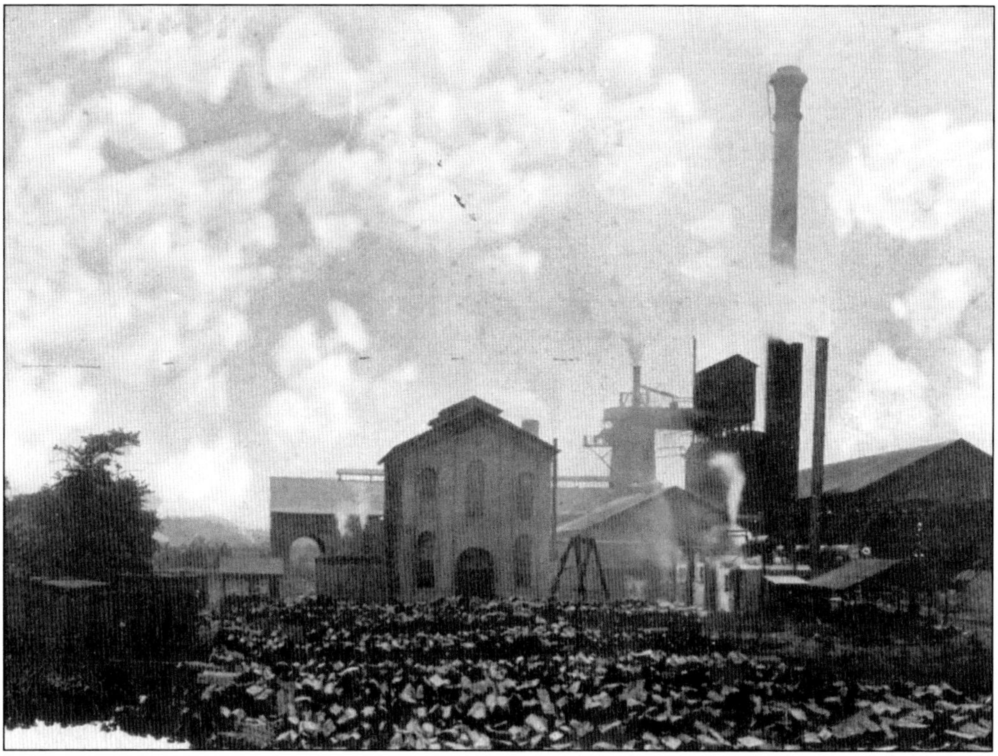

DeBardeleben next formed the Little Belle Iron Company and built his fifth furnace, "Little Belle," near Robertstown. In 1891, Little Belle became famous for producing the first basic iron in Alabama. Basic iron has very low silicon content and is much better for making steel than high-silicon iron. (Author's collection.)

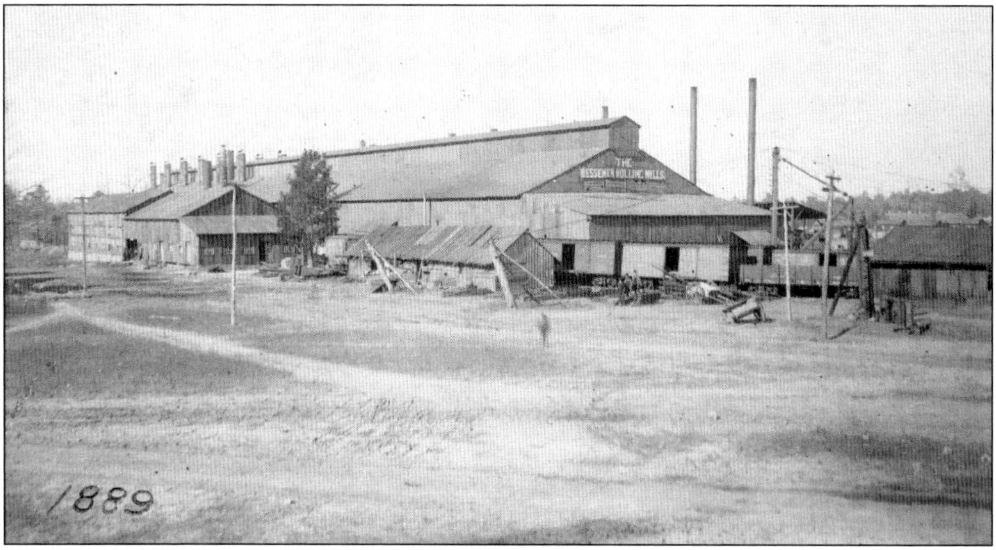

The first major industry in the city was not a furnace, but the Bessemer Rolling Mills. The company opened in 1887 adjacent to the site of furnaces No. 1 and No. 2. The Jamaica building from the New Orleans 1884 World's Fair was moved to Bessemer and incorporated into the Rolling Mills facilities.

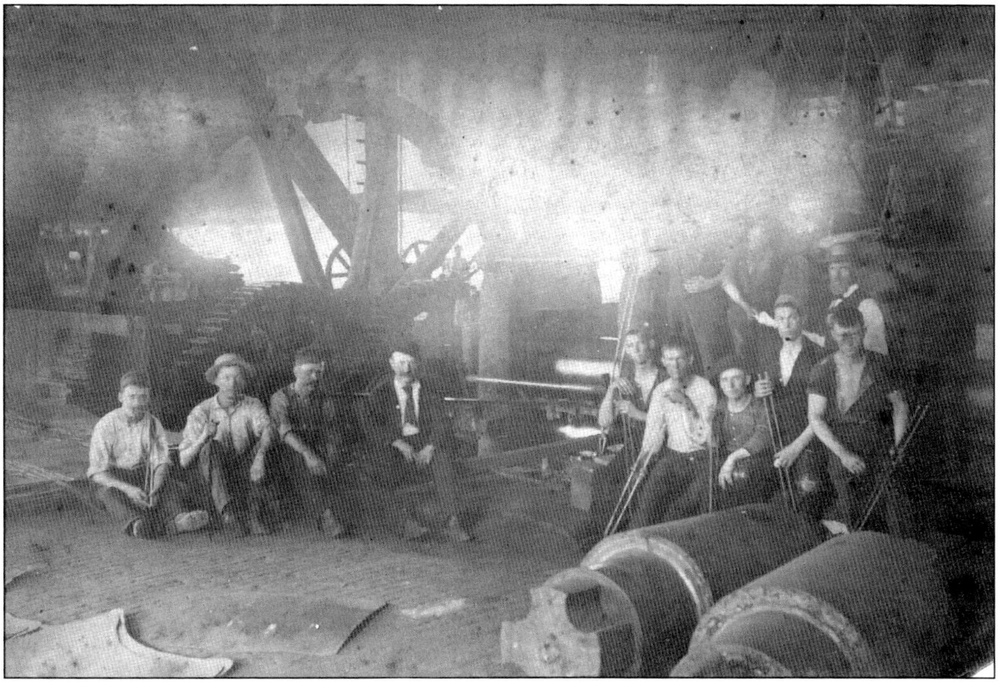

This 1890 photograph shows workers in the Bessemer Rolling Mills sheet mill. The mill was closed during the Panic of 1893, and was purchased and reopened by Tennessee Coal Iron and Railroad Company (TCI) in 1899. By 1900, there were 600 men working at the mill.

An 1890 view of the Bessemer Rolling Mills shows the billet yard. In addition to five trains of rolls, the mill operated 24 puddling furnaces, six heating furnaces, and three gas producers. When TCI took over production, the Rolling Mills' daily capacity was 80 tons of muck bar and 120 tons of finished iron and steel.

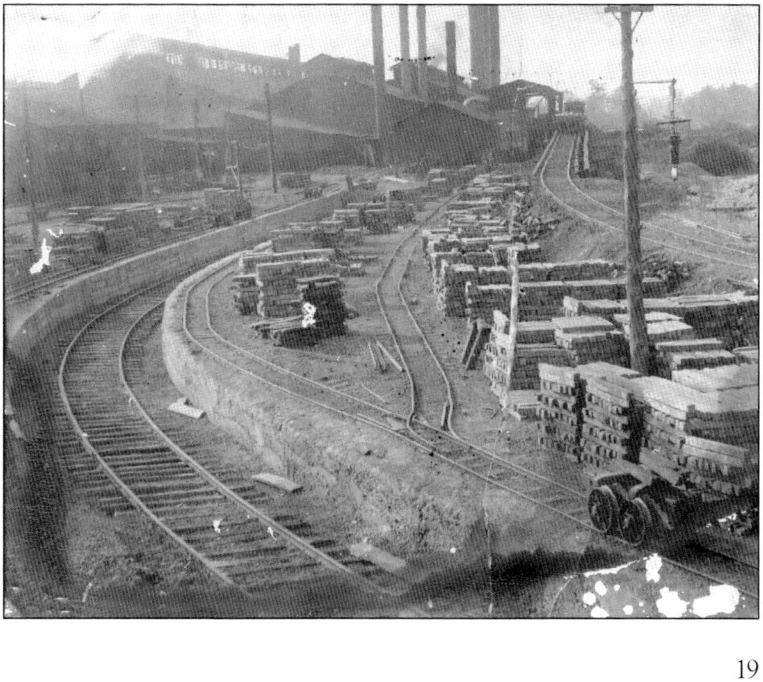

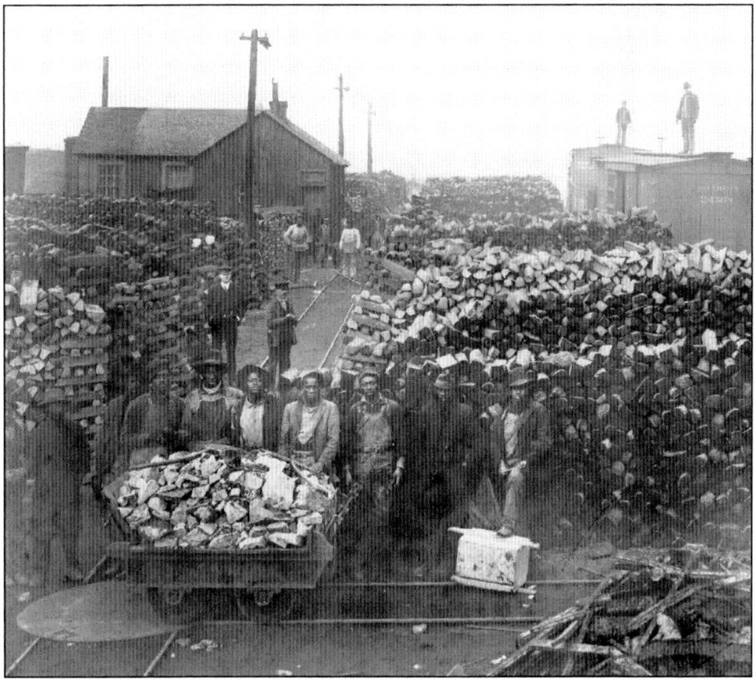

The most enduring of DeBardeleben's plans for Bessemer was locating a cast-iron pipe producer in the city. The Howard-Harrison Iron Company began production in 1889 and quickly became the largest producer in the South. This 1906 photograph shows workers with stacks of billets in the iron yard.

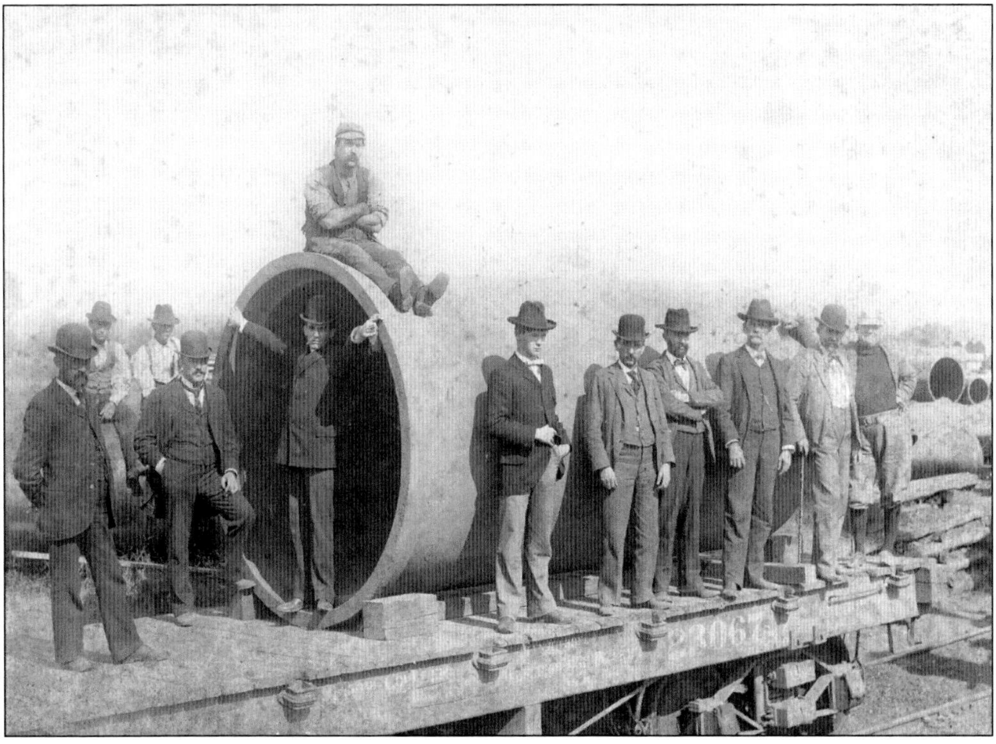

Plant managers and workers pose with (and inside of) a new 72-inch-diameter pipe in this 1900 photograph. US Pipe and Foundry Company purchased Howard Harrison and continues production at the Nineteenth Street and St. Louis Avenue plant today. In 2007, the company made a $45 million expansion to the Bessemer facility. (Author's collection.)

In 1887, George Pullman, of the Pullman Palace Car Company, and Robert Todd Lincoln, son of Abraham Lincoln and vice president of the Pullman Company, visited Bessemer. Pullman-Standard opened its Bessemer Plant in 1929. Pullman-Standard's Bessemer plant at Fifth Avenue and Twenty-fourth Street eventually employed as many as 1,800 workers and produced more than 40 freight cars a day.

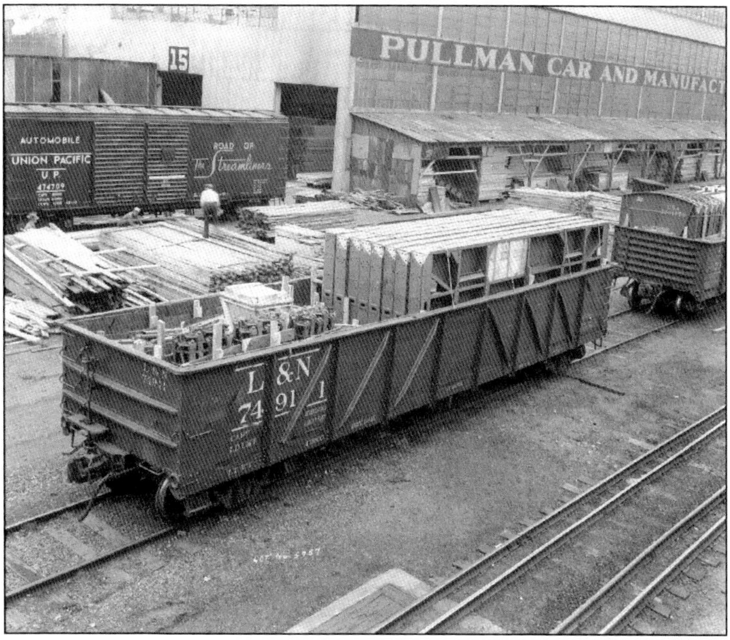

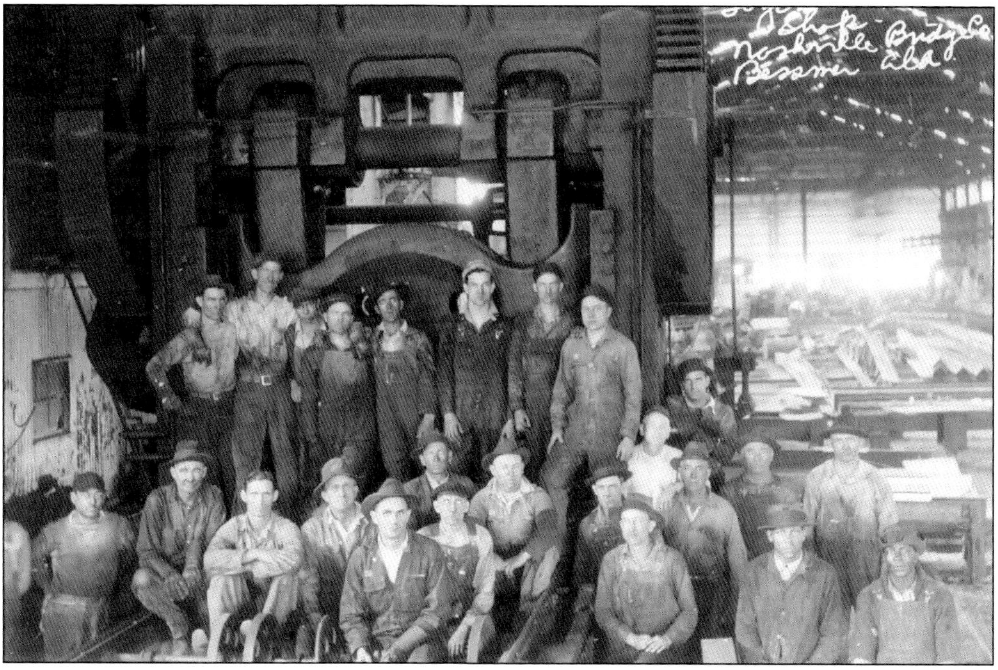

Nashville Bridge Company and Bessemer Galvanizing Works opened in 1923. The local plant produced steel bridge and ship parts and had the largest galvanizing kettle in the United States used to galvanize steel for transmission towers. This 1930 photograph is of employees in the layout and punch shop. The Nashville Bridge property is now part of the US Pipe plant.

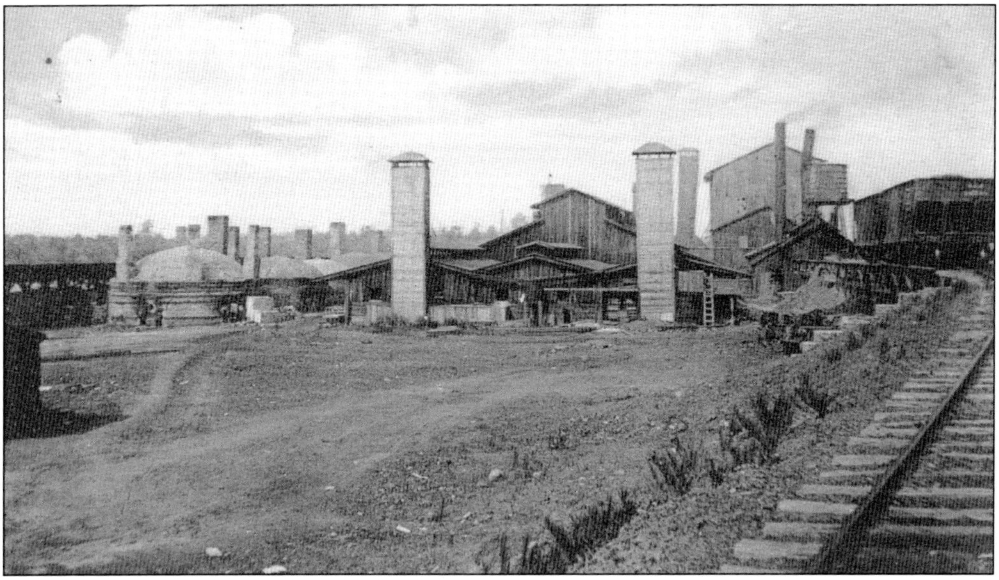

The Bessemer Fire Brick Company (later Alabama Clay Products Company) opened in 1888. In 1900, the plant employed 100 men and had an annual output of more than five million firebricks. Firebrick holds up to high-heat applications and is used to line furnaces, kilns, and fireplaces. The firebricks used to line steel-making furnaces withstand temperatures up to 3,000 degrees Fahrenheit.

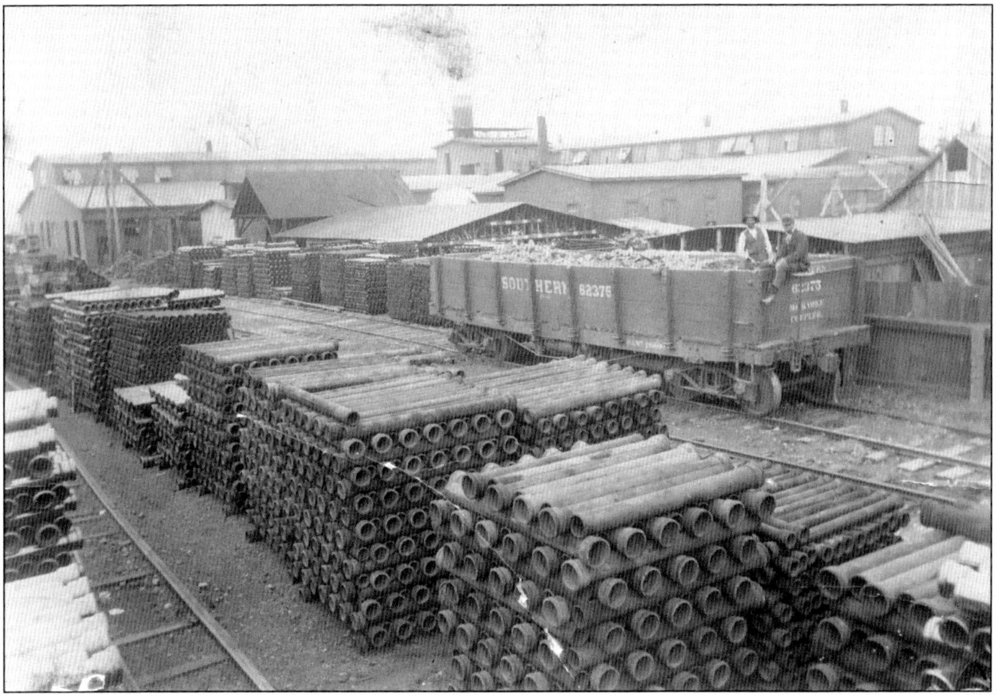

Bessemer was home to several soil pipe manufacturers including Nelson Foundry (seen here about 1925), Central Foundry Company, and Bessemer Soil Pipe Company. These companies employed more than 300 men by 1900 and distributed their brick, sewer pipe, and drainage pipe across the region.

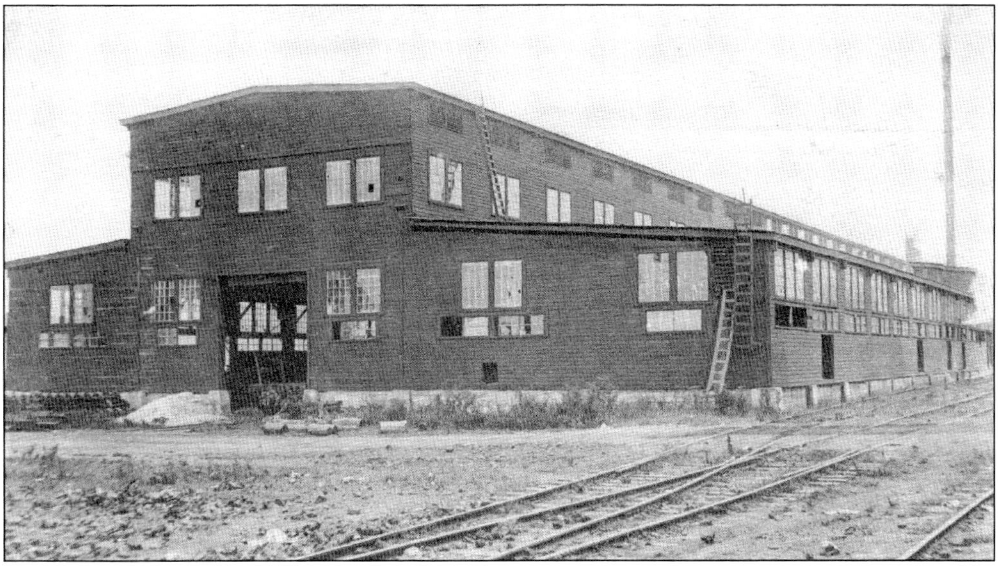

Bessemer Foundry and Machine Company opened in 1899, manufacturing all types of molding, castings, and machinery. The plant, located at Eighth Avenue and Twenty-fifth Street, had its own rail spurs connecting it to all of the rails of the city. Louis Hoster was president and treasurer of the company. The Hoster home remains a Jonesboro neighborhood landmark.

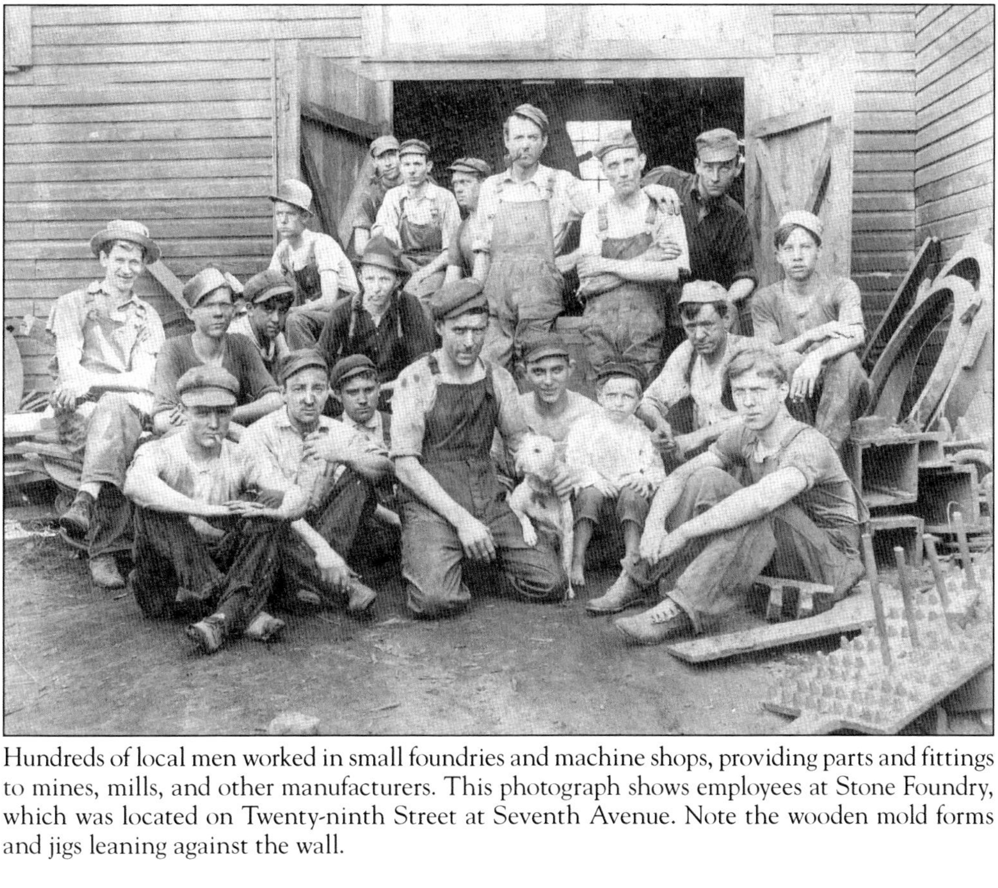

Hundreds of local men worked in small foundries and machine shops, providing parts and fittings to mines, mills, and other manufacturers. This photograph shows employees at Stone Foundry, which was located on Twenty-ninth Street at Seventh Avenue. Note the wooden mold forms and jigs leaning against the wall.

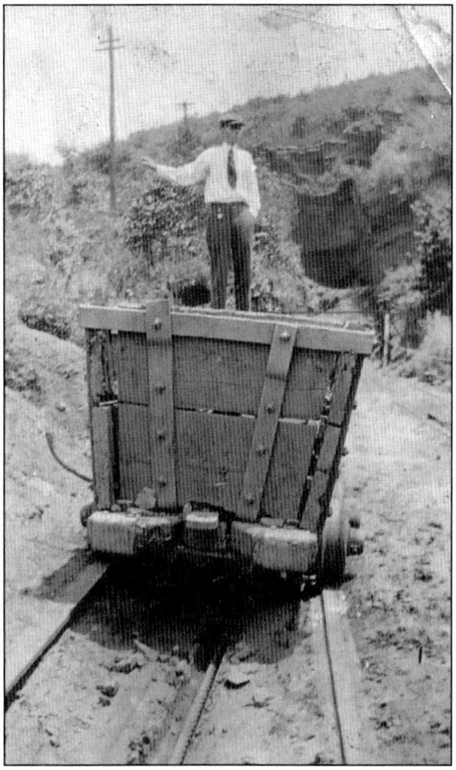

By 1930, the largest group of iron ore mines in the world was in Bessemer. The oldest of these were Sloss-Sheffield Steel & Iron Company's ore mines. Sloss No. 1 opened in 1882, before the city was founded. In this 1920 photograph, Sloss weighman William Andrew Crowson stands on one of the cars that were lowered into the mine and pulled back out via large steel cables. Some of the oldest portals into Sloss No. 1 can be seen in the hillside behind Crowson. (Courtesy of William Eiland.)

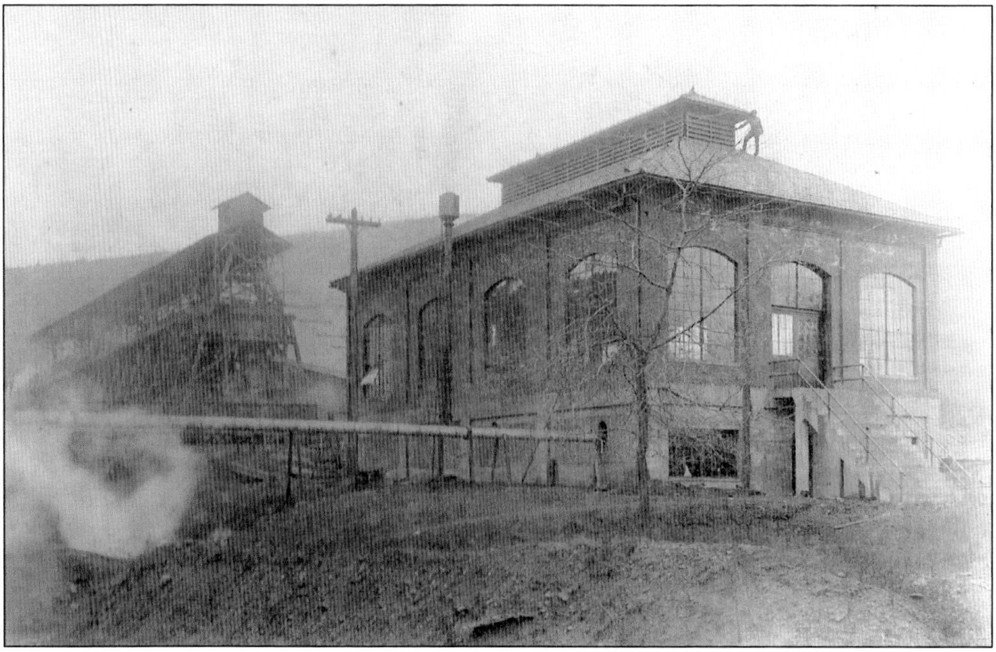

When mining first stared at Sloss, mules pulled mine cars filled with ore. Later, the enormous motor-driven hoist used to pull cars out of Sloss Mine No. 1 was in this building—the hoist-house. The hoists pulled tons of ore and slag from the mine. For a sense of the scale of the structure, photographed in 1913, note the man standing atop the building beside the roof vents.

Sloss Mine Village had its own park and playground. The two children in the foreground on the swing are Mary and Gene Williams. Their father, William Thomas Williams, was superintendent at Sloss Mines from about 1901 to 1922. The back of this 1913 photograph notes that the dog's name is Karo, and that the large tank in the background is an "indoor swimming pool."

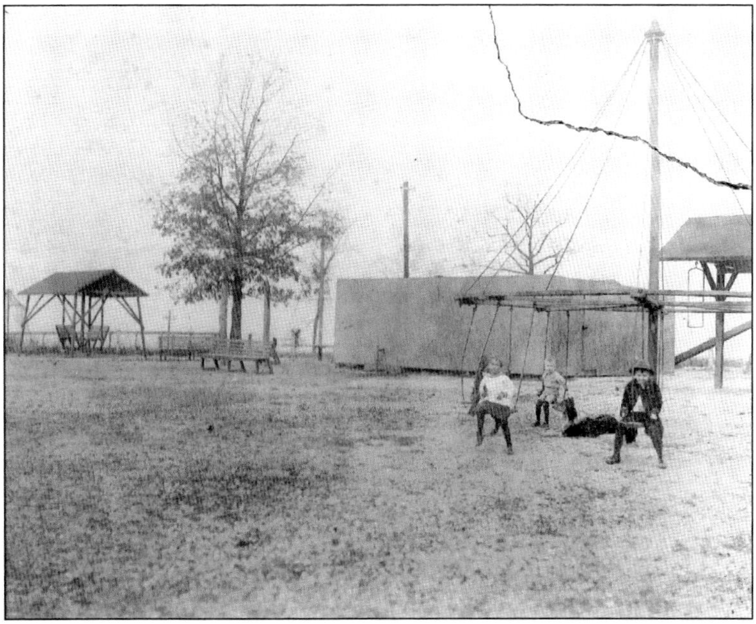

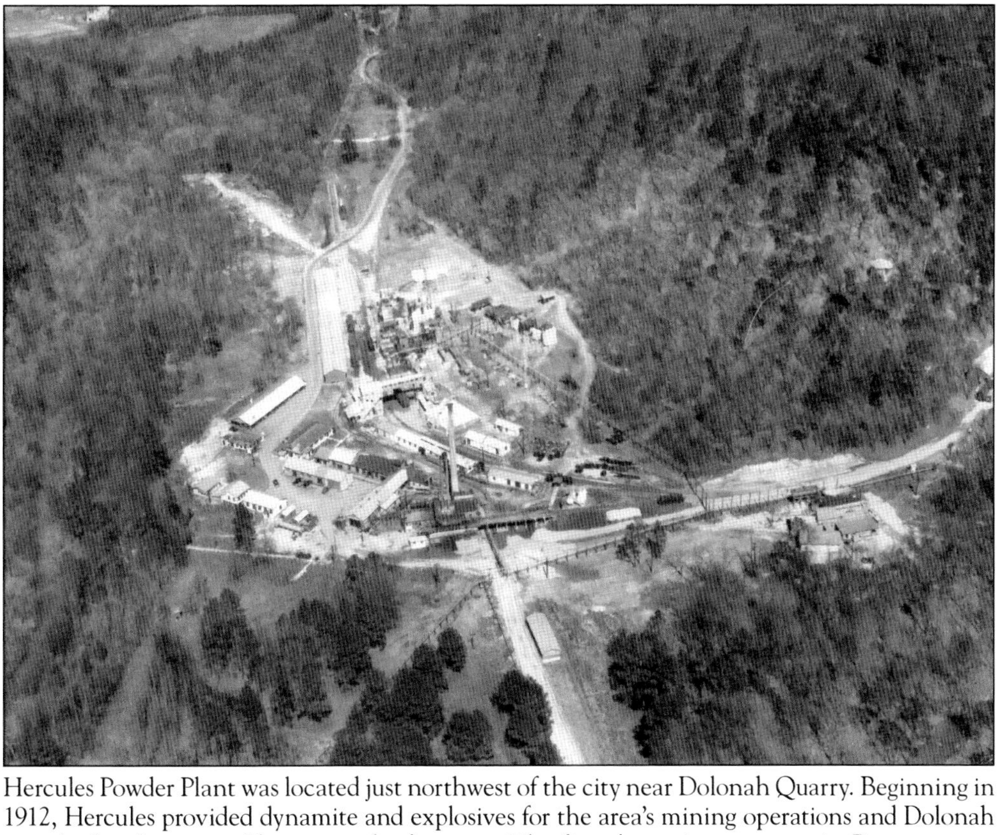

Hercules Powder Plant was located just northwest of the city near Dolonah Quarry. Beginning in 1912, Hercules provided dynamite and explosives for the area's mining operations and Dolonah was the local source of limestone for furnaces. The first dynamite company in Bessemer was Standard Dynamite. It opened in 1889 and was located on Nineteenth Street at Valley Creek, near Lee's Junction.

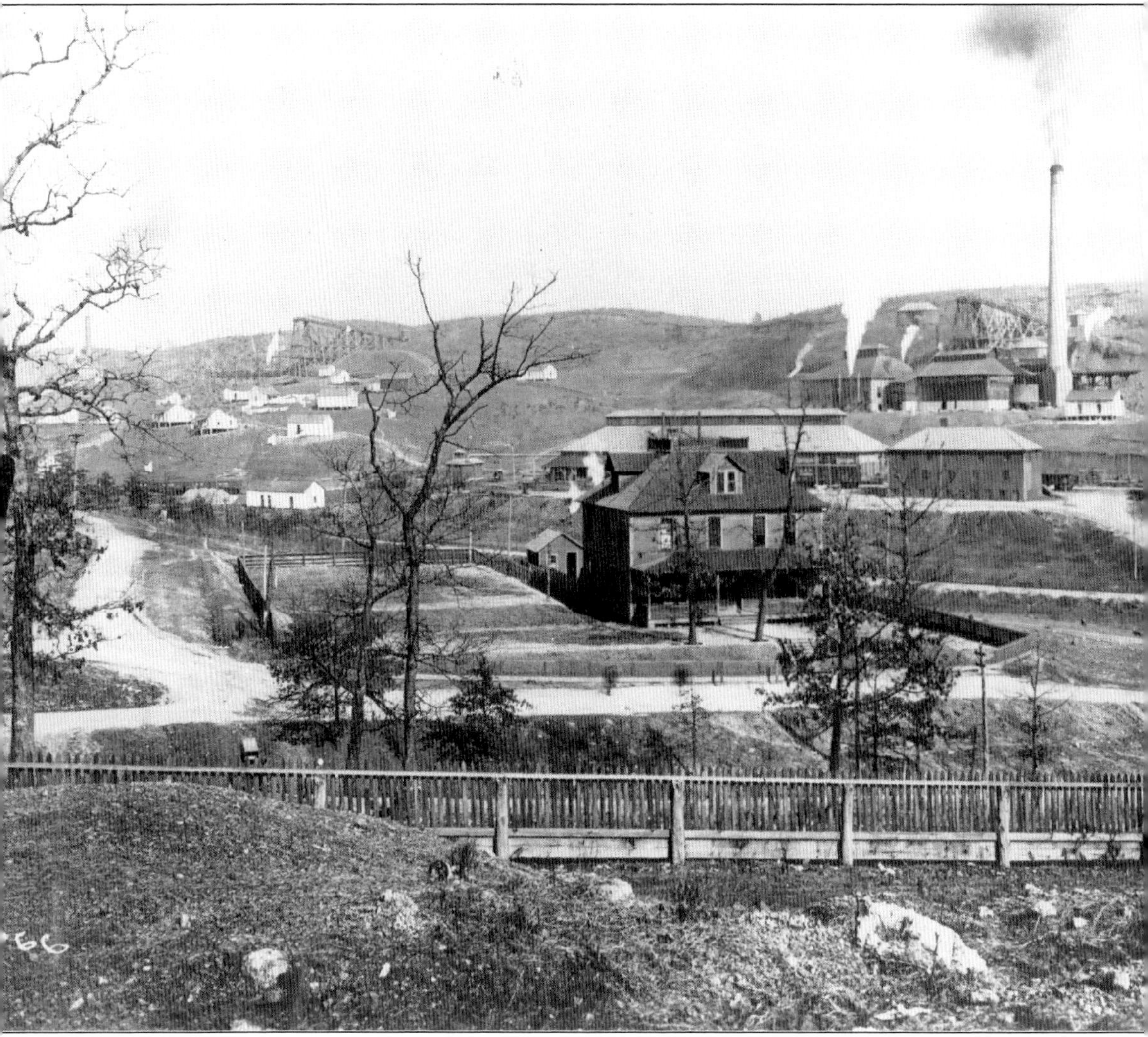

This view of TCI's Muscoda Mines was photographed from Reeder's Hill about 1915. The two-story building with hipped-roof and dormers is the old mine offices. Smith Mining Company began mining the area in 1888 and found so many arrowheads that they named the place Muscoda for the Muskogee Indians that they believed had lived there. By the 1920s, Muscoda was the largest mining operation owned by TCI. There is a neighborhood of distinctive mine workers' houses on the western side of Reeders Gap. The square homes with central chimneys and pyramidal roofs cost $385 each and were designed by Birmingham architects Wheelock, Joy, and Wheelock.

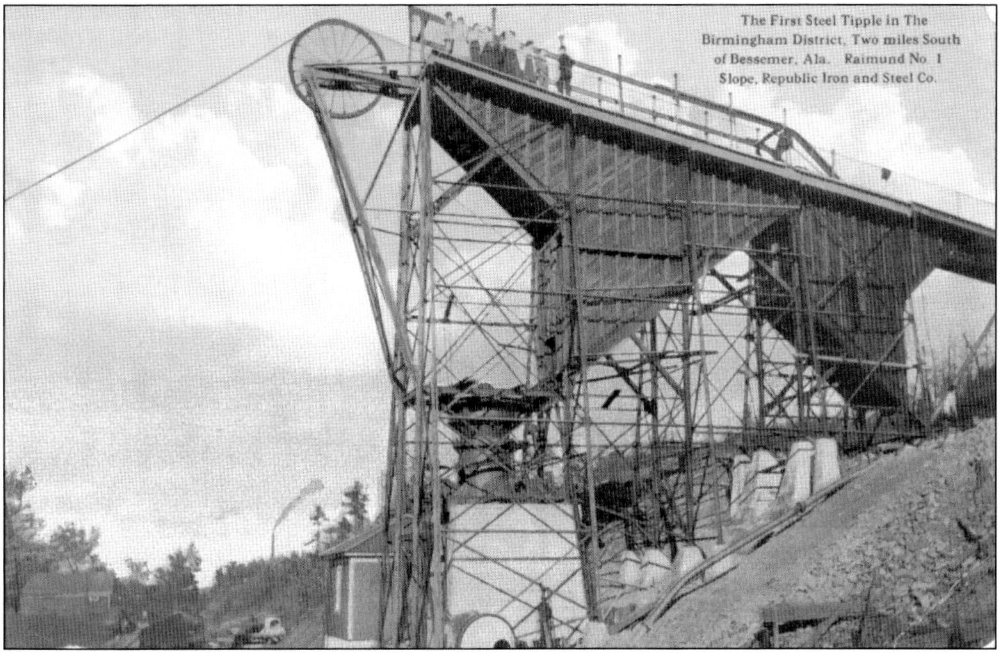

Raimund mine was first opened and named in 1894. The Republic Iron and Steel Company bought the property from the Pioneer Mining and Manufacturing Company in 1899. Republic built the first steel tipple in the area (seen in this postcard view from about 1915). The mine had produced 12 million tons of ore by 1938.

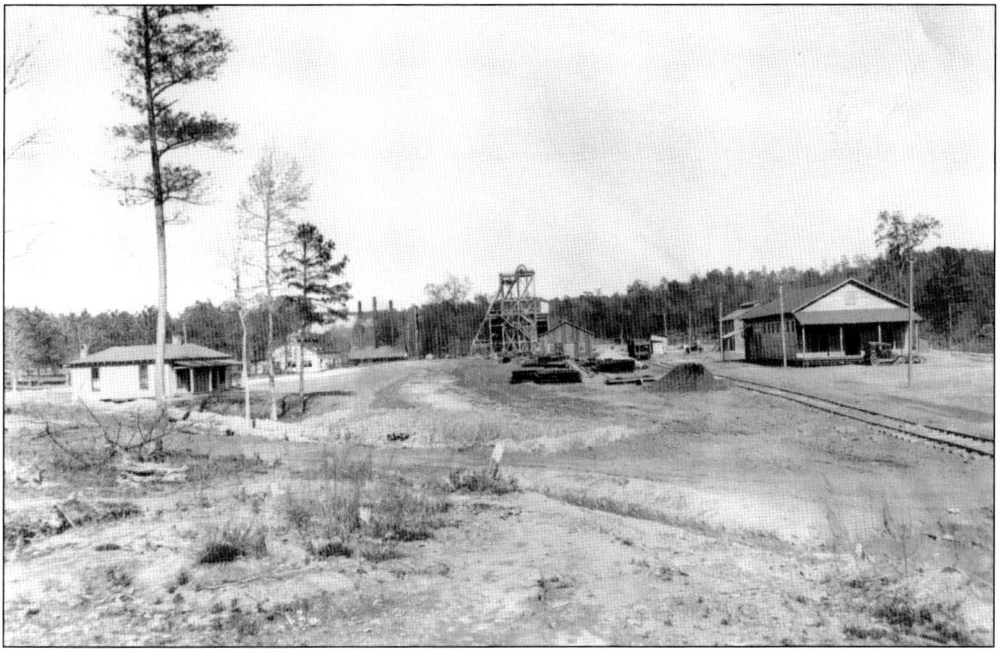

The 1,280-foot shaft at Pyne Mine made it the deepest ore mine in the United States. This image from April 11, 1919, documents the sinking of the first shaft. TCI and Woodward Iron Company expanded operations until Pyne was the largest ore producer in the nation. Pyne Mine did not close until 1971, making it the last mine to operate on Red Mountain.

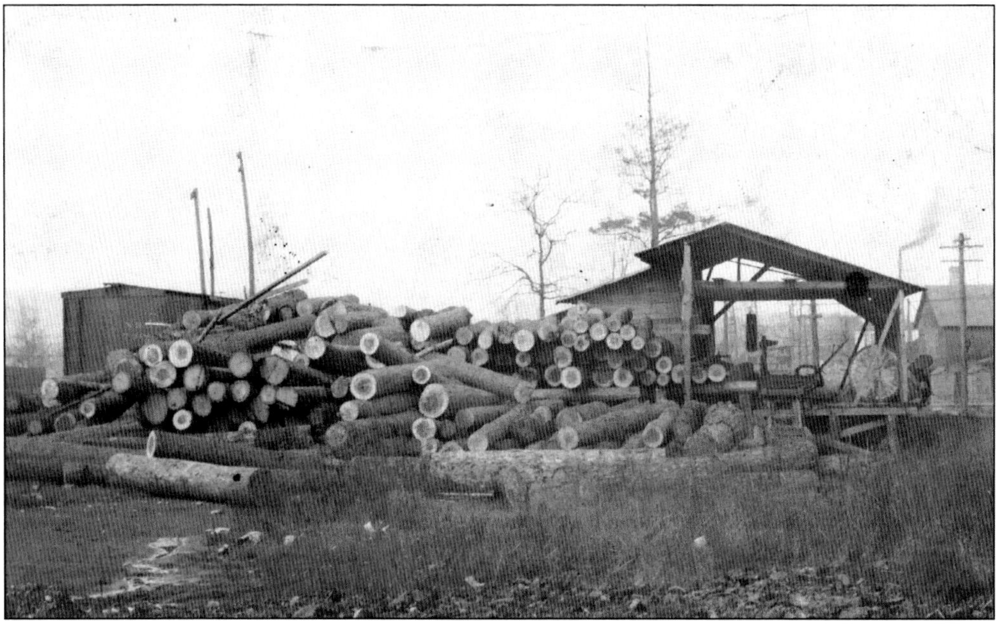

Not all of the area's natural resources were mined. Timber was also an important industry in the Bessemer area. In nearby Adger, Johns, and Shades Valley, virgin stands of yellow pine were cut and milled at lumber mills like the one seen above. Some of the earliest lumber companies in the city were Ratliff Lumber Yard, Fitzpatrick Lumber Company, Krebs Manufacturing Company, and G.B. Edwards Lumber and Coal (seen below in 1902). The Edwards yard was located on Twentieth Street between Sixth and Seventh Avenues. G.B. Edwards founded the nearby town of Brighton.

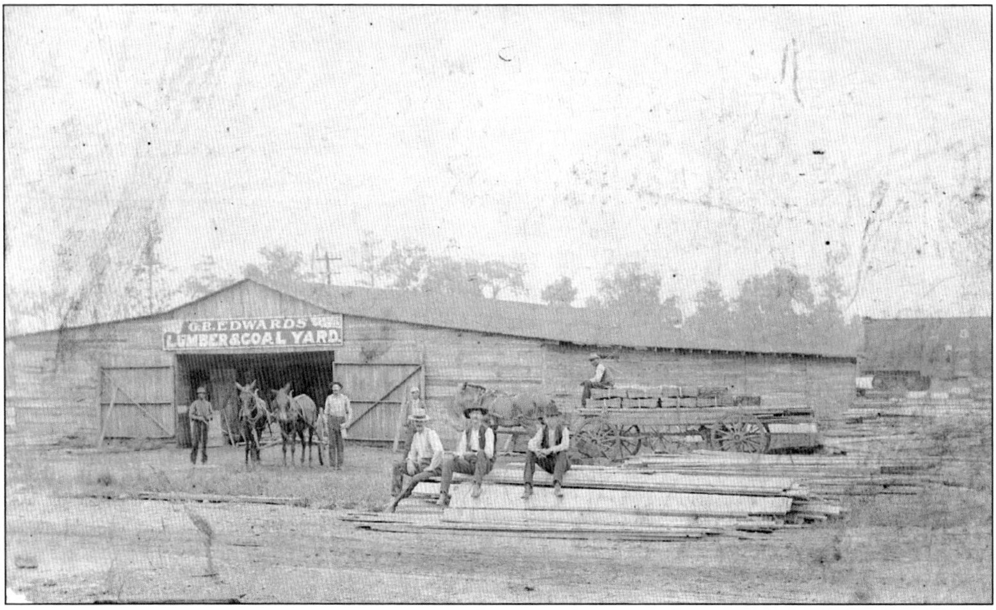

Three

RAILROADS

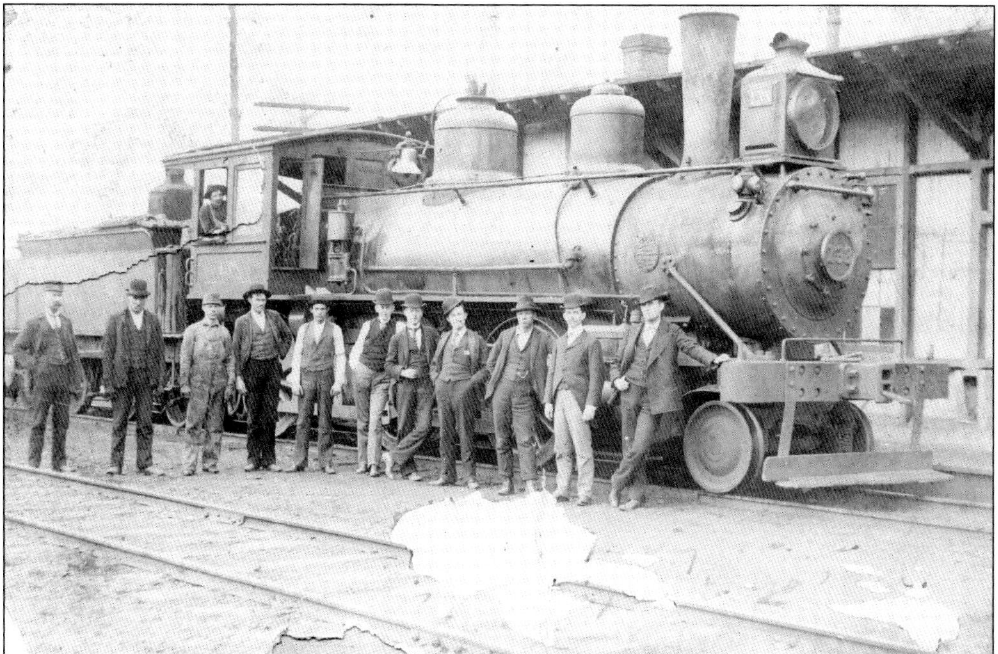

Knowing the importance of trains for bringing men and materials in and out of the city, DeBardeleben planned Bessemer along the Alabama Great Southern Railroad (AGS). In 1888, AGS had four northbound and four southbound trains stopping in Bessemer each day. The Louisville and Nashville line was completed though the city within a few weeks of its founding. By 1900, the city was served by two commuter lines and four major railroads handling more cars than any city in Alabama with the exception of Birmingham. This photograph from 1900 shows a steam engine stopped in front of the city's original wood-frame AGS Depot.

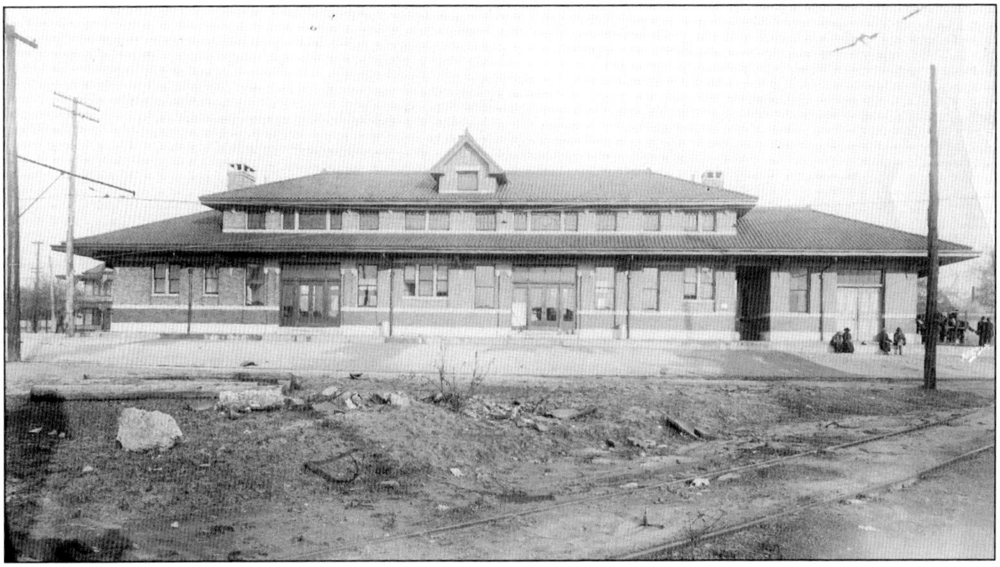

A new Alabama Great Southern passenger depot was opened on Wednesday, March 1, 1916 (above). The building was constructed by AGS employees at a cost of $30,000. The 170-foot-long building is constructed of buff-colored brick and concrete with copper trim and a heavy tile roof. The interior is finished with plaster, terrazzo wainscot, and Circassian walnut wood. This was the only building south of Ohio with vapor heating, which allowed the entire building to be heated with a single pound pressure of steam. The station has been beautifully preserved and remains one of the most recognized landmarks in the city.

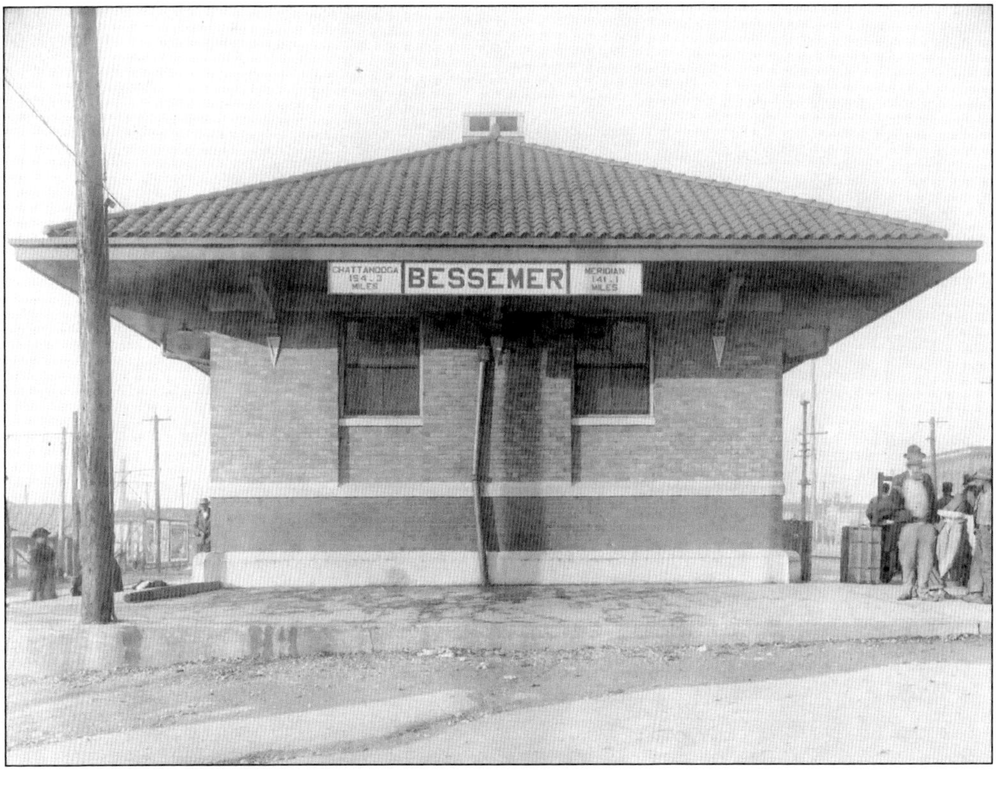

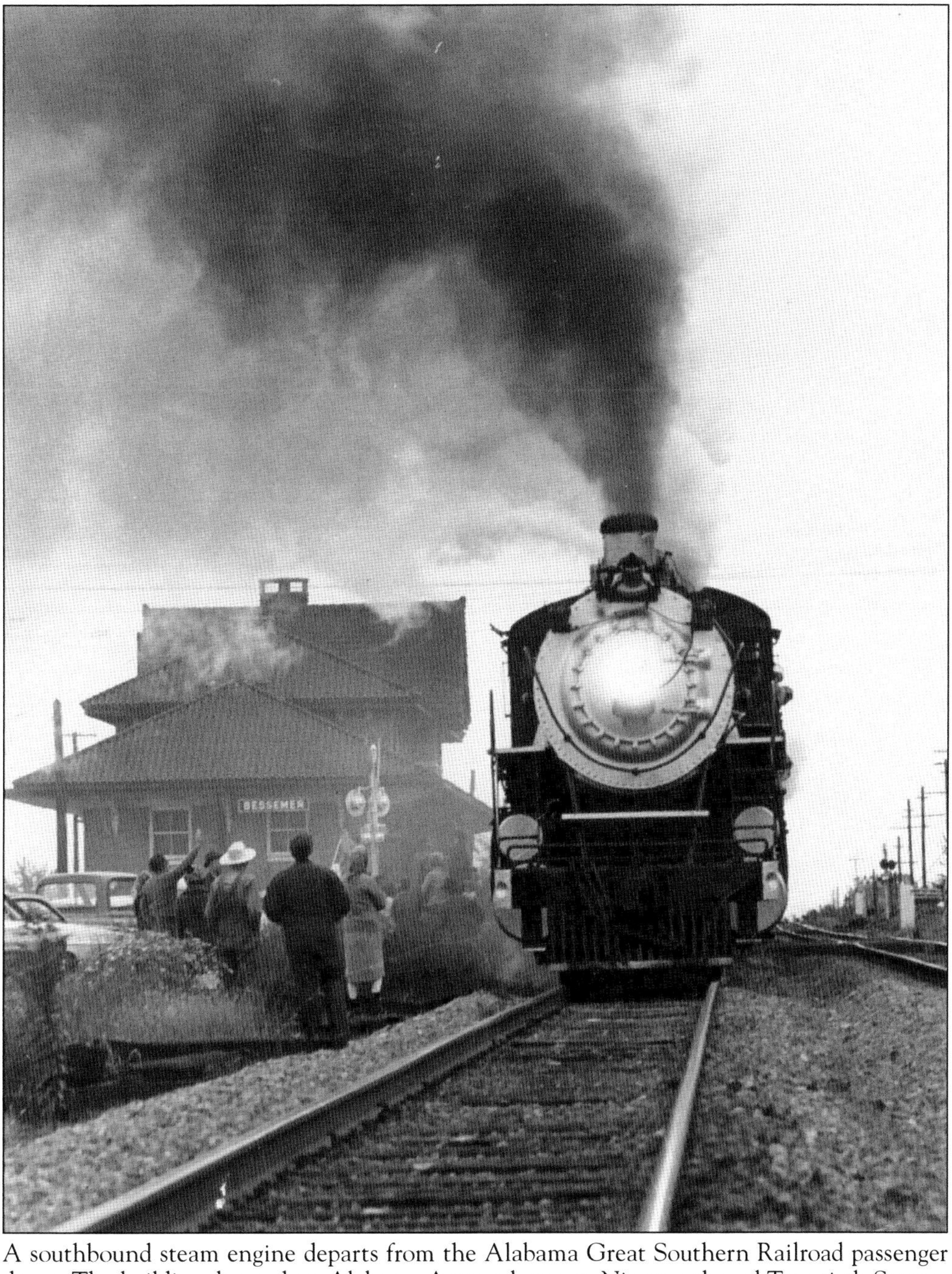

A southbound steam engine departs from the Alabama Great Southern Railroad passenger depot. The building, located on Alabama Avenue between Nineteenth and Twentieth Streets, was placed in the National Register of Historic Places in 1973. The Bessemer Hall of History Museum moved into the depot in 1985.

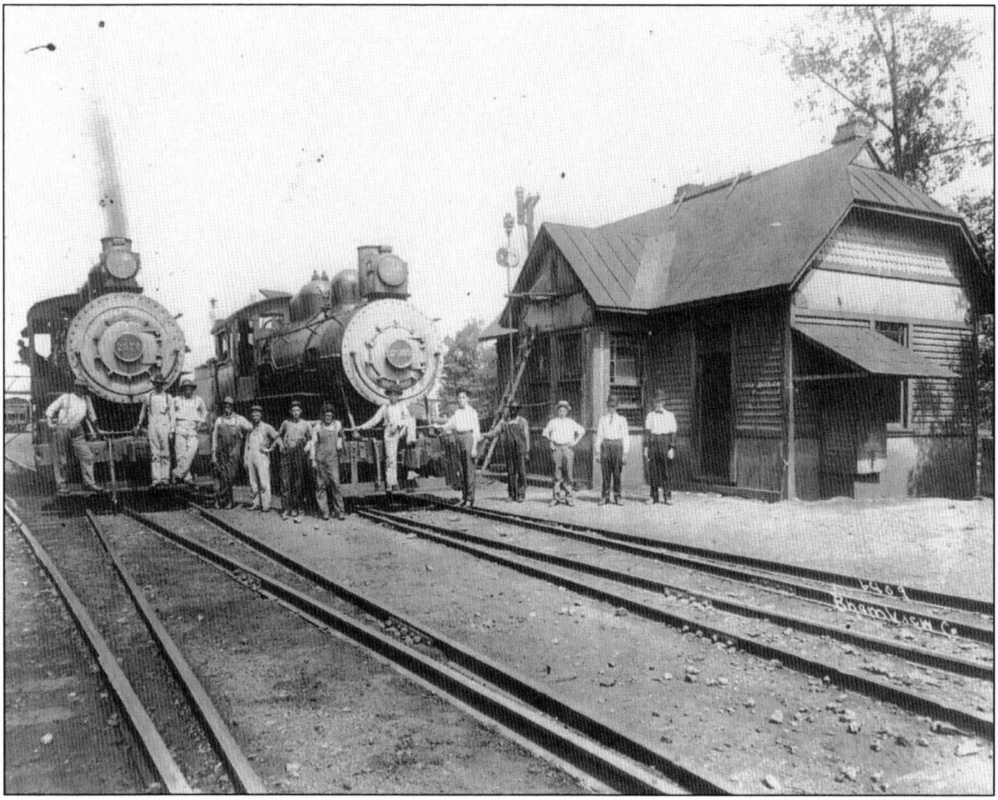

Rail workers pose with two steam locomotives stopped in front of the Alabama Great Southern Burstall Depot near Center Street at Jonesboro. The Burstall station was about a mile southwest of downtown Bessemer and served Jonesboro and neighboring communities. Following the completion of the AGS Railroad in the 1870s, many families moved from Old Jonesboro to this area.

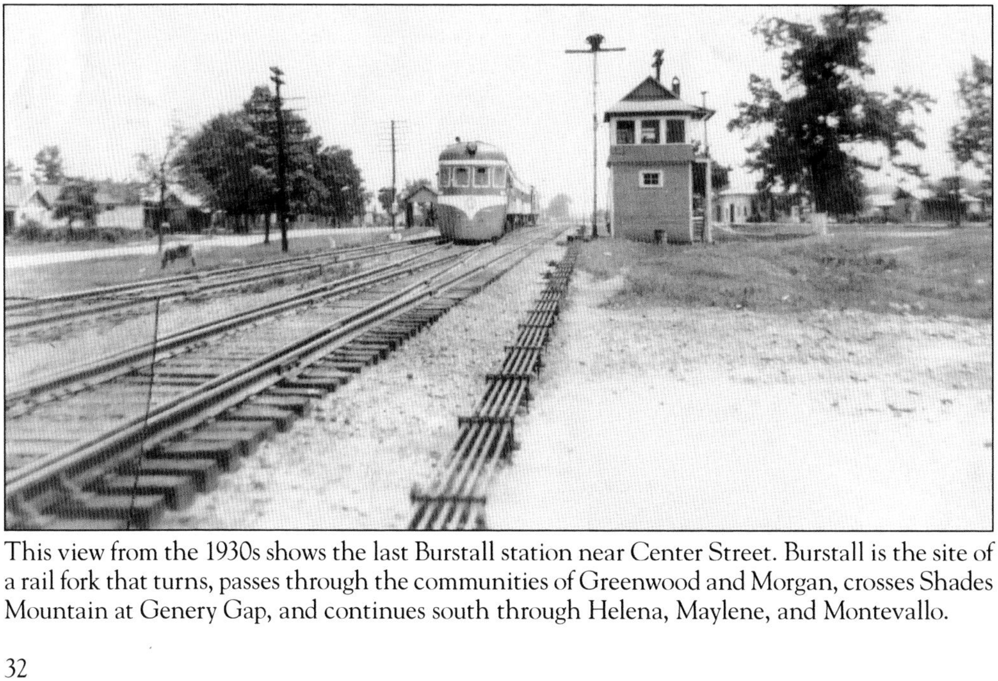

This view from the 1930s shows the last Burstall station near Center Street. Burstall is the site of a rail fork that turns, passes through the communities of Greenwood and Morgan, crosses Shades Mountain at Genery Gap, and continues south through Helena, Maylene, and Montevallo.

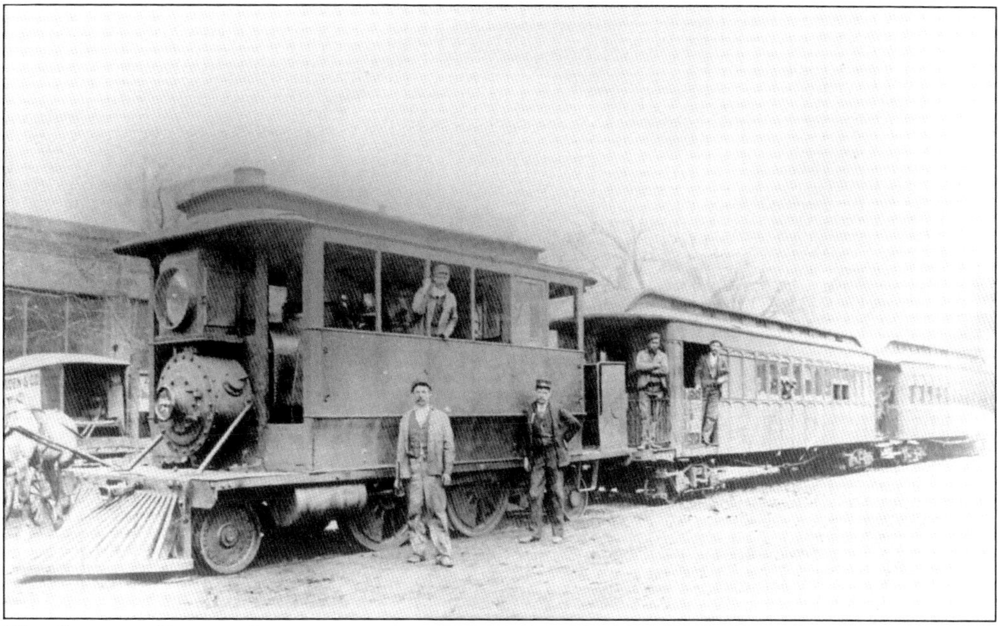

The Bessemer Dummy Line commuter train connected Bessemer with Birmingham. A round-trip ticket cost 40¢. In 1889, the line had 19 miles of track, five steam engines, and 15 cars. Dummy Line trains ran every 85 minutes. The company changed its name to the Bessemer and Birmingham Railroad Company in 1899. The ticket office for the Dummy Line was located in the Bessemer Rifles building, which used to stand on the northwest corner of Nineteenth Street and First Avenue.

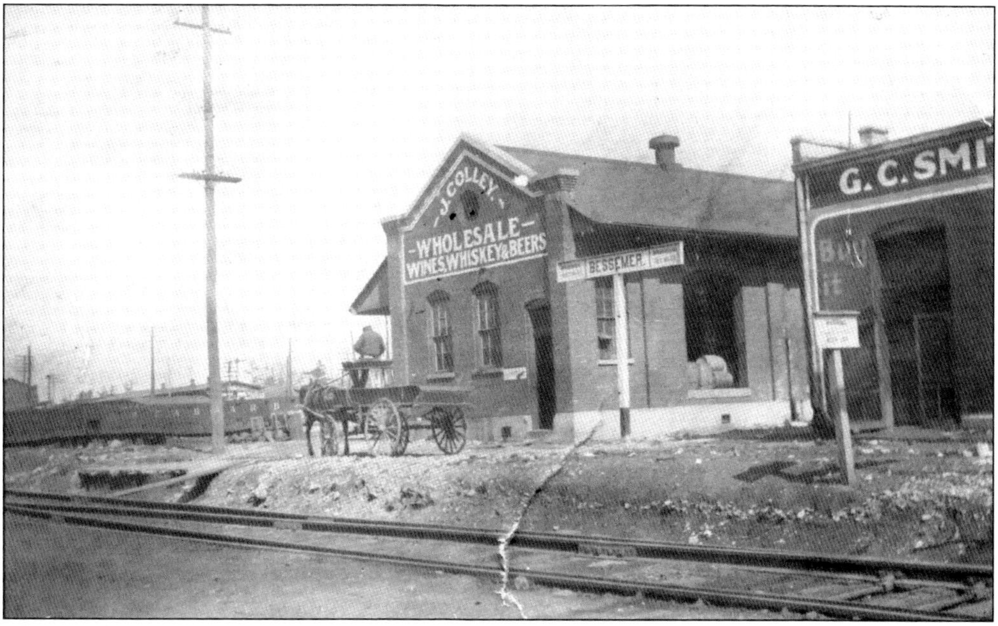

The J. Colley building, originally a repair house for the Dummy Line, still stands across Alabama Avenue from the AGS passenger depot. Over time the structure served as a liquor warehouse, a produce market, and the Railway Express Agency office. At the time of this image (sometime before 1916) it housed J. Colley's Wholesale Wines, Whiskey & Beers.

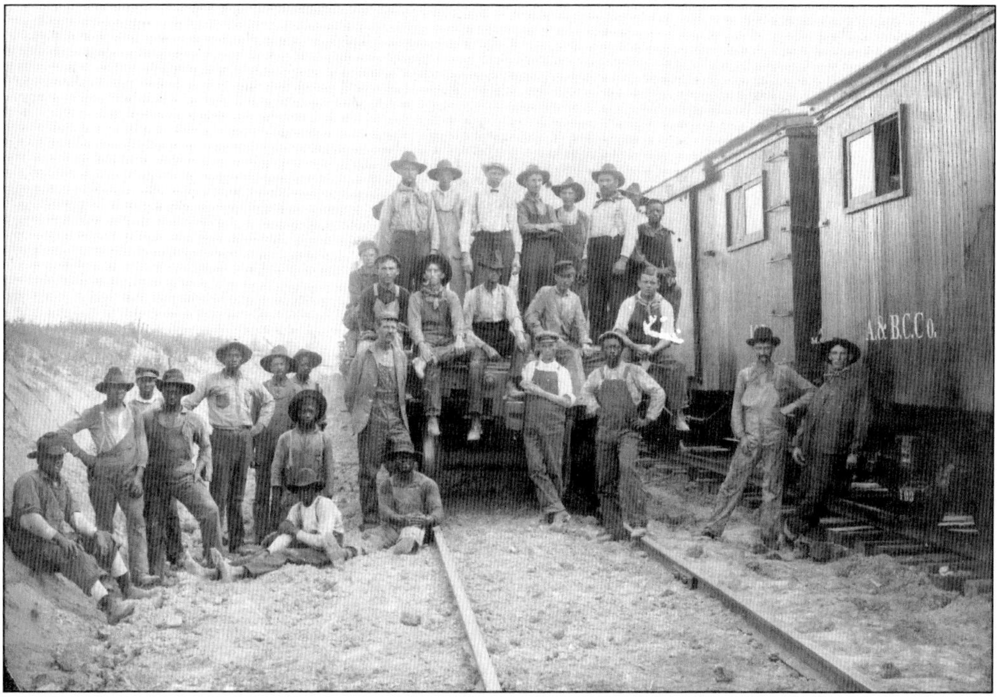

Above, the Atlantic & Birmingham Construction Company crew stops work for a portrait while laying track near Bessemer. The A&BCCo was a subsidiary of the Atlanta, Birmingham, & Atlantic Railway that eventually became the Atlanta, Birmingham & Coast (AB&C). Below, steam shovel No. 2 was used for the line's heavy excavation work. The second man from the left is John Rheuby.

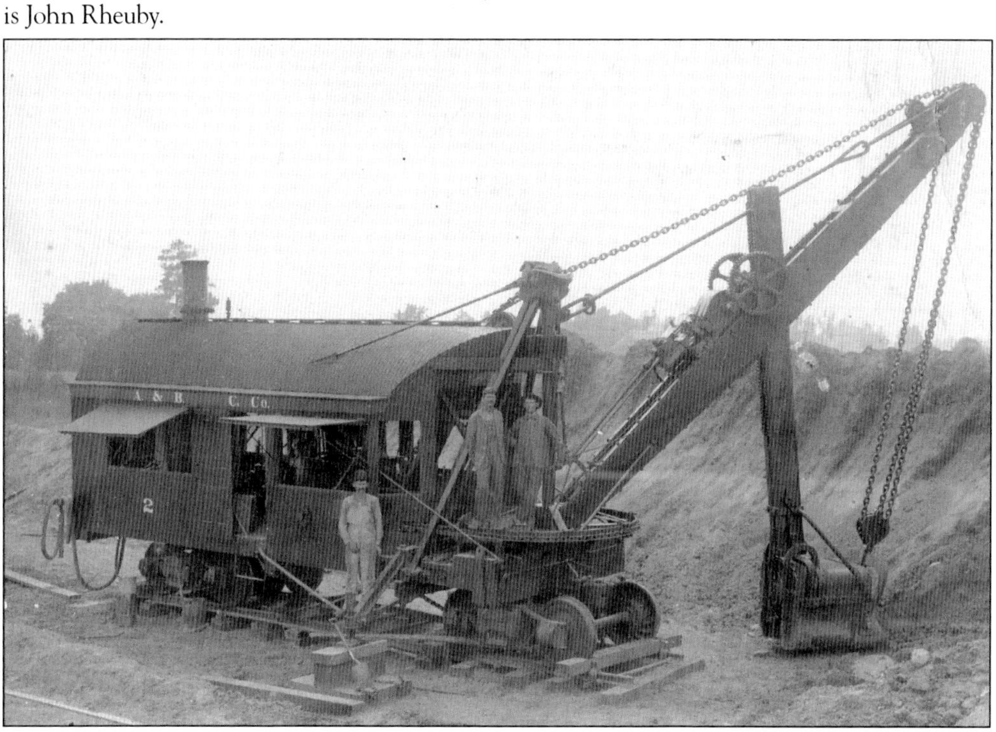

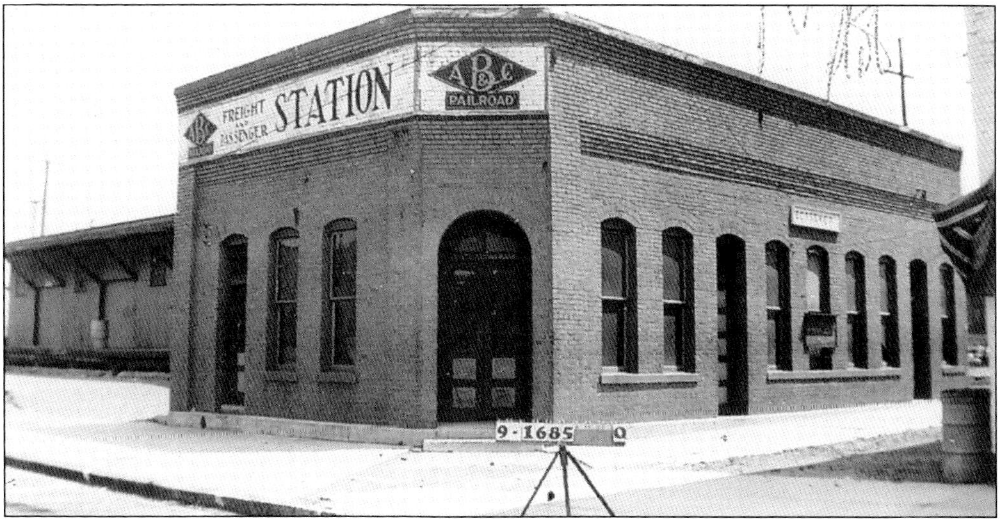

The AB&C railroad passed through Reeders Gap at Muscoda, and then ran atop a berm paralleling Fourteenth Street, and crossed the AGS tracks and Carolina Avenue on a curved trestle. The AB&C passenger station and hotel buildings still stand on First Avenue between Nineteenth and Twentieth Streets.

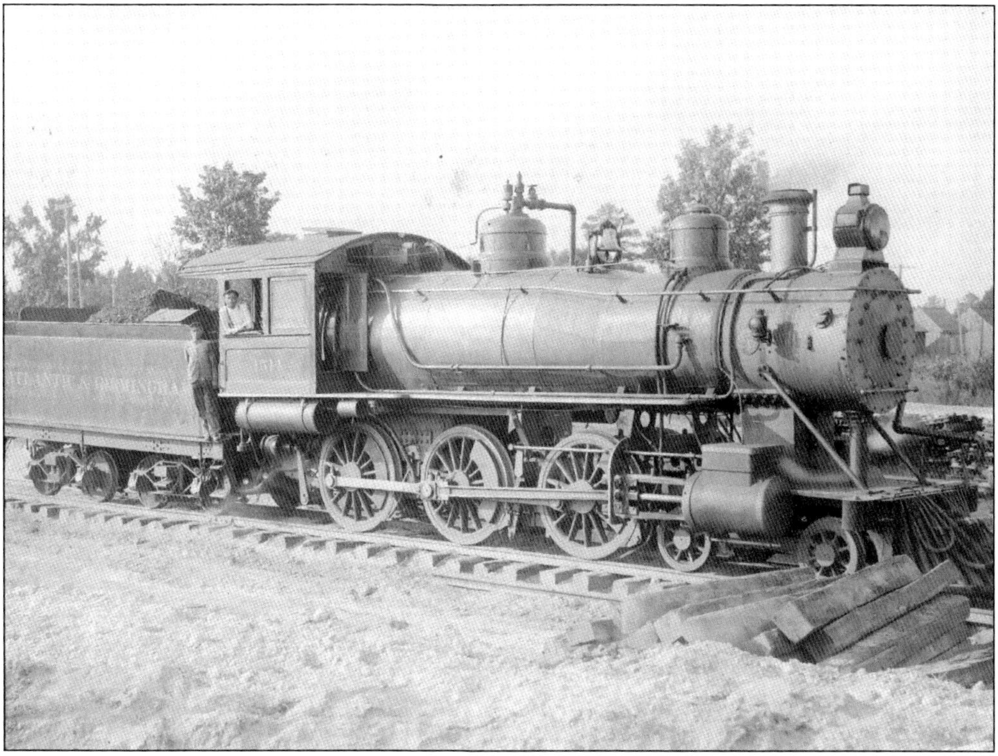

Following several expansions in 1903 and 1904, the Atlantic & Birmingham Railway Company purchased several new locomotives. This 10-wheeler 1514 photographed near Bessemer was one of the most powerful that the A&B (later Atlanta, Birmingham, & Coast) bought new.

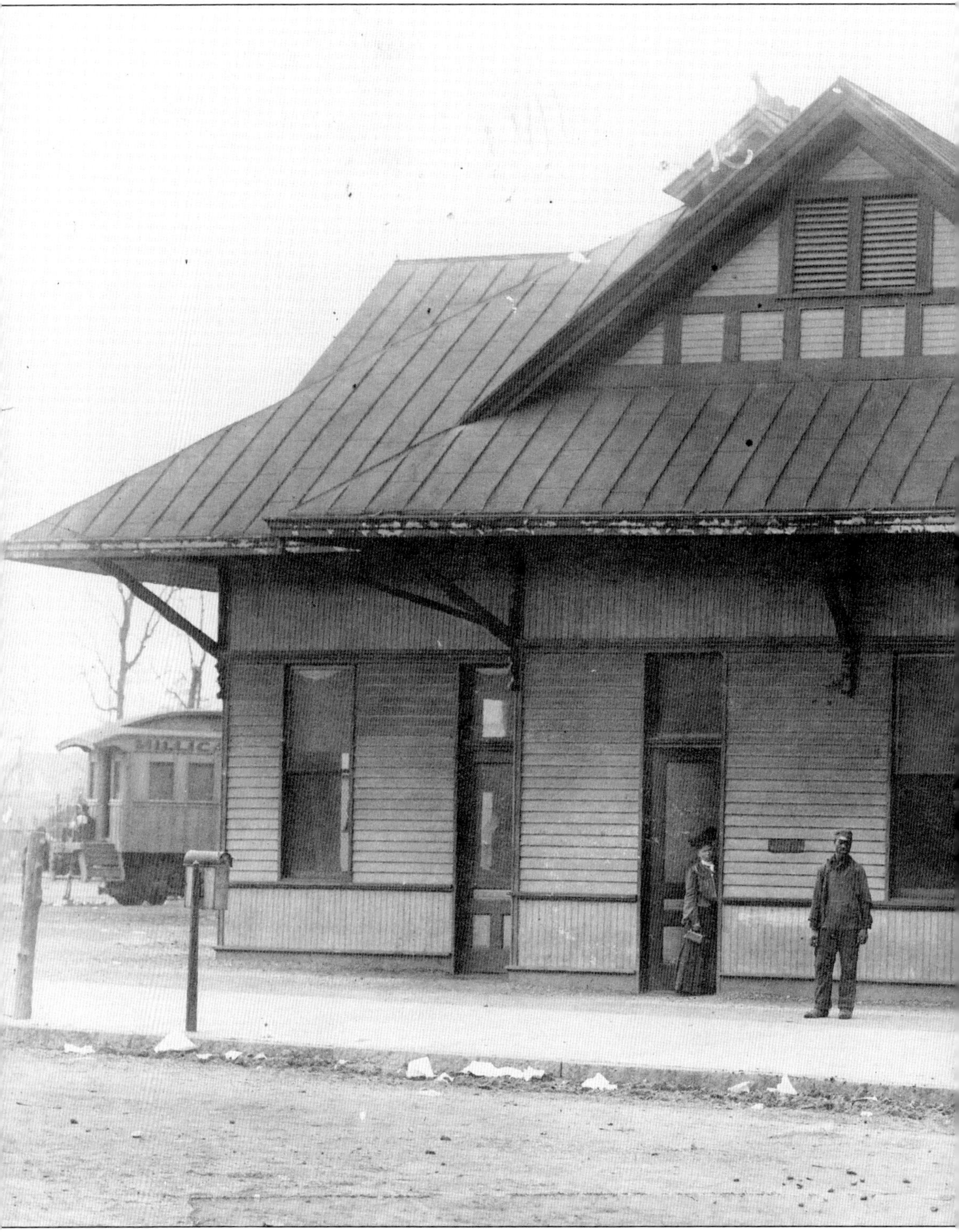

The Louisville and Nashville Railroad depot was built at the corner of Third Avenue and Twentieth Street in the 1880s. This view shows the building and employees in 1907. Within weeks of

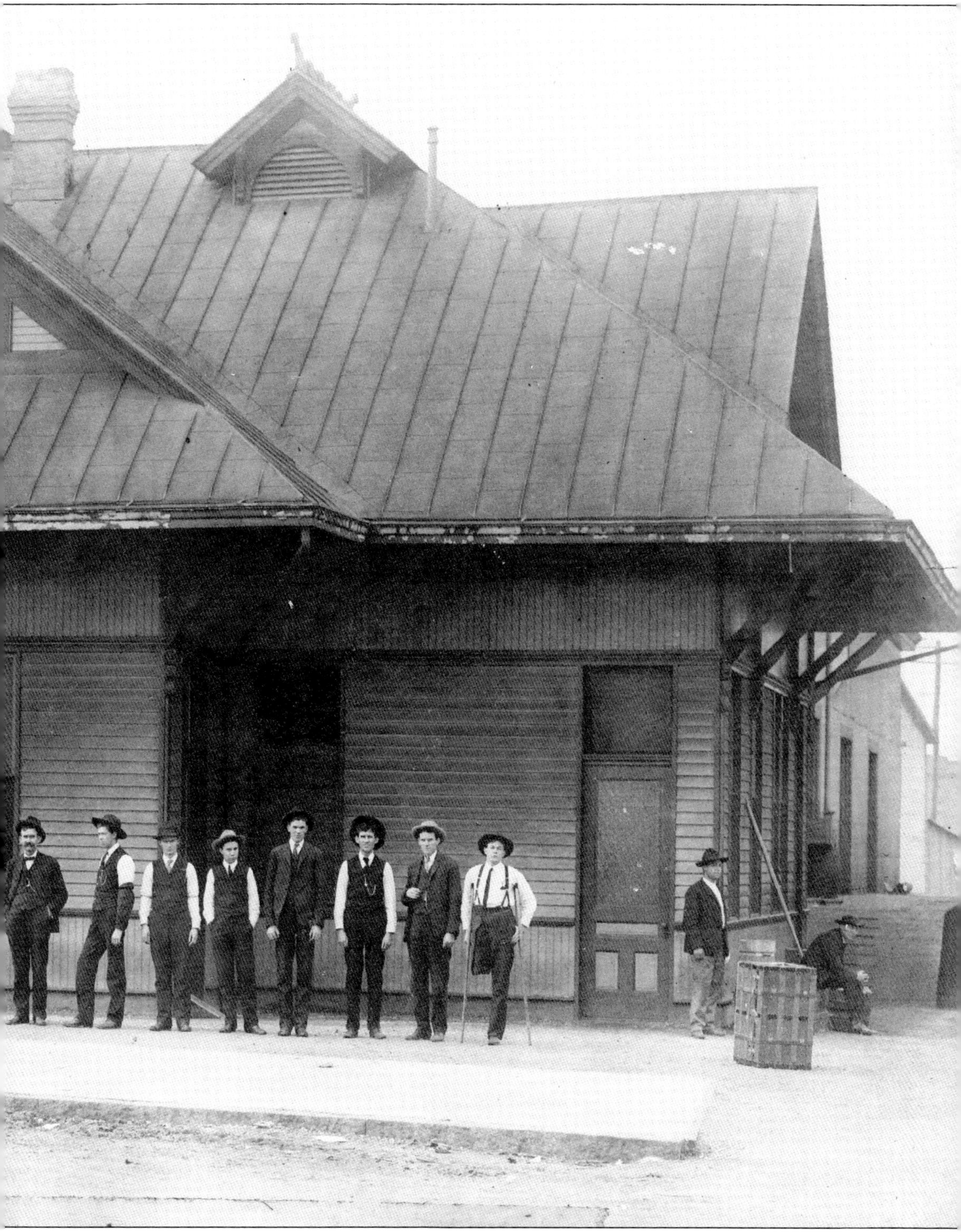

Bessemer's founding in 1887, the L&N completed lines then known as "the three Bs"—Bessemer to Blocton Junction, Bessemer to Boyles, and Bessemer to Brookwood.

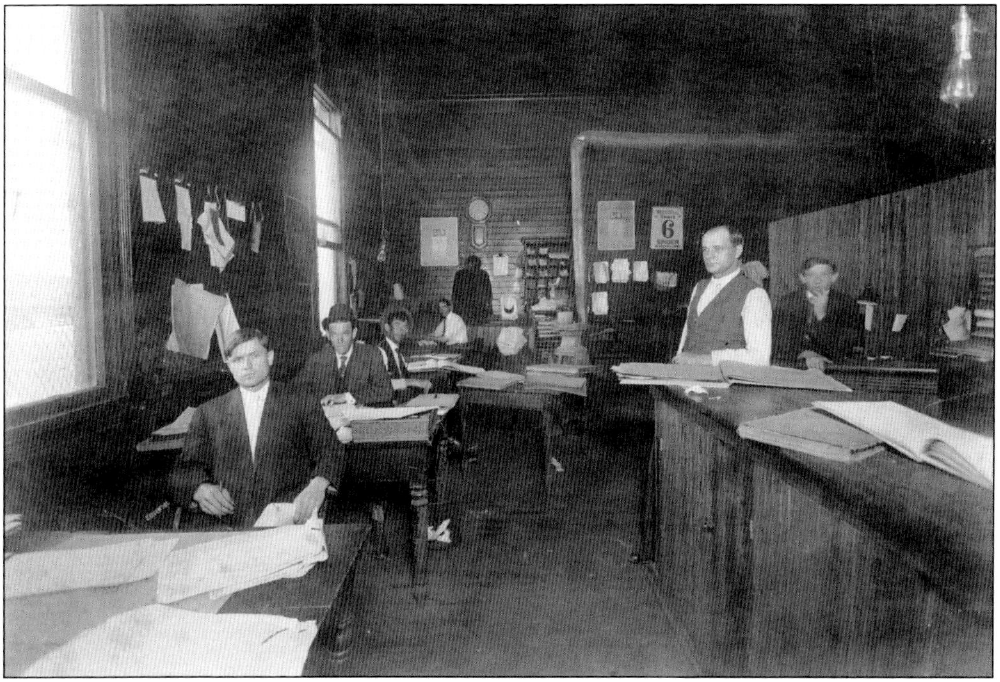

In addition to passenger service, the Louisville and Nashville Railroad depot managed freight shipments. The view above shows the interior and employees of the freight office in April 1910. The 1925 photograph below shows L&N management in the "new" freight office completed around 1915: chief clerk Joseph Willis Wiles, agent John McEniry, and executive secretary Lucille Hamner. McEniry served as Bessemer's mayor from 1895 to 1899.

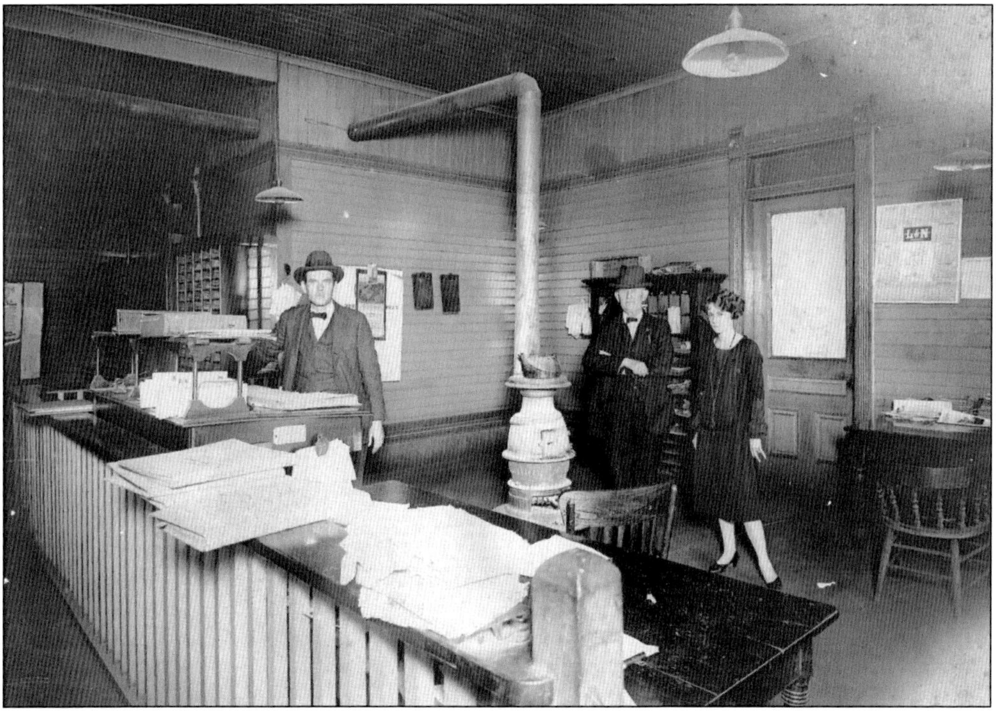

Four

BUSINESSES

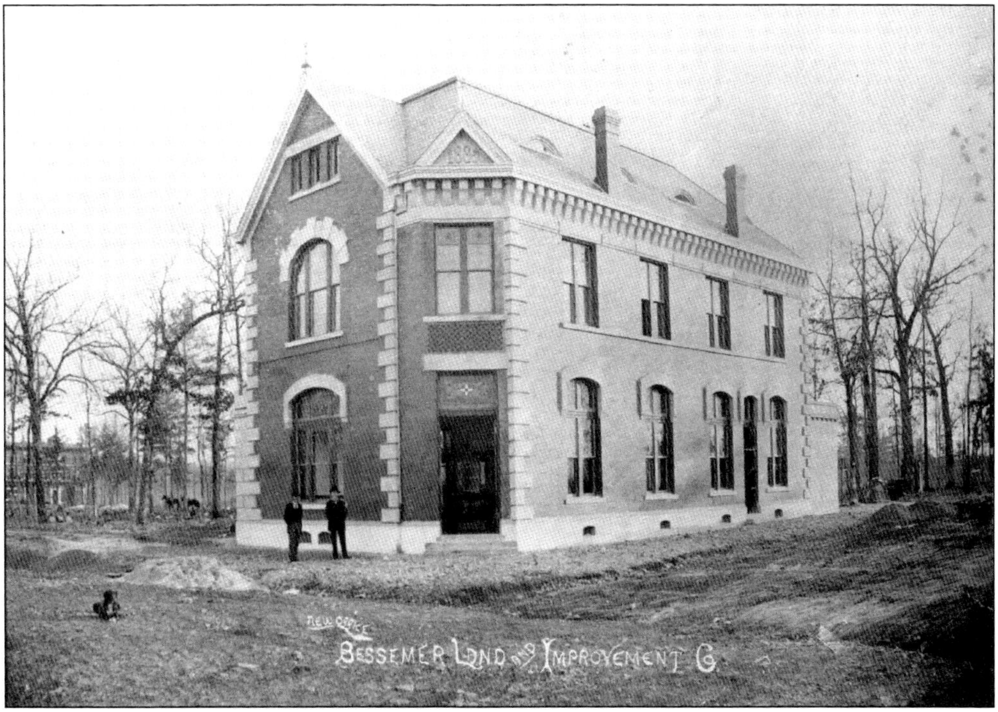

Henry DeBardeleben and Andrew M. Adger of Birmingham, along with David Roberts, Moses E. Lopez, and A.T. Smythe of Charleston, South Carolina, chartered the Bessemer Land and Improvement Company (also known as the Town Company) on January 7, 1887. The company used cash bonuses, company stock, land grants, and loans to attract businesses to Bessemer. Some of their earliest successes included the Bessemer Rolling Mills, Bessemer Fire Brick Company, and Howard-Harrison Iron Company (now US Pipe). The company also built the first public schoolhouse in the city and set aside lots for churches. The Bessemer Land office building, shown above in 1889, was based on a design by G.M. Torgerson and stood at the corner of Nineteenth Street and Fourth Avenue. (Birmingham Public Library archives, File No. 1556.20.61.)

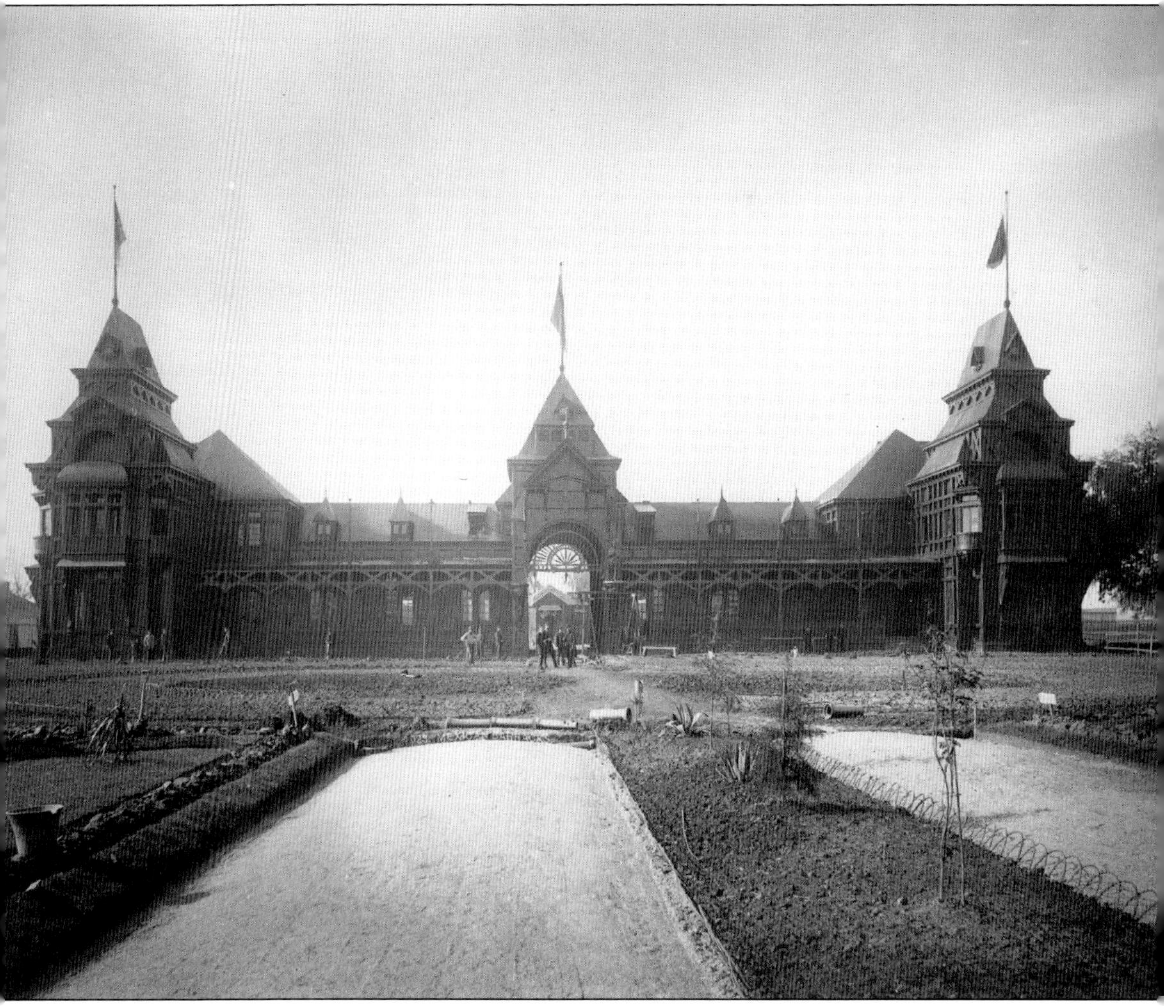

DeBardeleben purchased buildings from the 1884 World's Fair site in New Orleans and had them dismantled, shipped by rail, and reconstructed in Bessemer. The most notable of these was the fabulous Queen Anne–style Montezuma Hotel. The three-story building had been part of Mexico's entry at the World's Industrial and Cotton Centennial Exposition. DeBardeleben situated the timber-frame structure in the highlands overlooking the town, on Arlington Avenue between Twenty-third and Twenty-fourth Streets. Several town founders called the hotel home and it hosted industrialists and financiers brought in on L&N excursions to see the booming town. Here, the building is shown in New Orleans before it was dismantled. (Historic New Orleans Collection, accession No. 1982.127.94.)

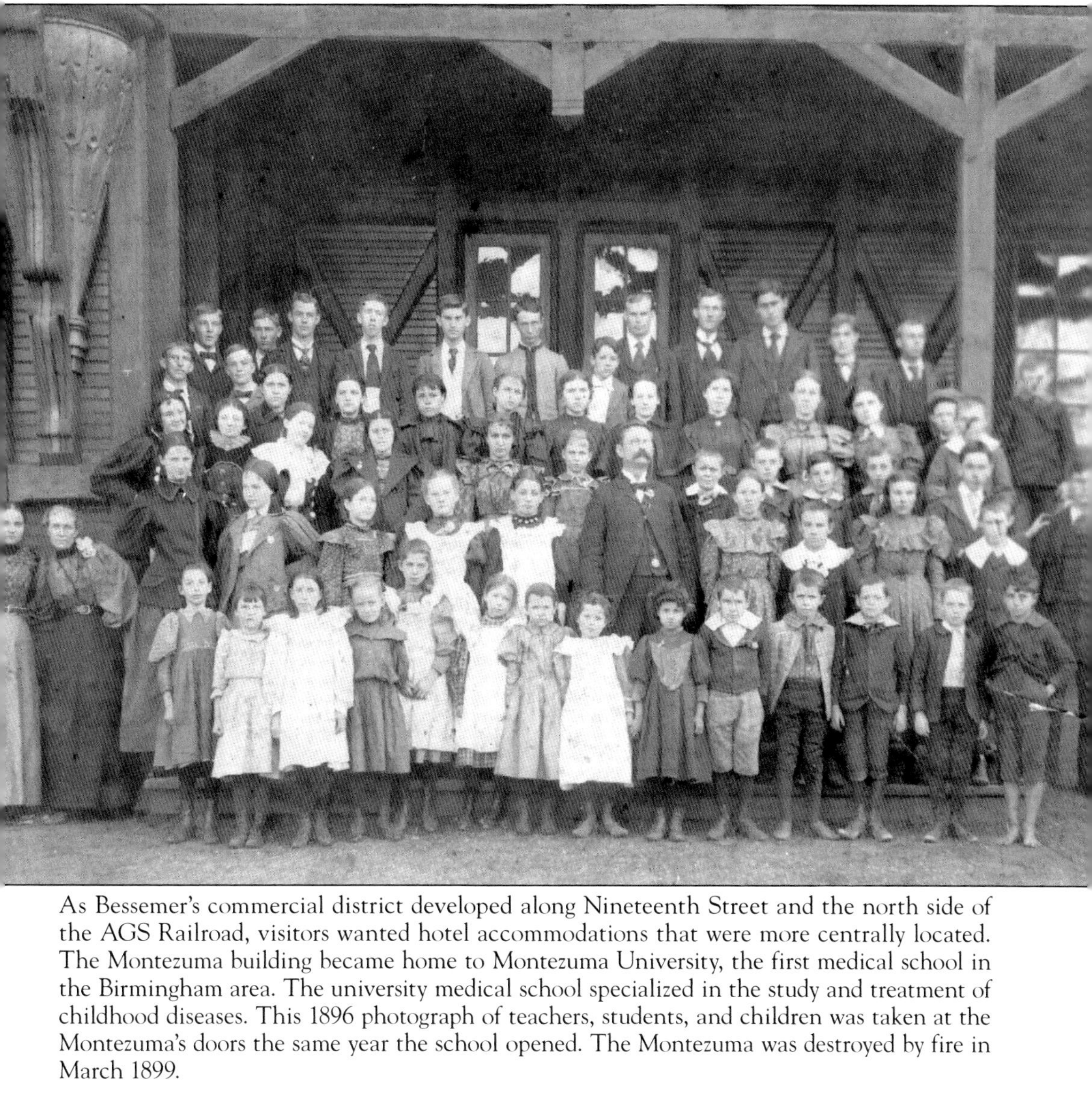

As Bessemer's commercial district developed along Nineteenth Street and the north side of the AGS Railroad, visitors wanted hotel accommodations that were more centrally located. The Montezuma building became home to Montezuma University, the first medical school in the Birmingham area. The university medical school specialized in the study and treatment of childhood diseases. This 1896 photograph of teachers, students, and children was taken at the Montezuma's doors the same year the school opened. The Montezuma was destroyed by fire in March 1899.

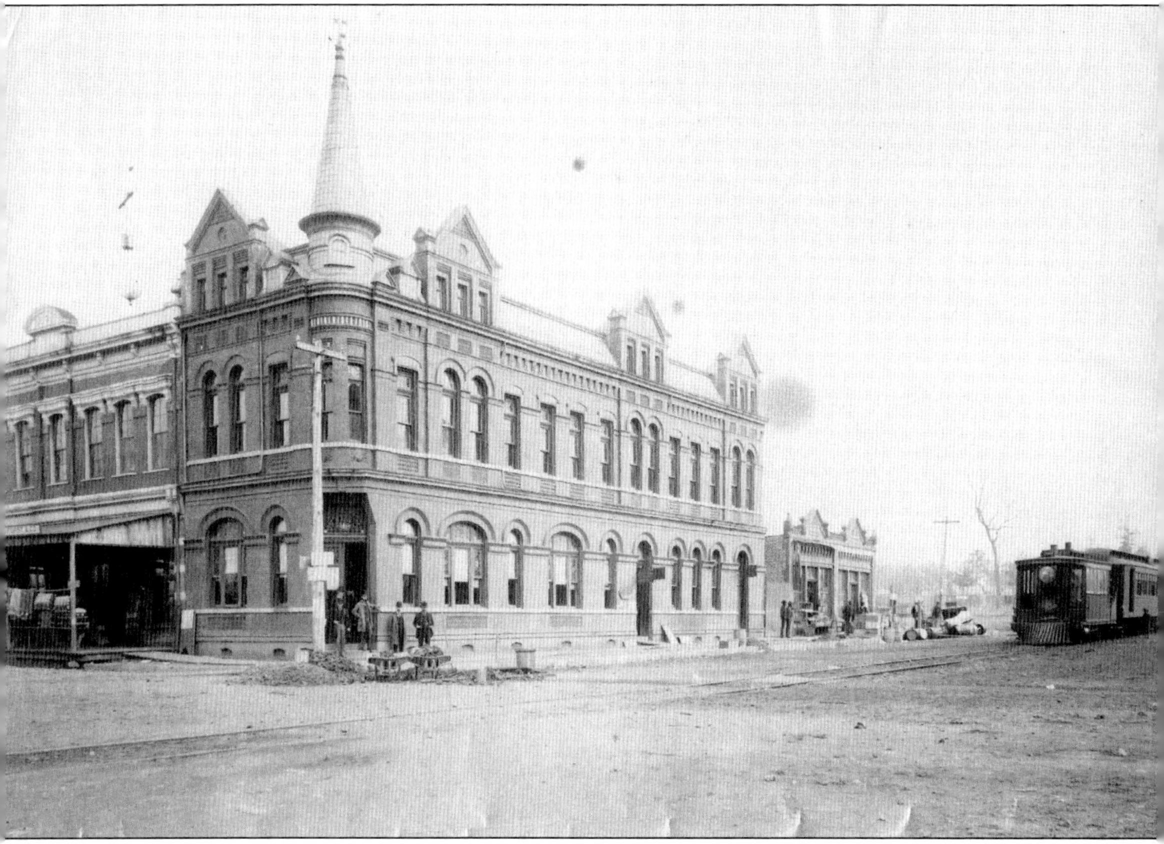

William Berney, treasurer of the Bessemer Land and Improvement Company, hired G.M. Torgerson to design a business block and home for the Berney Bank of Bessemer. Torgerson, designer of the Cotton Centennial Exposition building, created the beautiful, red brick Berney Brothers Block at the corner of Nineteenth Street and Second Avenue. In this early view, Forst Mercantile Company can be seen to the left of the Berney building, and the Dummy Line is approaching the building on the right. (W.S. Hoole Special Collections Library, the University of Alabama.)

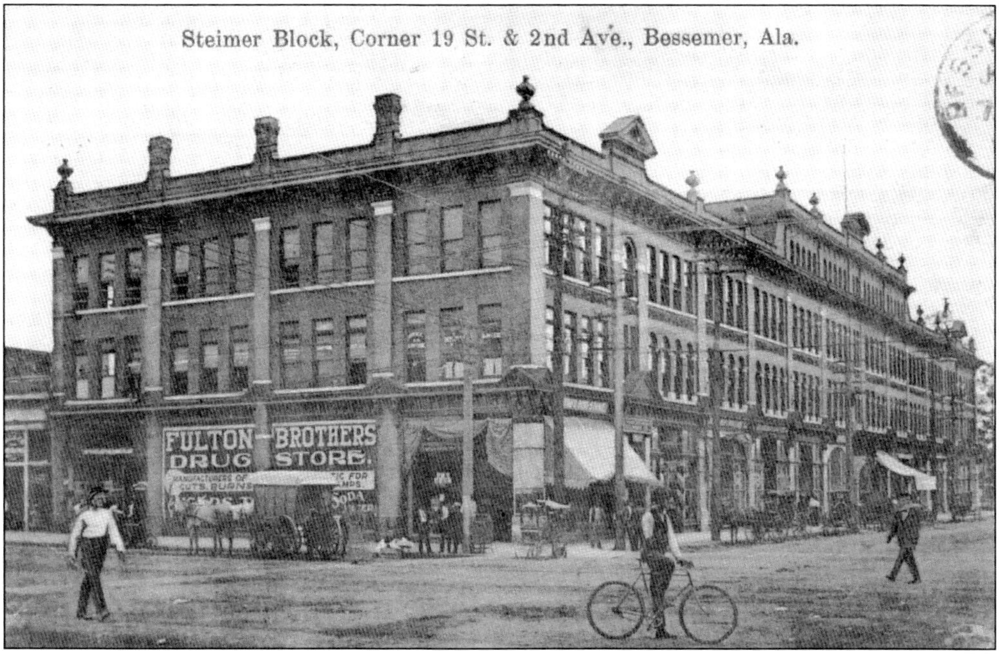

A group of South Carolina investors built the Charleston Block at the corner of Nineteenth Street and Second Avenue in the late 1880s. By 1900, Birmingham bankers, the Steiner Brothers, bought the building and renamed it the Steiner Block. It remained the largest office building in Bessemer for many years. This postcard view from about 1910 misidentifies it as the "Steimer" Block. (Author's collection.)

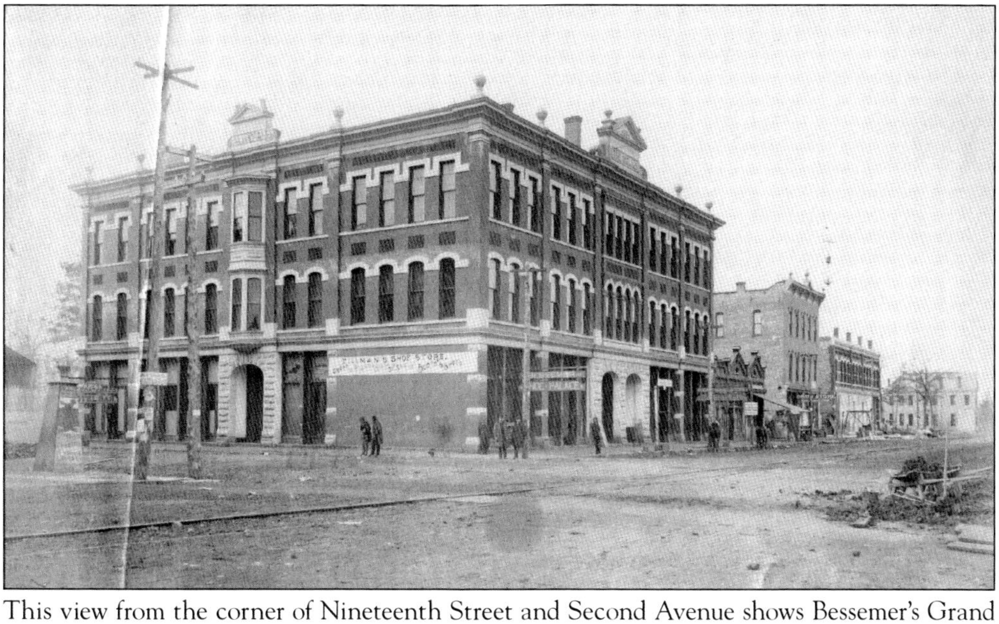

This view from the corner of Nineteenth Street and Second Avenue shows Bessemer's Grand Hotel. The Grand was opened in 1887 and stood until 1987. During its 100 years, the building was home to many shops, the Gary Hotel, and the Grand Theater. The building at the far right of the photograph is the Bessemer Land and Improvement Office. (W.S. Hoole Special Collections Library, the University of Alabama.)

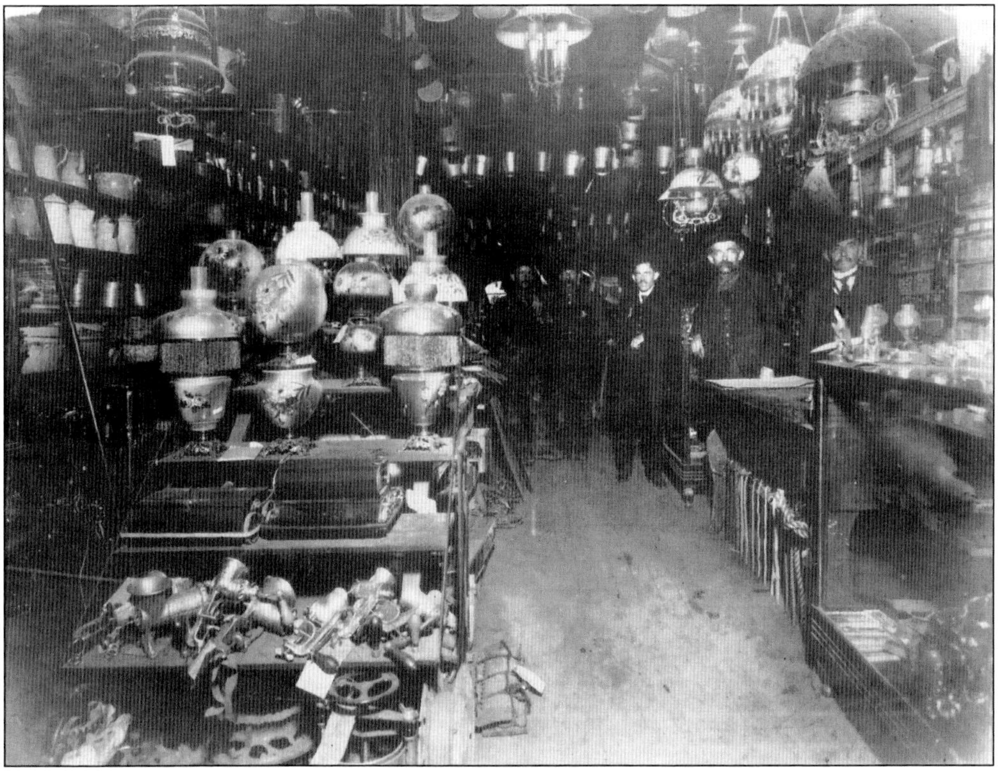

The Bessemer Cornice Works was one of the city's earliest businesses and the start of two of the area's longest lasting. W.J. Long opened the company in 1887, producing tin and iron roofing, storefronts, cornices, and ornamental metal work. By 1900, the Cornice Works was also serving as a carriage and wagon repository and selling stoves and household furnishings, as seen above. In 1890, the cornice works was developed into the general contracting firm Sullivan, Long, and Haggerty. The company merged with I.A. Lewis's hardware store and changed its name to Long-Lewis Supply Company. The buggy wagon department became Alabama's first Ford dealership, Long-Lewis Ford. Below, Gordon Fritz, A.L. Saunders, Marvin Vassar, and H.B. Barrett pose with a Ford Model A in the Long-Lewis Hardware auto parts department.

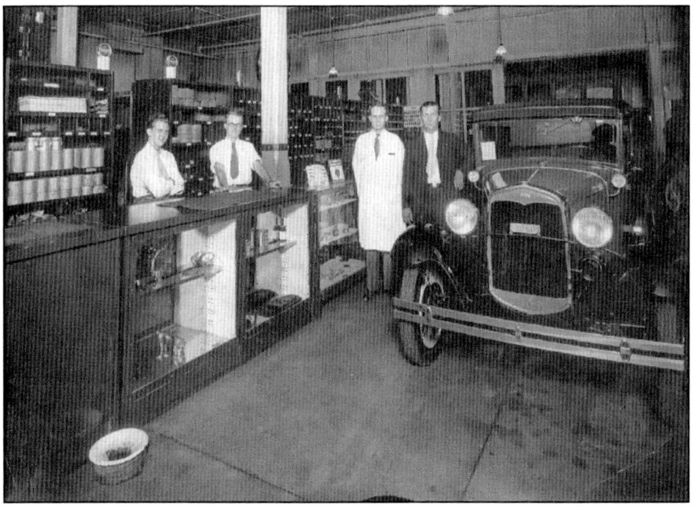

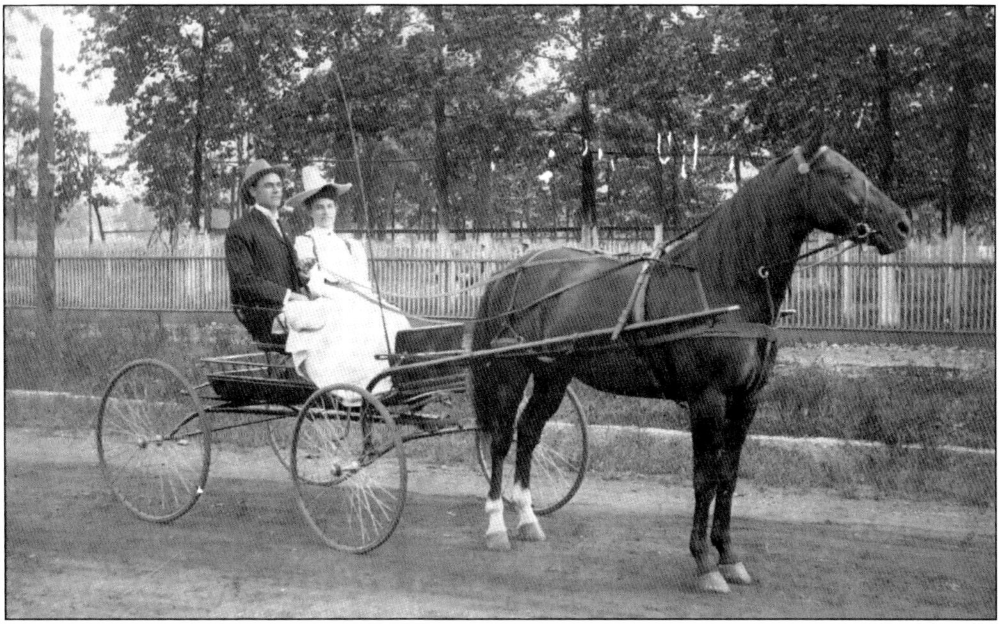

Barton Patridge and Amelia Renner were photographed in Patridge's carriage on September 14, 1905, before they married. Barton died young, leaving Amelia to raise two children and help her family manage their business, J&P Renner General merchants.

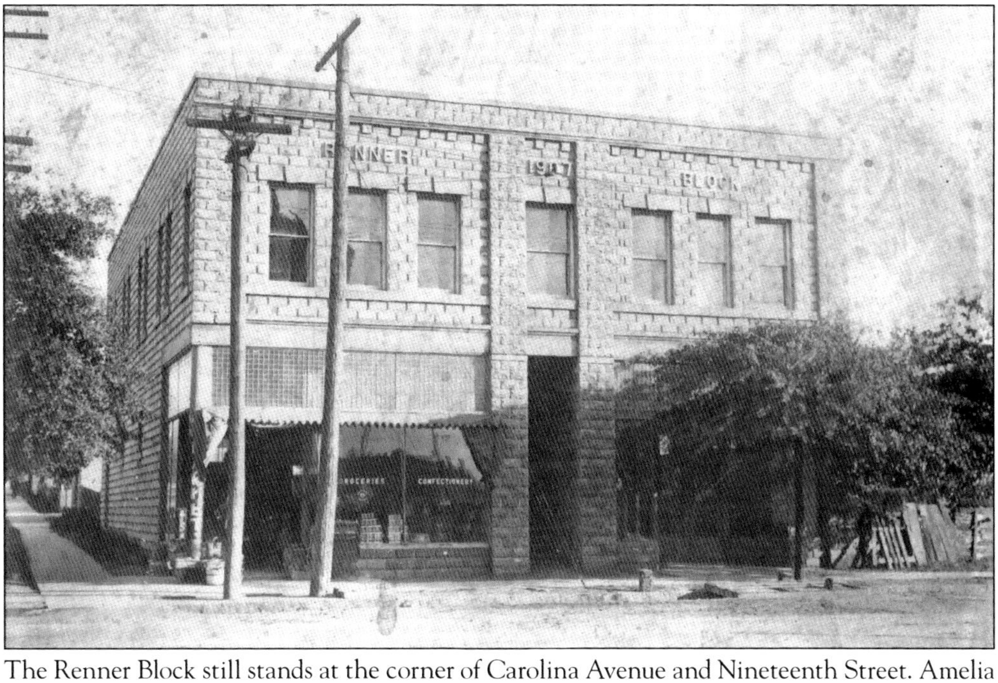

The Renner Block still stands at the corner of Carolina Avenue and Nineteenth Street. Amelia ran the family store here for many years. This building was the second Renner Block in Bessemer. The first was a three-story brick building located two blocks west on Carolina at Seventeenth Street. The older building burned in what is remembered as one of the most stubborn fires the fire department fought. The temperature that night was 10 degrees below zero, and most of the fireplugs in town were frozen.

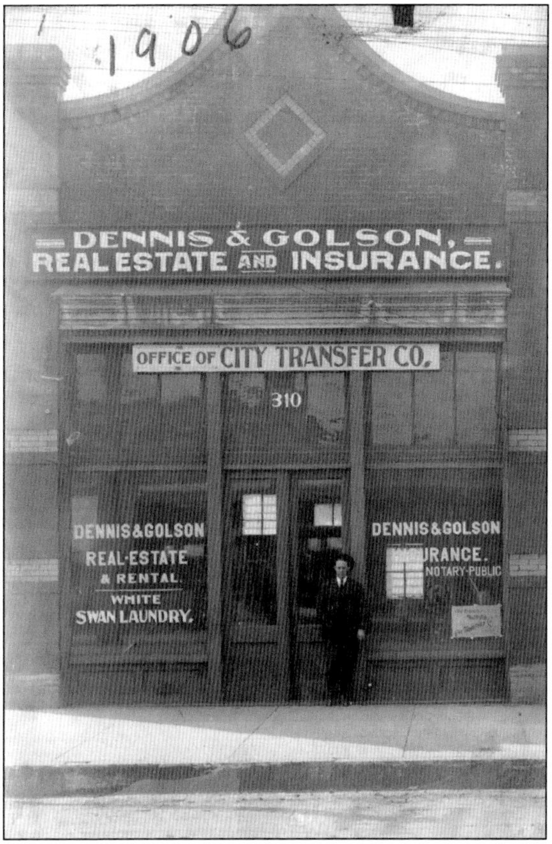

William H. Dennis and William Pendleton "W.P." Golson bought out Percy T. Whilden & Company and started Dennis and Golson Real Estate and Insurance in the late 1890s. Before starting their partnership, Dennis had been an agent of the Southern Express Company and Golson learned the real estate business working for Charles F. Hard. Here, Golson stands in front of the company office on Nineteenth Street.

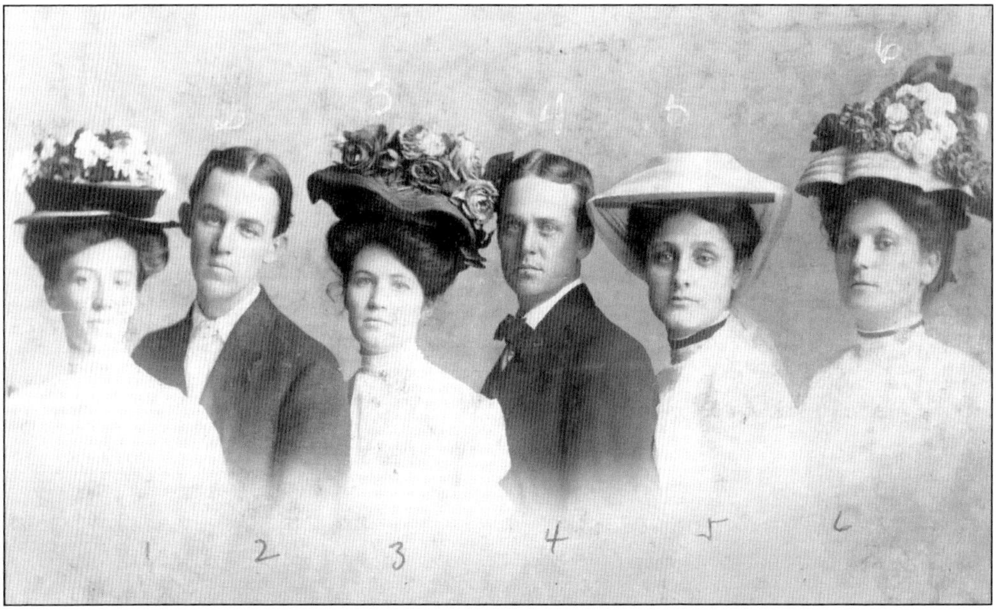

This portrait of young Bessemer residents in their finery includes, from left to right, Rhoda Dennis (wife of William H. Dennis), Leo Golson, Mrs. I.J. Perkins, William Pendleton Golson (partner in Dennis and Golson Real Estate and Insurance), Mrs. J.C. Berry, and Mrs. W.P. Golson.

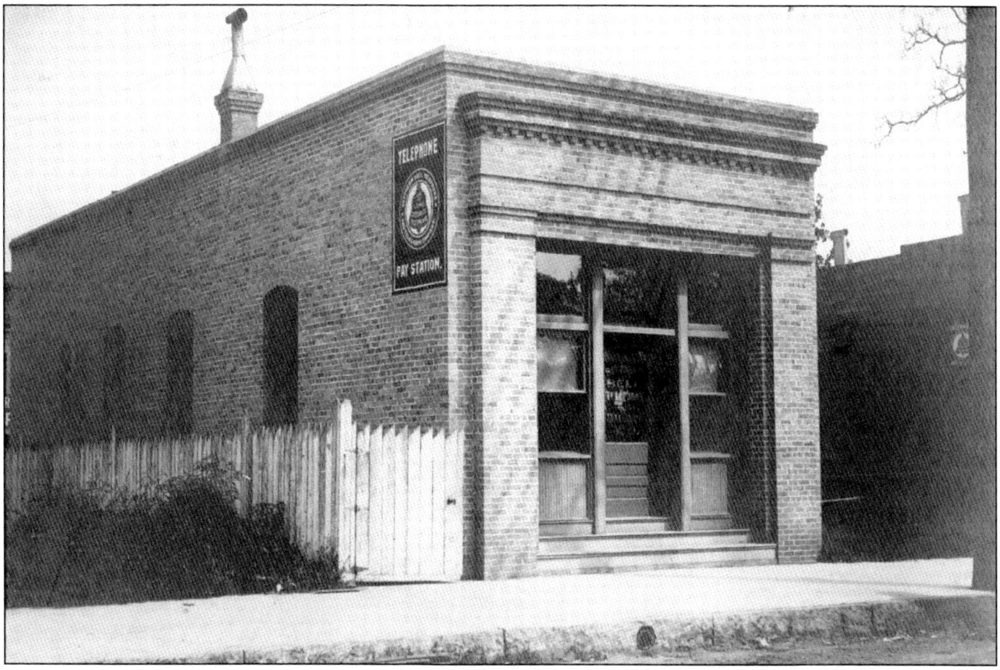

The Southern Bell Telephone and Telegraph Building is located on Third Avenue between Eighteenth and Nineteenth Streets. Telephone operators connected calls using manual exchange switchboards with cords and buttons. The operators called these "cordboards." Below, chief operator Minnie Ward is standing at the desk. The four nearest operators are, from left to right, Nora Bell Salter, Kate Givens, unidentified, and Audrey F. Burnett. The Southern Bell building, renamed the "Judy Building," has been beautifully restored and now houses law offices.

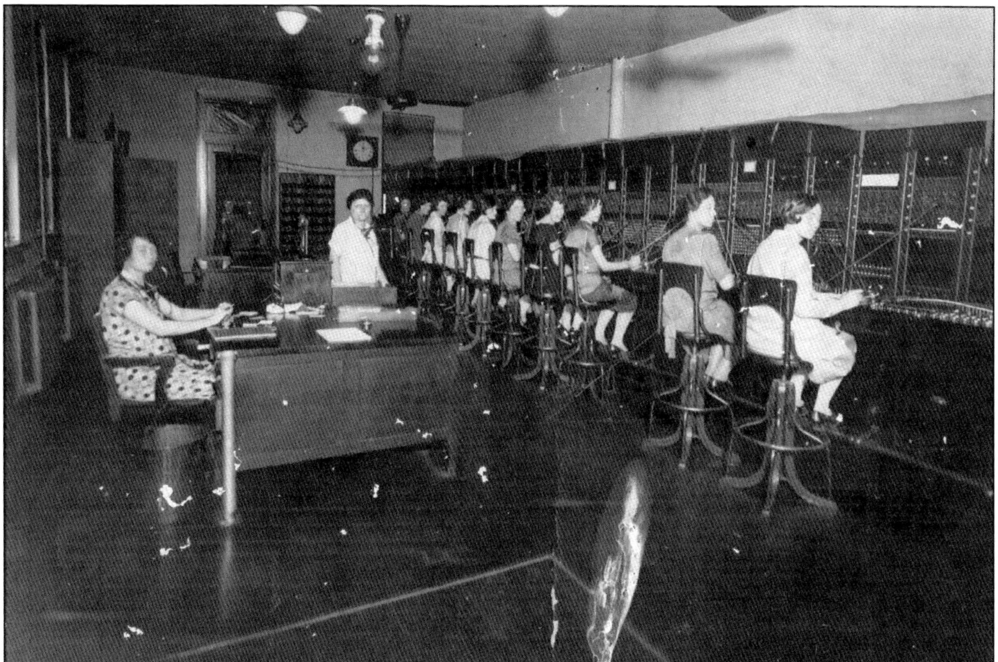

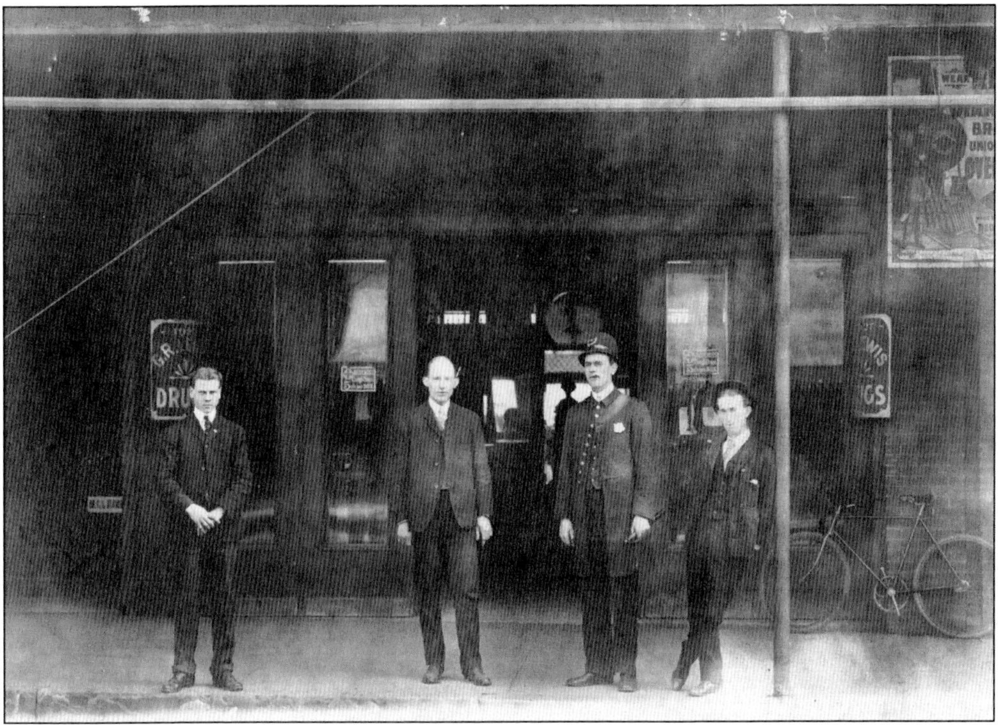

William Harper "W.H." Lewis, Dr. George Roland Lewis, Bessemer Police Officer Glenn, and Harry Grigsby stand in front of G.R. Lewis Drugs in 1897. That same year W.H. and George formed a partnership and changed the company name to W.H. Lewis & Bro Druggists. The company was located on Second Avenue near Nineteenth Street.

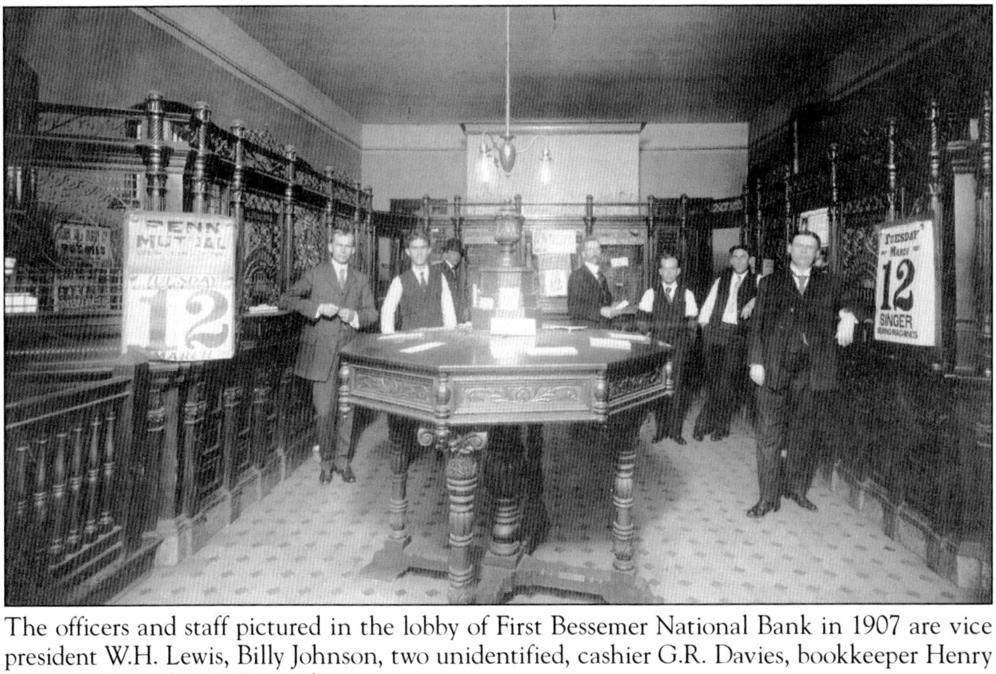

The officers and staff pictured in the lobby of First Bessemer National Bank in 1907 are vice president W.H. Lewis, Billy Johnson, two unidentified, cashier G.R. Davies, bookkeeper Henry Hurd, and president R.F. Smith.

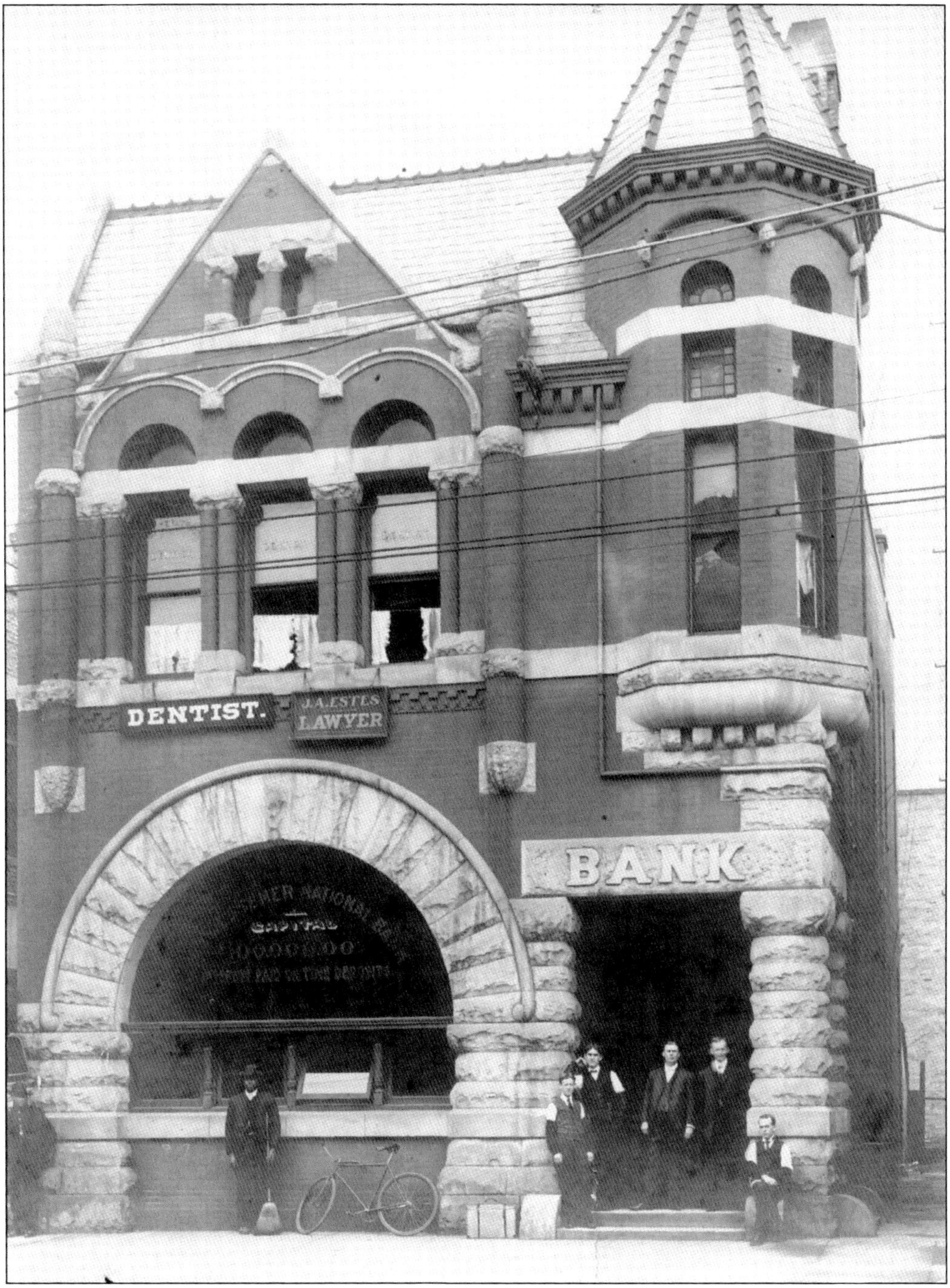

In 1890, the Bessemer Savings Bank was organized and began construction of this building on Nineteenth Street between Second and Third Avenues. By 1907, when this photograph was made, the building was home to First Bessemer National Bank and the office of James Albert Estes, who began practicing law in Bessemer in 1893. From left to right, Billy Johnson, Henry Hurd, R.F. Smith, W.H. Lewis, and George Davies pose in the bank doorway.

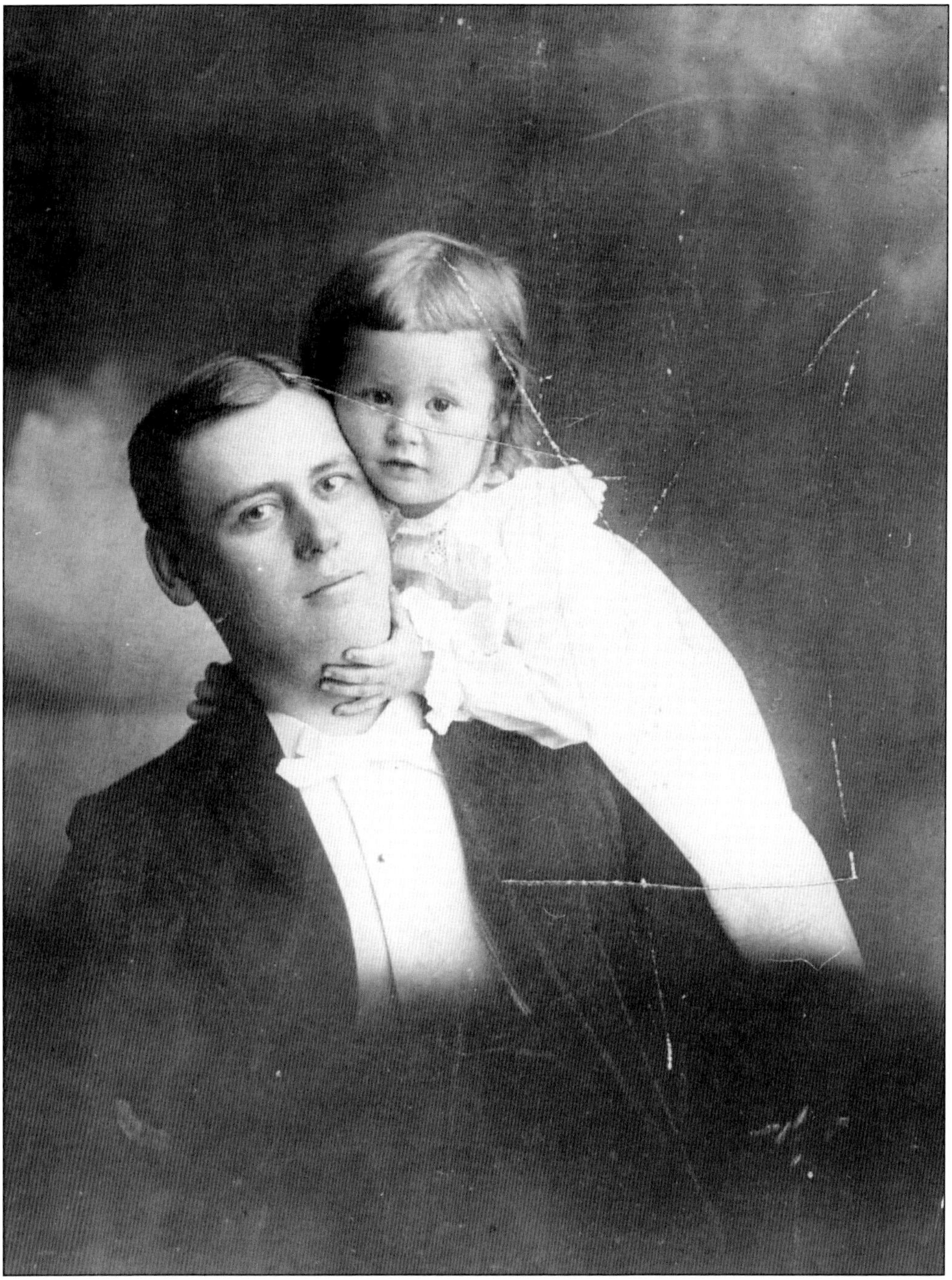

This portrait of W.H. Lewis with his daughter Marguerite was originally published in a May 18, 1901, special edition of the *Bessemer Weekly* newspaper. Lewis was born in Giles County, Tennessee, and grew up in Athens, Alabama. He attended Huntsville High School and apprenticed at Dr. Moreland's Drug Store in Athens. He married Exor May of Bessemer in June 1896.

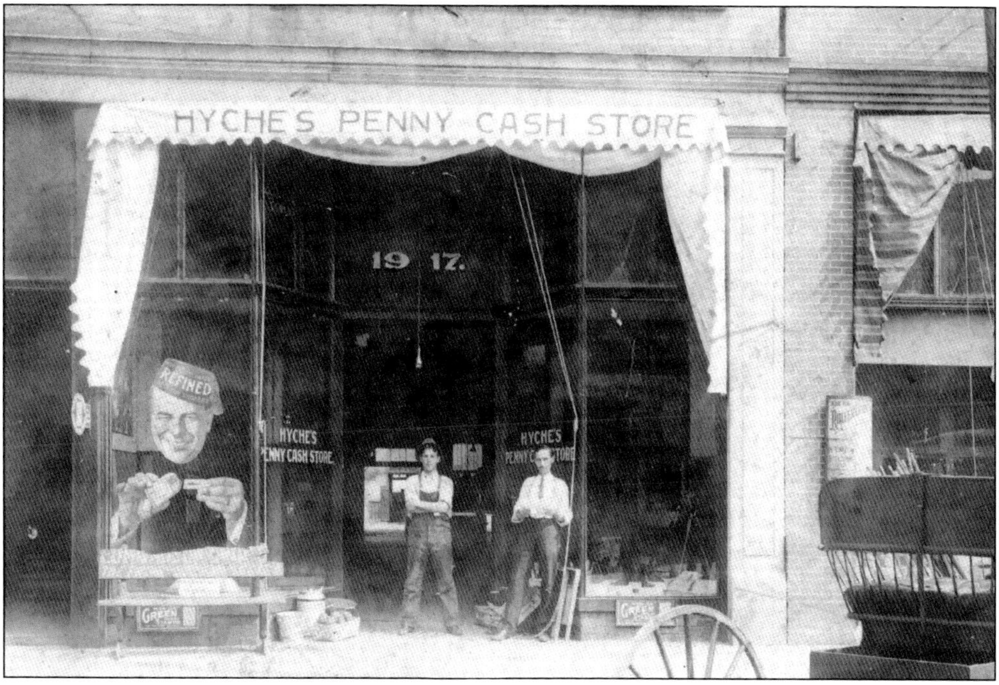

Walter and Ebb Hyche pose in front of Hyche's Penny Cash Store on Third Avenue between Nineteenth and Twentieth Streets. This building still stands next door to the McAdory Building and is part of a furniture store. Hyche's was typical of many dry-goods stores of the period, selling everything from tobacco and sweet potatoes to washboards.

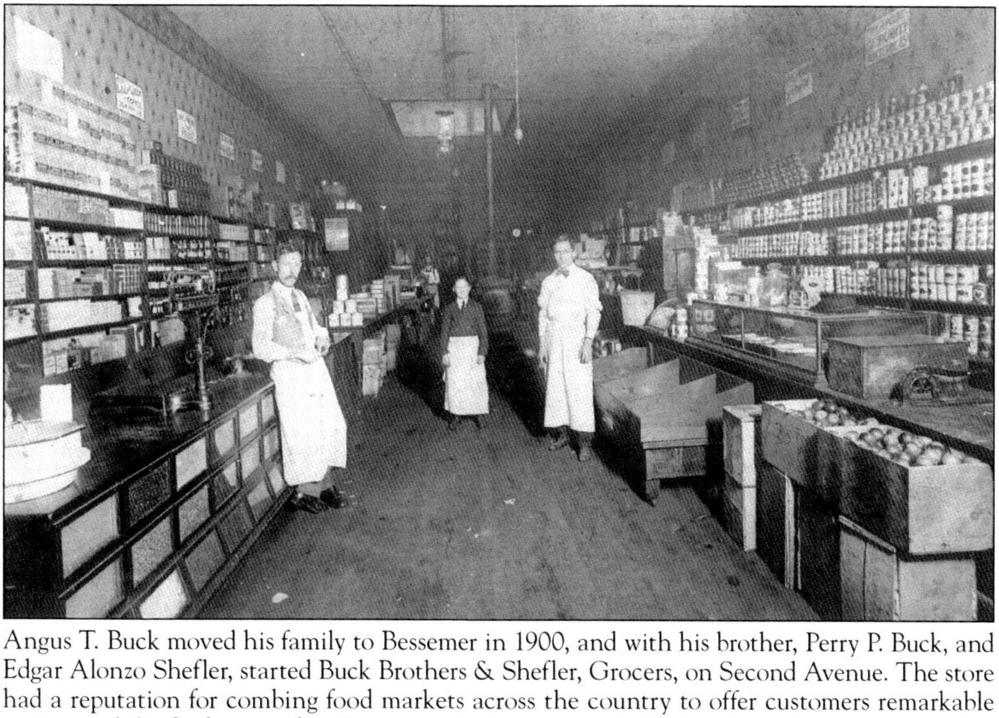

Angus T. Buck moved his family to Bessemer in 1900, and with his brother, Perry P. Buck, and Edgar Alonzo Shefler, started Buck Brothers & Shefler, Grocers, on Second Avenue. The store had a reputation for combing food markets across the country to offer customers remarkable variety and the freshest produce in town.

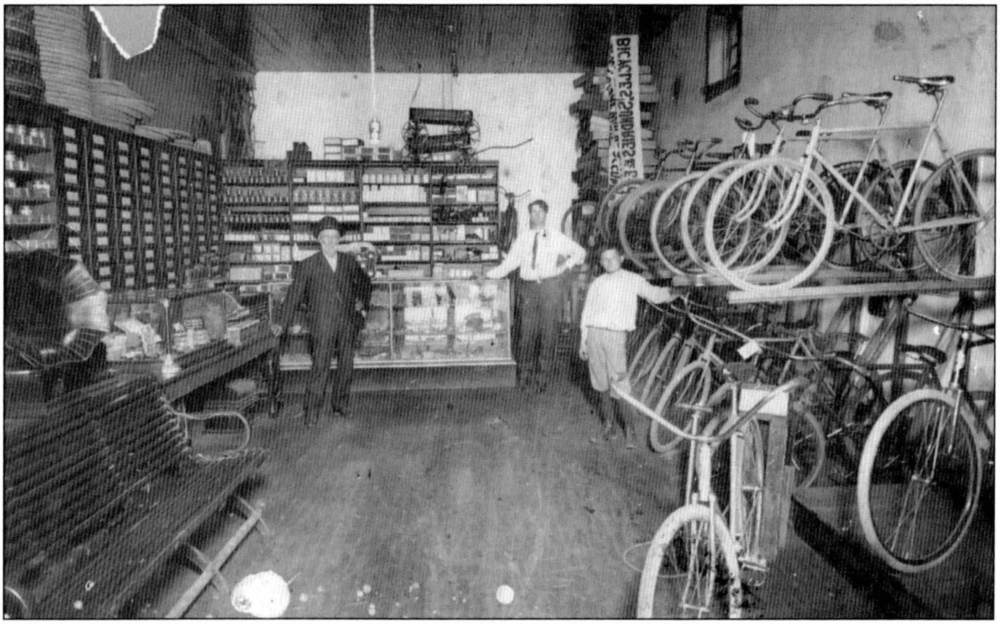

Houston "Hou" Montgomery Bryant (left) founded Bryant' s Bicycle Merchant, Repair, and Rental about 1895. By 1900, his bicycle shop on Second Avenue in the Steiner Block had grown to one of the most successful in North Alabama. Hou's son, Jasper "Jap" Bryant (center) took over the family bicycle business and eventually served as mayor of Bessemer from 1935–1947 and again from 1950 to 1956.

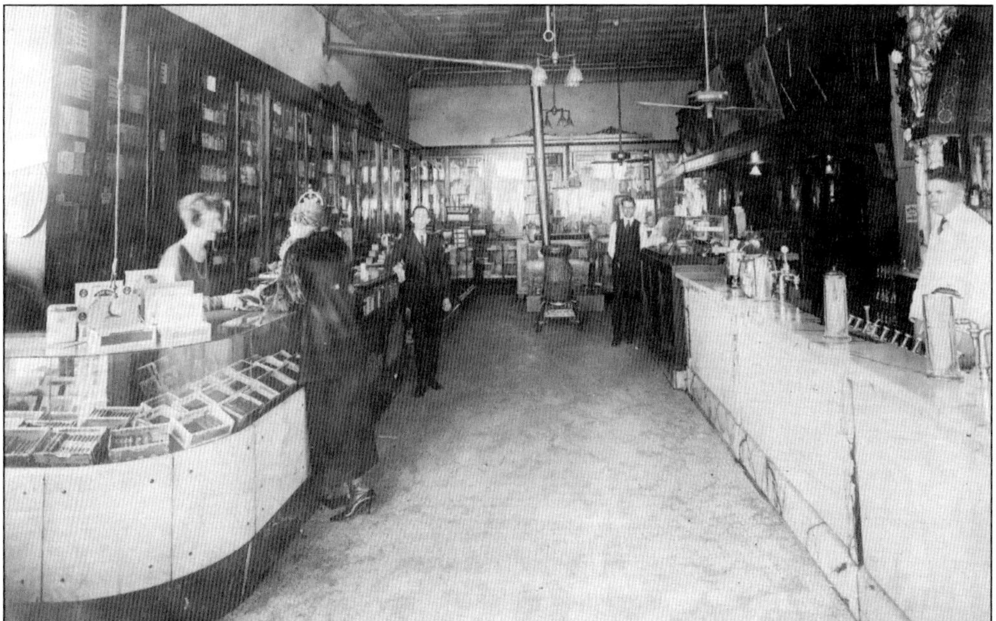

Turner Read Fulton founded Fulton Brothers Drugstore in 1900. By 1910 when this photograph was made, Fulton had sold the business to the McDowell Brothers, but they kept the Fulton name. Pictured from left to right are 16-year-old Daisy Hayes Pridmore talking to a customer; George McDowell; Walter McDowell; and an unidentified soda jerk.

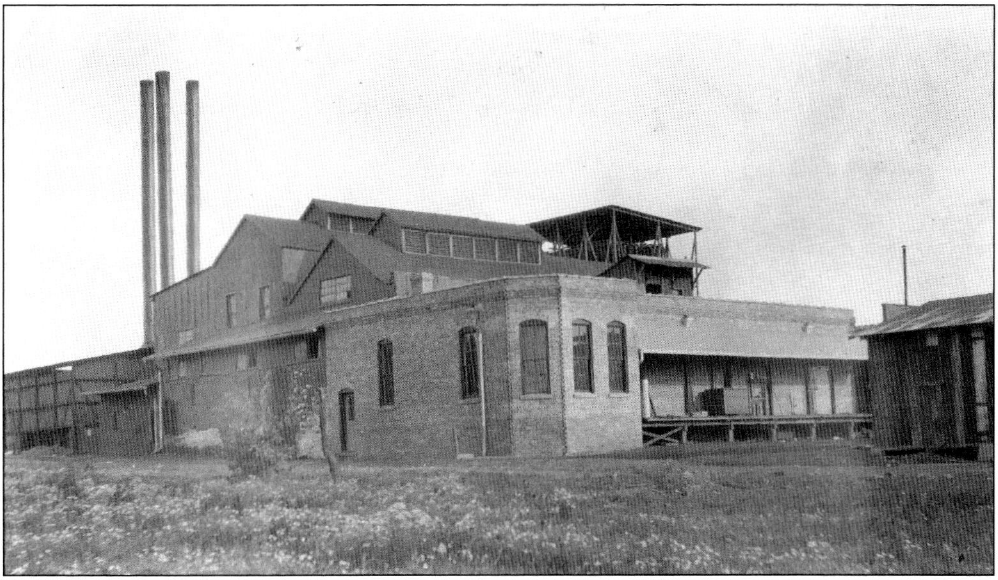

Bessemer Ice Delivery Company (later Bessemer Ice & Coal Company) had the capacity to produce 18 tons of ice each day and store 500 tons. Ice from the plant was shipped throughout the South by the train carload. One building from the original 1890 plant, above, still stands at the corner of Arlington Avenue and Twenty-fifth Street. The company also delivered ice and coal to businesses and residents in the Bessemer area, using mule-drawn carts, below. Early company advertisements note that they specialized in "Famous Cahaba Coal" and "Superior Export Montevallo Coal."

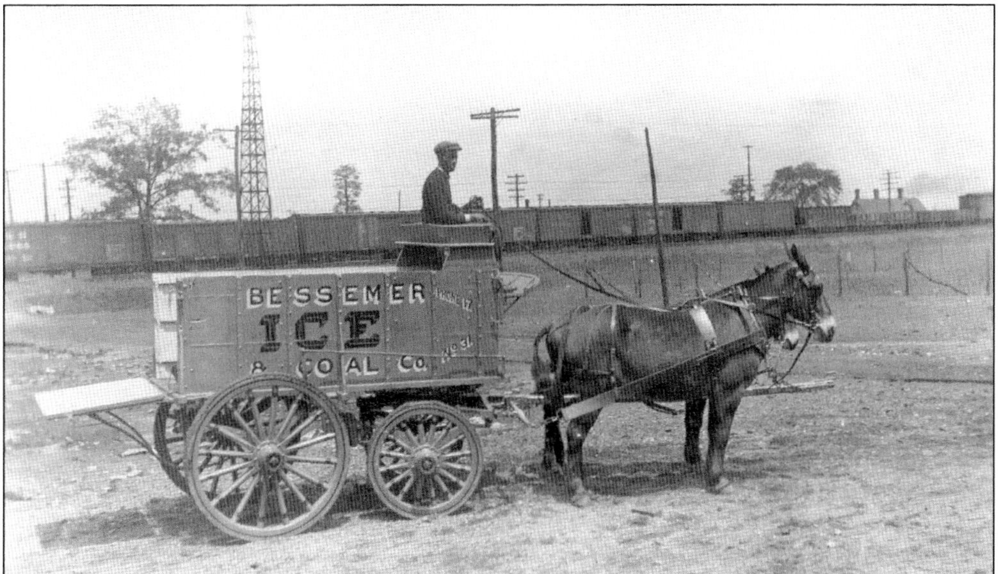

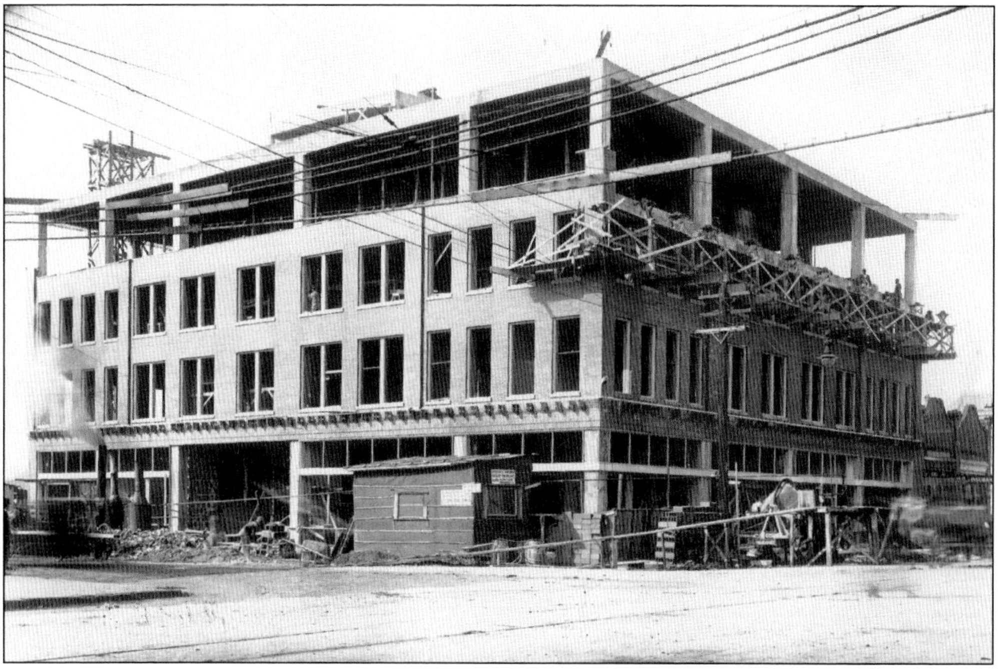

The Rebie Hall building, an 1890 office block, burned in March 1914, leaving a large, empty lot on the corner of Nineteenth Street and Third Avenue. Above, a February 1915 photograph captures construction of the Realty Building on the Rebie site. Below, a postcard view from 1916 shows the finished building with its signature Bright Star Café sign on the Nineteenth Street side. Lewis Read Drug Store was located on the Third Avenue side of the building. In recent years, the Realty Building has been extensively renovated and still provides office space for Bessemer businesses.

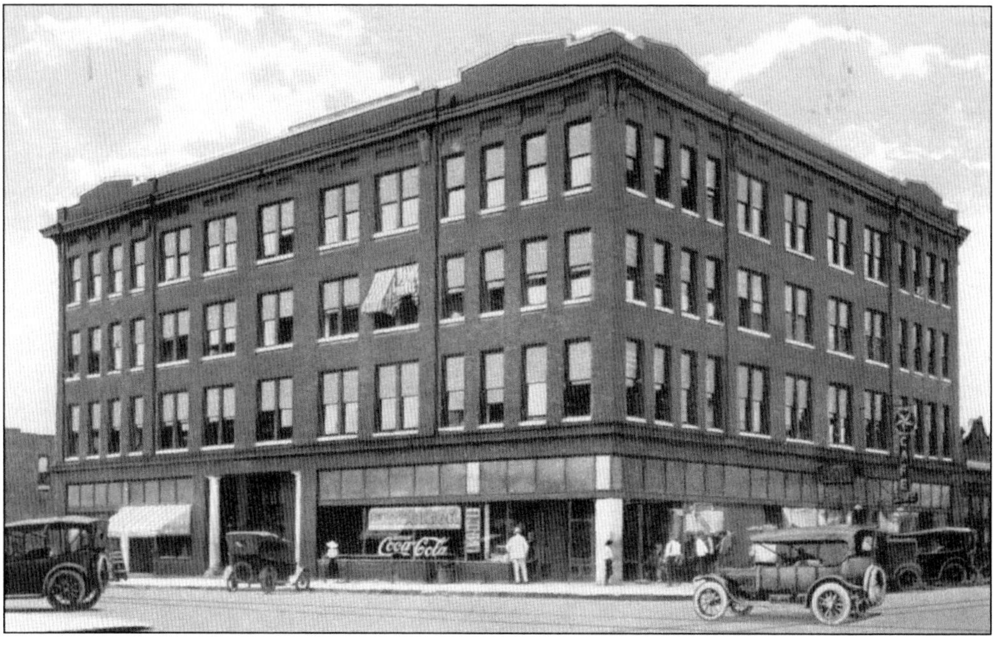

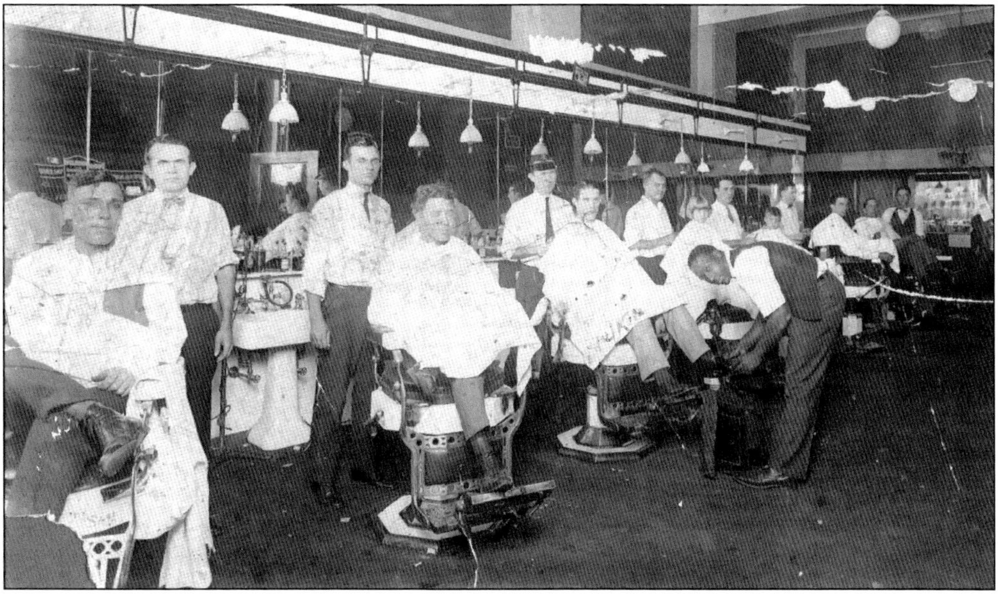

The Realty Barber Shop was in the basement of the Realty Building. On this day in 1926, some notable citizens were in the chairs: Sam Romano (first chair), who opened a grocery and fruit market in 1889—the Romano Block still stands at the corner of Carolina Avenue and Twentieth Street; Jim Mulkin (third chair); Pete Parsons (sixth chair); and Randolph Hodge (seventh chair). The shoe shiner was "Boots," and the barbers were Sam Cain, Paul Cain, Ben Evans, Bill Ammons, Dick Crouch, Floyd Stewart, and T.J. Smitherman.

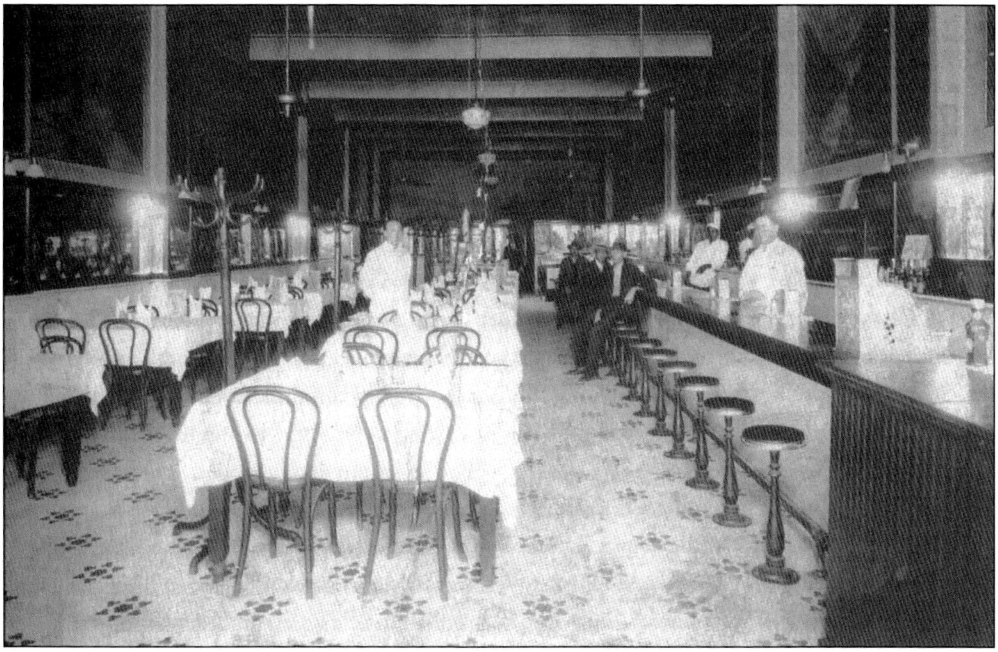

Since its construction, the Realty Building has housed the famous Bright Star restaurant, the oldest restaurant in Alabama and winner of James Beard Foundation "American Classics" recognition. The restaurant opened in 1907 and has remained in family hands throughout the years. The Bright Star's interior contains murals that were painted by European artists in the 1920s.

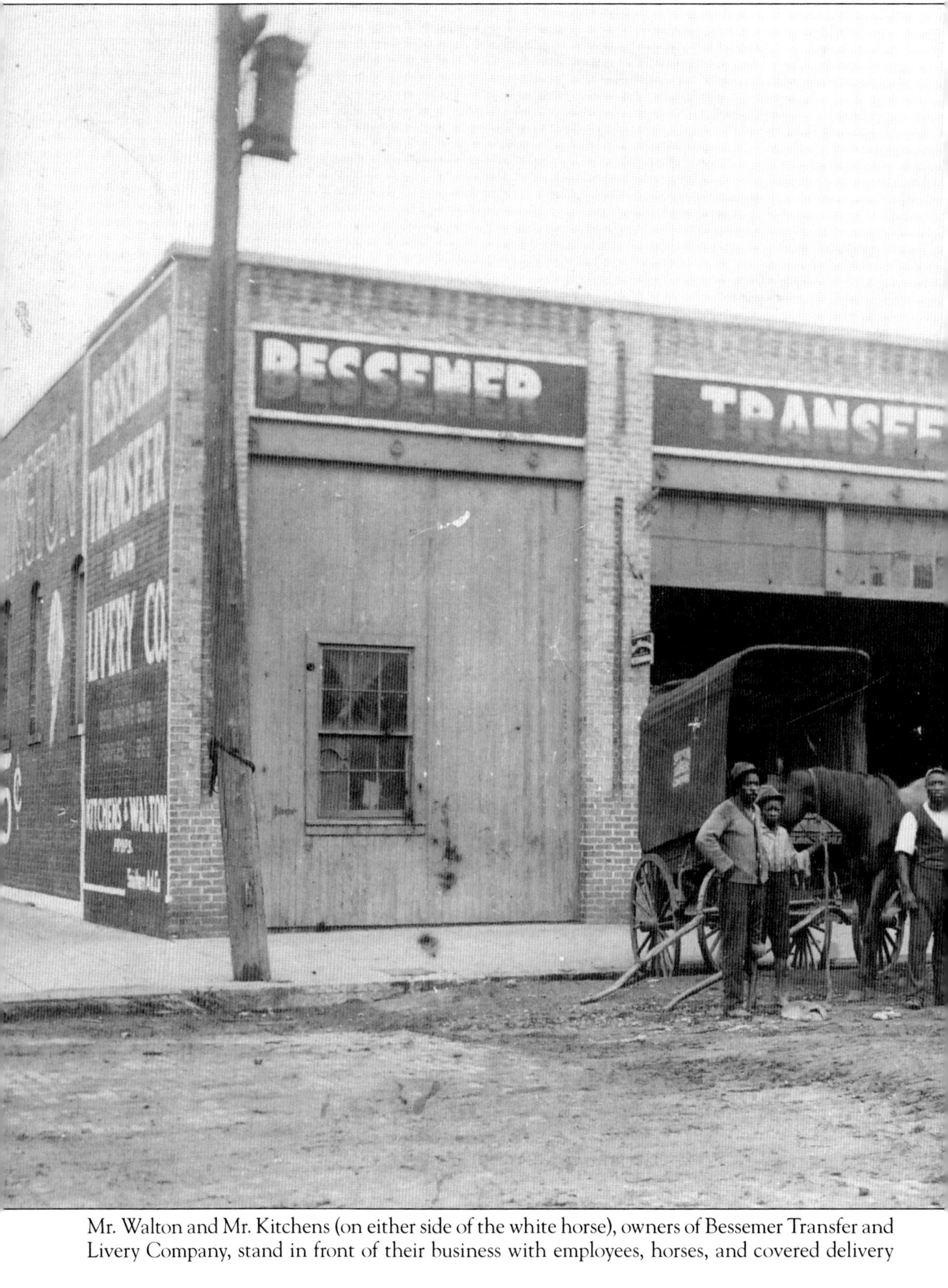

Mr. Walton and Mr. Kitchens (on either side of the white horse), owners of Bessemer Transfer and Livery Company, stand in front of their business with employees, horses, and covered delivery

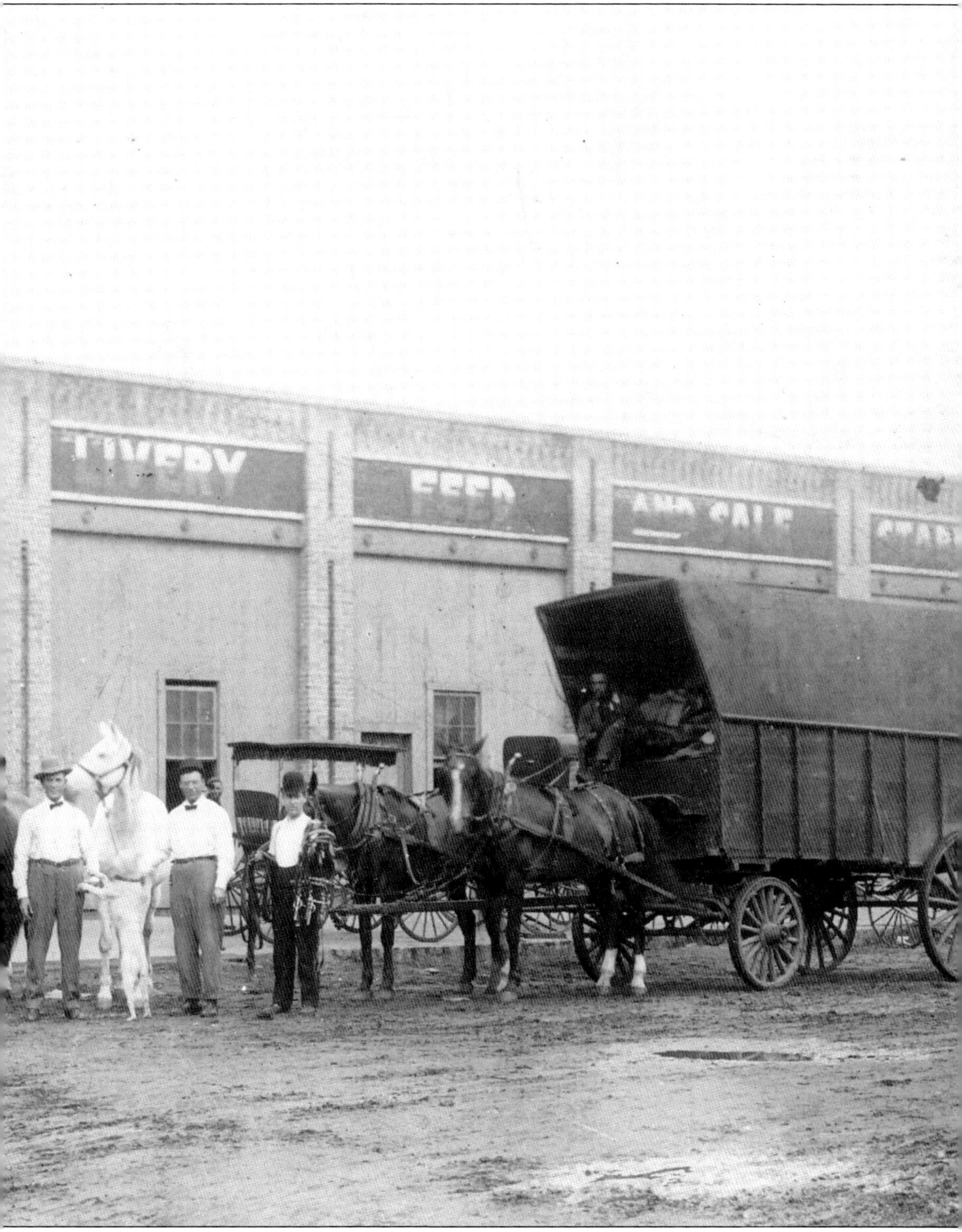

wagons around 1910. One of several liveries in town, the Bessemer Transfer building opened in 1890 and was on the corner of Twentieth Street and First Avenue.

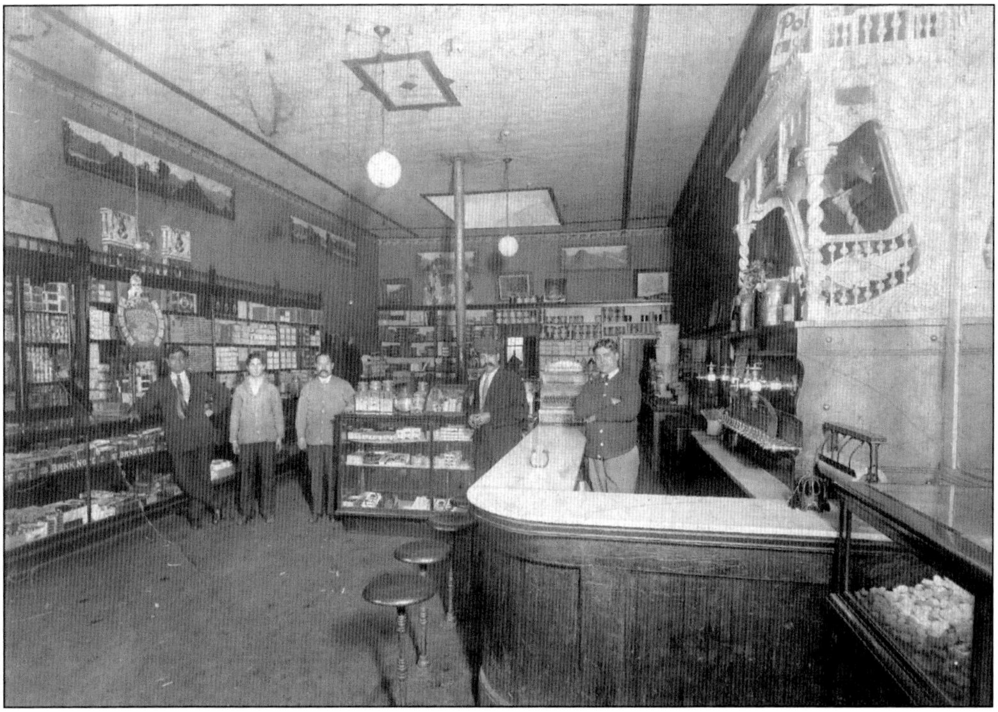

The Schilleci family, founders of Superior Ice Cream Company, started building their ice cream empire at the Schilleci Fountain Drug Store. Pasquale Schilleci, Tom Manzella, Joe Contariespre, Charlie Schilleci, and Sam Schilleci stand in the drugstore in this photograph from about 1910.

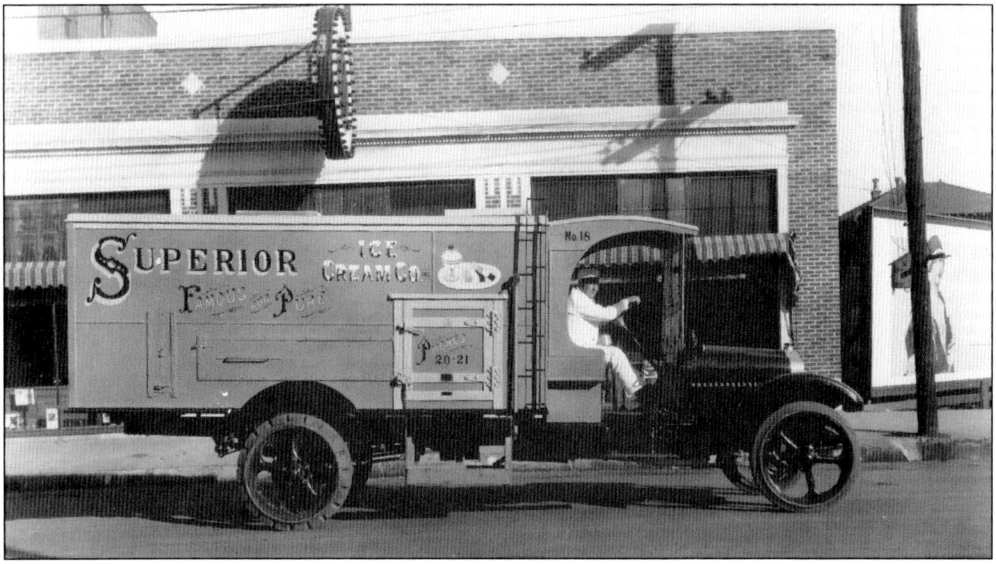

This Superior Ice Cream delivery truck, driven by longtime employee Wilson Hall, was photographed on a delivery in front of Birmingham Electric Company in downtown Birmingham. The truck worked on the same principal as a home ice cream freezer. The door on the right (with phone numbers) was to the ice cream box. A mixture of salt and ice surrounded the ice cream box. The salt and ice were added in a door at the top of the truck. The doors on the side of the truck held containers to catch the saltwater melt.

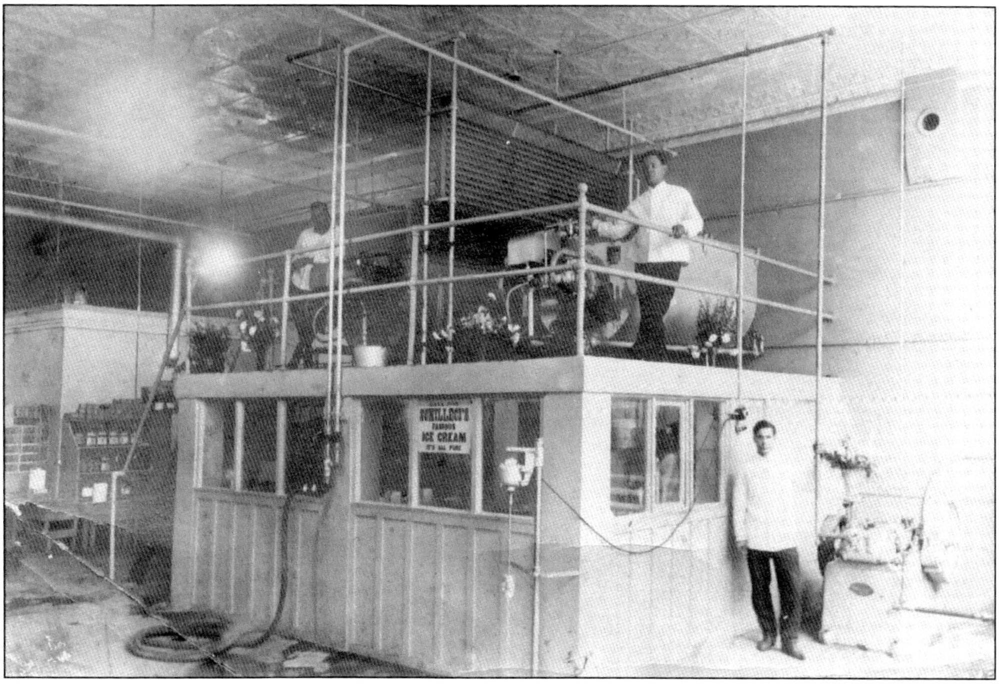

The Schilleci brothers' Superior Ice Cream Company was located on Second Avenue between Eighteenth and Nineteenth Streets for many years. Ice cream delivery trucks could drive into a refrigerated room through a bay door, have ice cream loaded without worrying about it melting, and then exit the freezer.

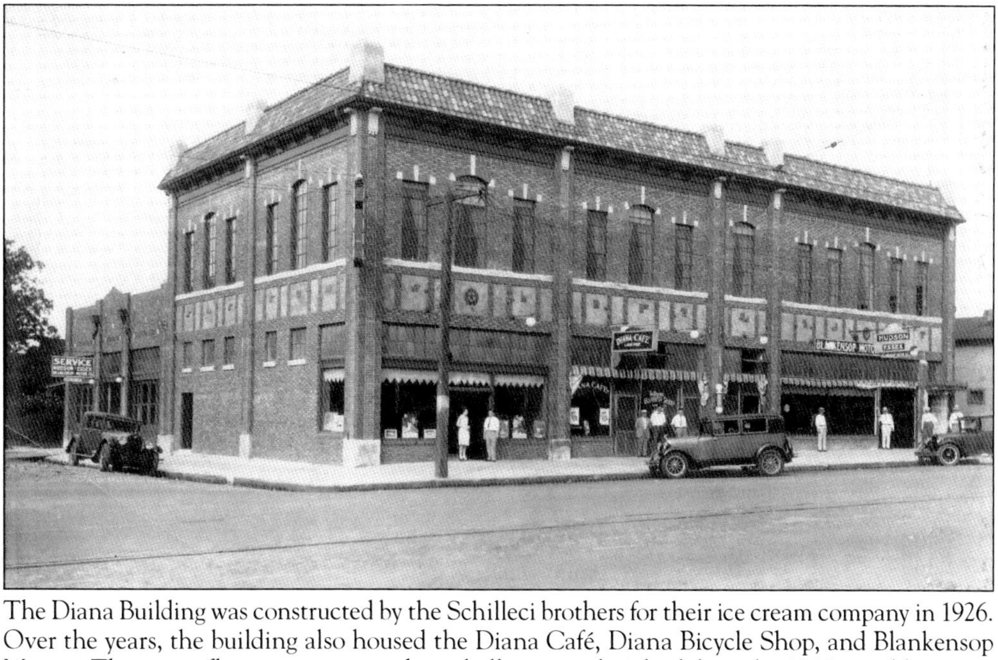

The Diana Building was constructed by the Schilleci brothers for their ice cream company in 1926. Over the years, the building also housed the Diana Café, Diana Bicycle Shop, and Blankensop Motors. The upper floor was once used as a ballroom and nightclub in the 1920s, and later as a hall for civic and school dances. During World War II, it was known as Teen Town, a center for youth activities.

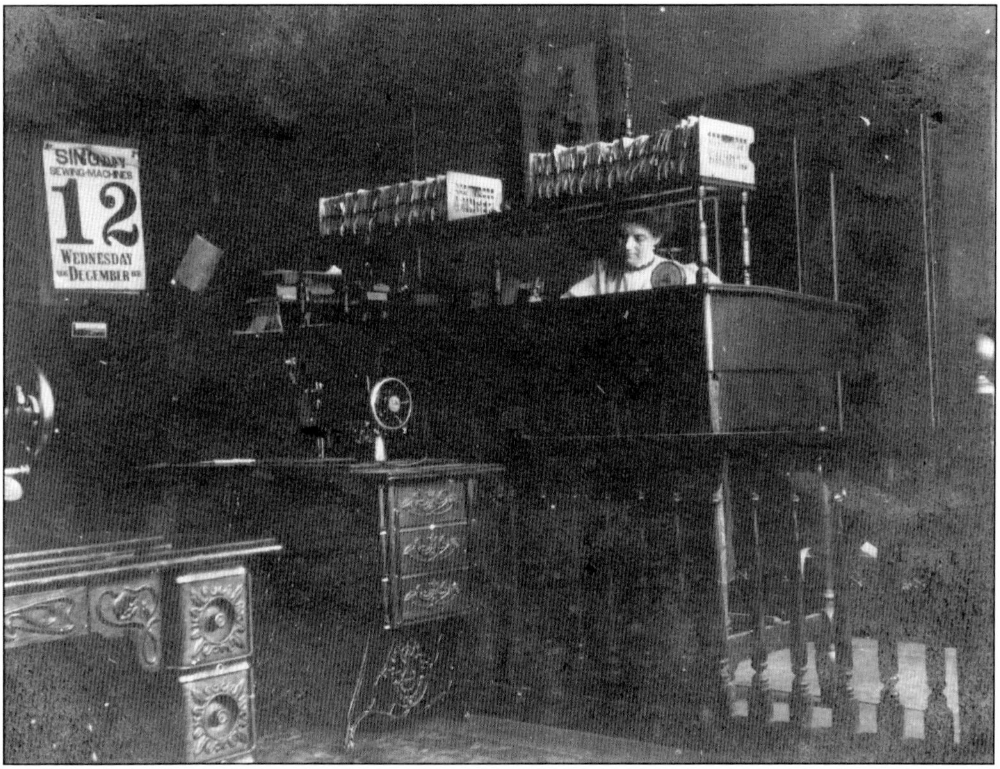

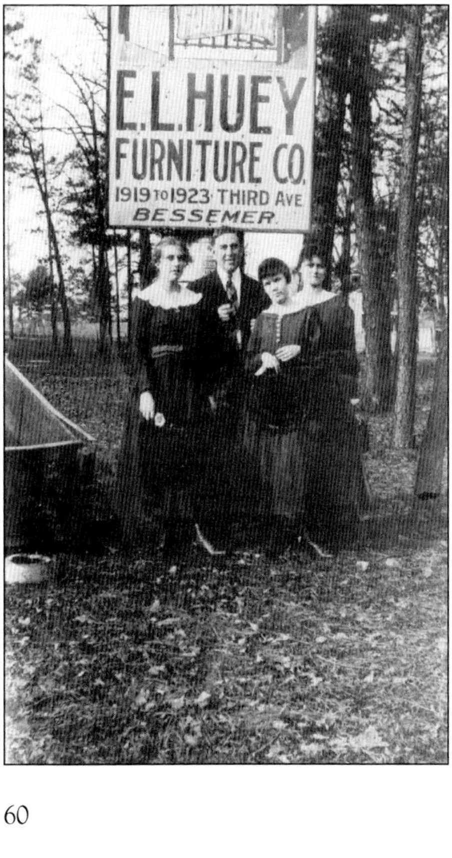

E.L. Huey with his father-in-law, Chambers McAdory, founded the E.L. Huey Furniture Company in 1905. Above, "Sister" Elizabeth Phelps works behind the counter at the company's first location on Second Avenue between Nineteenth and Twentieth Streets in 1906. The store was later moved to the McAdory Building on Third Avenue. At left, employees pose with a sign showing the store's new address. Huey's home, "Hillcrest," in the Jonesboro neighborhood, is used for weddings and events.

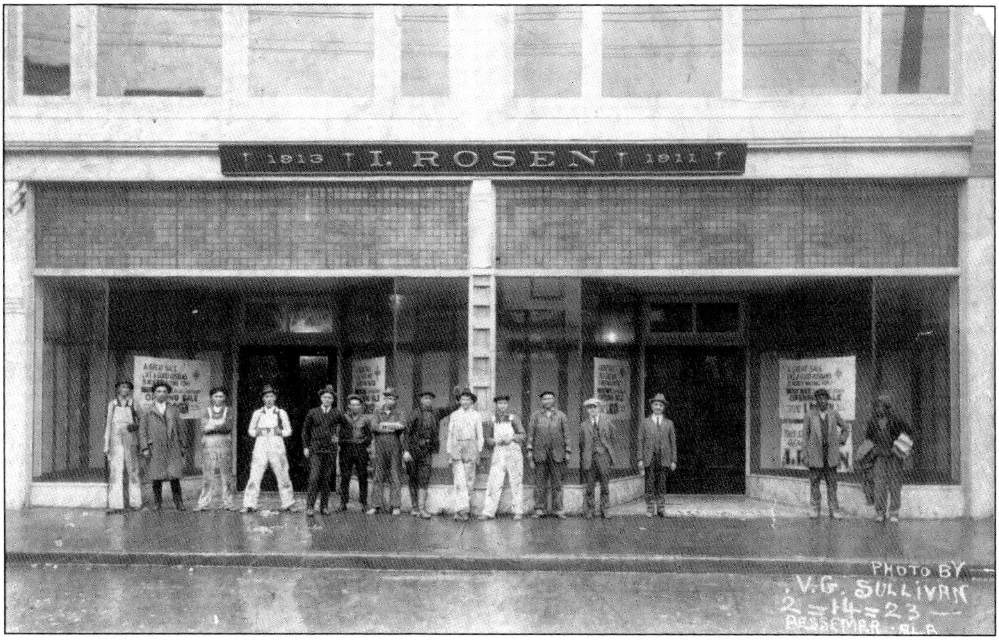

Isaac Rosen established one of the city's first fine department stores on Second Avenue in 1916. These photographs were made when the I. Rosen store reopened after a remodeling in February 1923. Above, standing with the painters and plasterers who completed the work, Rosen is third from the right. Below, from left to right, a shopper, five sales clerks, and Rosen present the updated shoe and accessories department in this press photograph for the grand reopening. By the 1930s, other fashionable department stores, including Lovemans, Pizitz, and Sokols, were located along Second Avenue between Nineteenth and Twenty-first Streets.

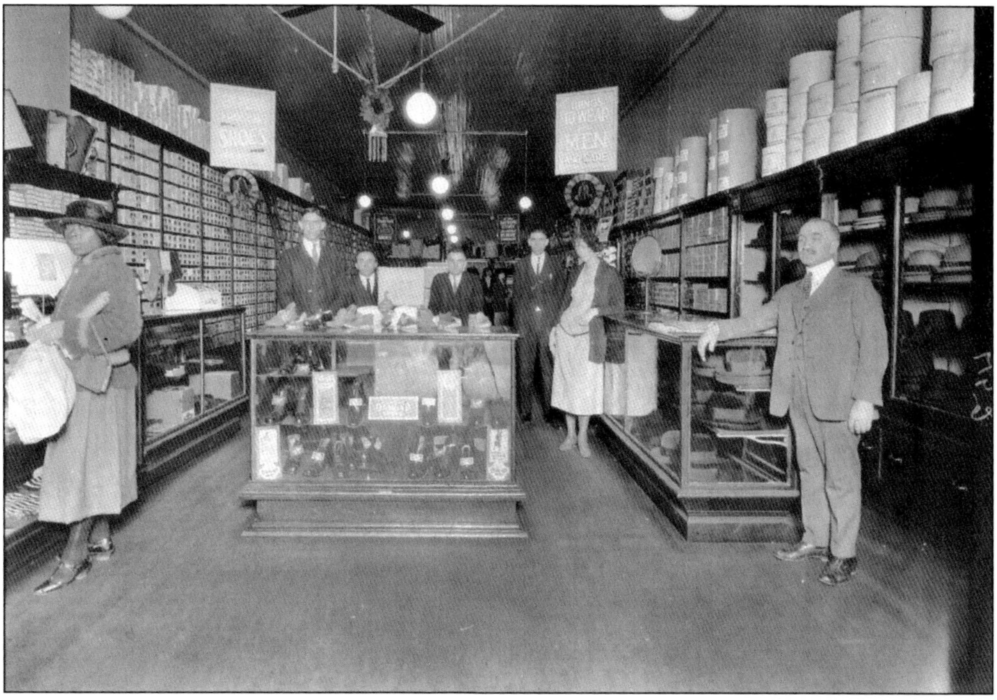

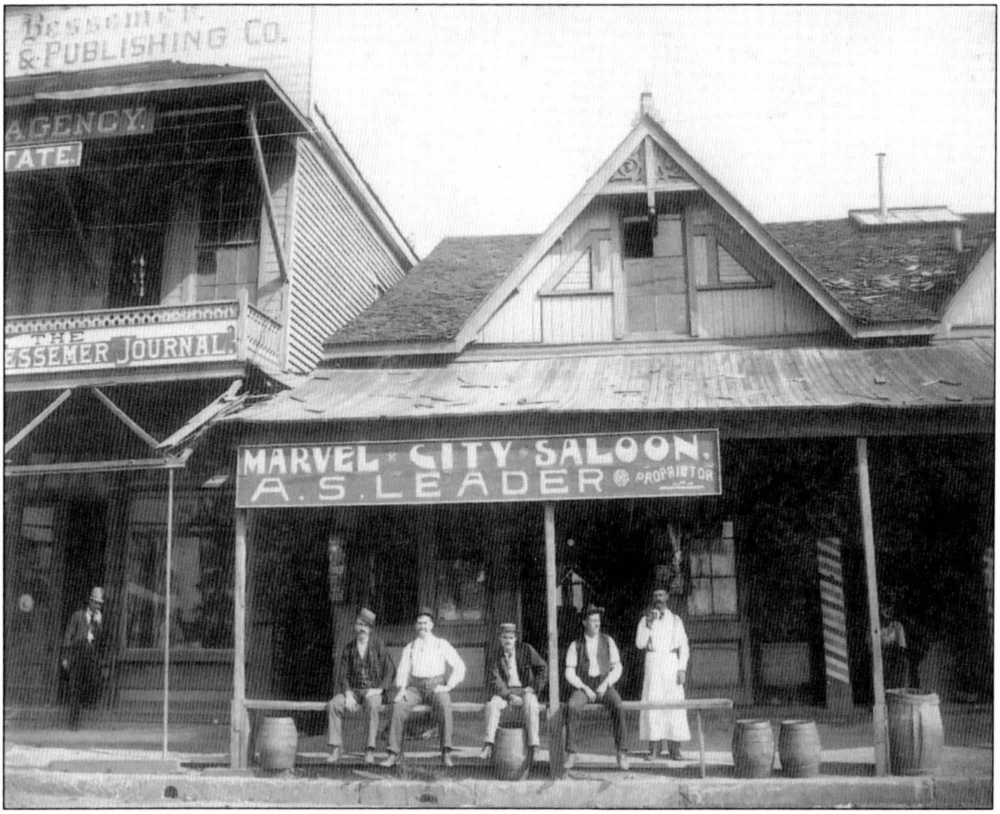

The *Bessemer Weekly* reported on March 17, 1894, that A.S. Leader moved his Marvel City Saloon into the Voelkel building on Carolina Avenue. The saloon sat directly opposite the original Alabama Great Southern rail depot, welcoming thirsty travelers. Leader later owned a dry goods store in Bessemer, and was active in the development of the neighboring town of Brighton. He encouraged Hill's Grocery, one of the first chains out of Birmingham to locate at Brighton, and he started a residential real estate development along the Bessemer & Birmingham Railway in Brighton. Leader's Brighton home has been featured on HGTV's *If These Walls Could Talk* program.

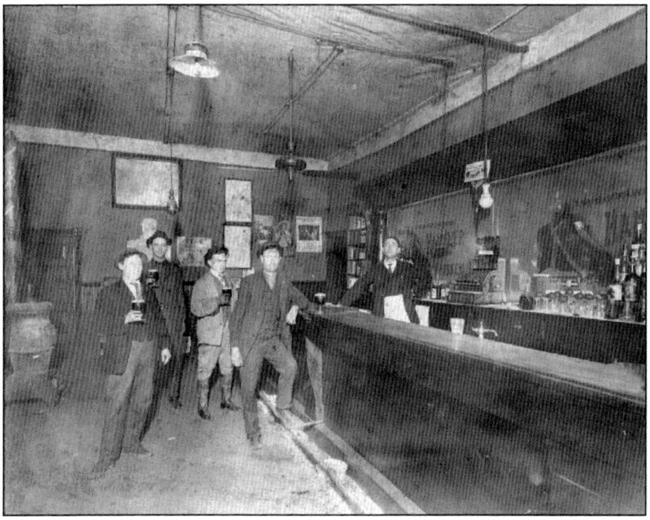

Four men enjoy a glass of beer at the Monark Saloon about 1913. The Monark was on Twenty-first Street between First and Second Avenues. From the wild-west atmosphere of bars in the eastern section of the city known as "Whiskey Town," to more refined establishments like downtown's Bank Saloon, Metropolitan Bar, and Palace Saloon, Bessemer had a booming liquor business from its earliest days. In 1901, the *Bessemer Weekly* reported 15 saloons in the city limits.

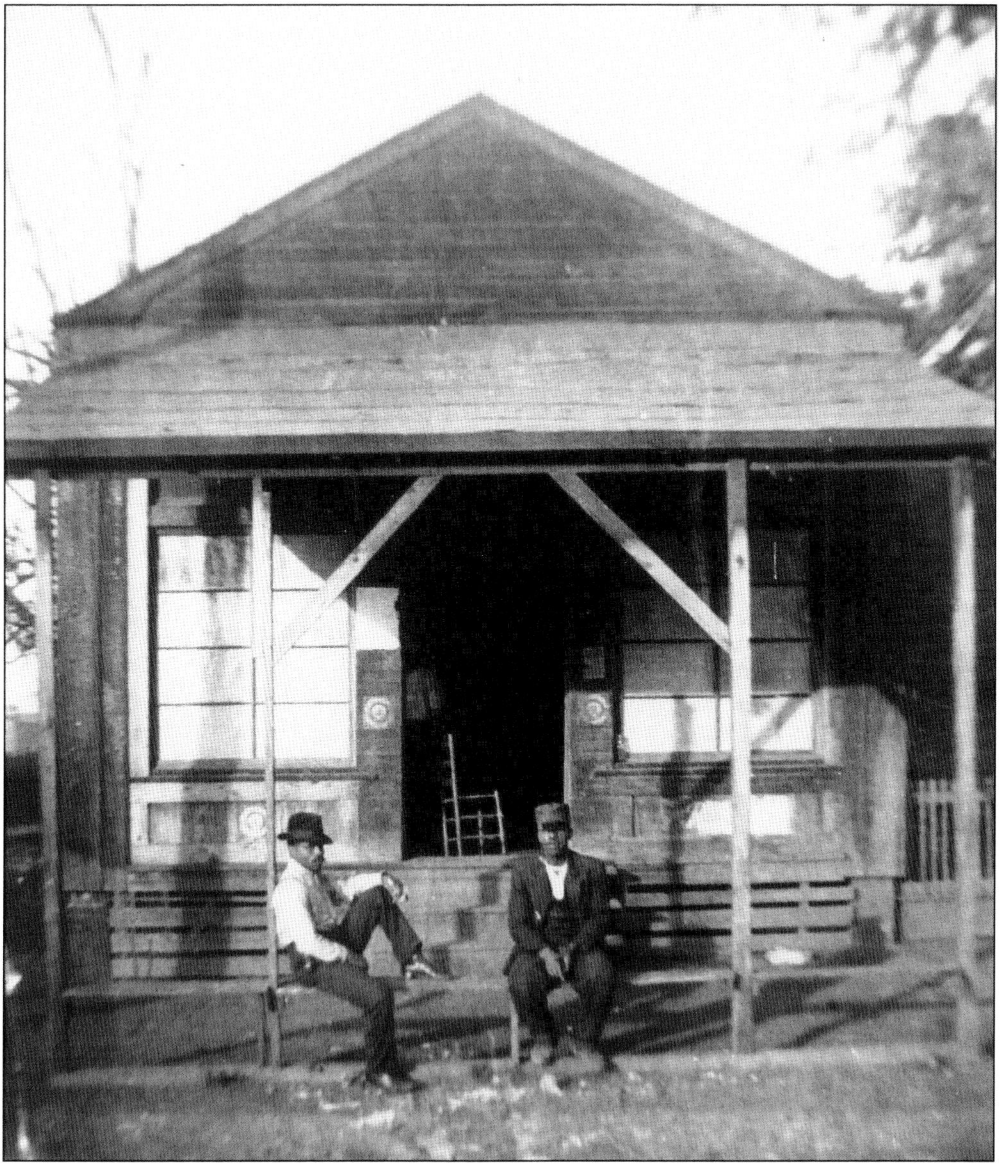

Jim Henderson's Pool Room was located at Nineteenth Street and Eighteenth Avenue, near US Pipe and Foundry, about 1915. Henderson (left) owned the poolroom and a check cashing service. His father, Ed Henderson, was among Bessemer's earliest residents and blacksmiths. He brought his family to the city from Stylesboro, Georgia, in 1888. (Henderson family pictures, Bessemer Hall of History.)

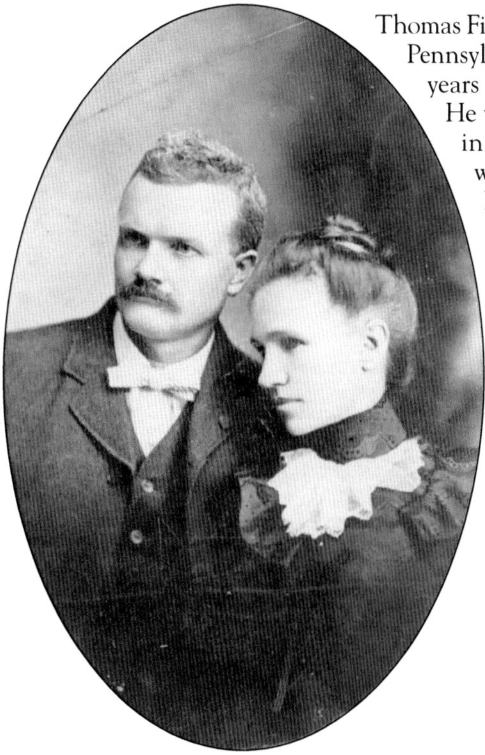

Thomas Fitzpatrick began his working life as a coal miner in Pennsylvania. He also studied photography, and after nine years of mining, started a new career with his camera. He worked in Baltimore until he moved to Bessemer in 1889 and opened the Fitzpatrick Gallery. This wedding self-portrait from November 1891 shows him with his bride, Mary Woltersdorf.

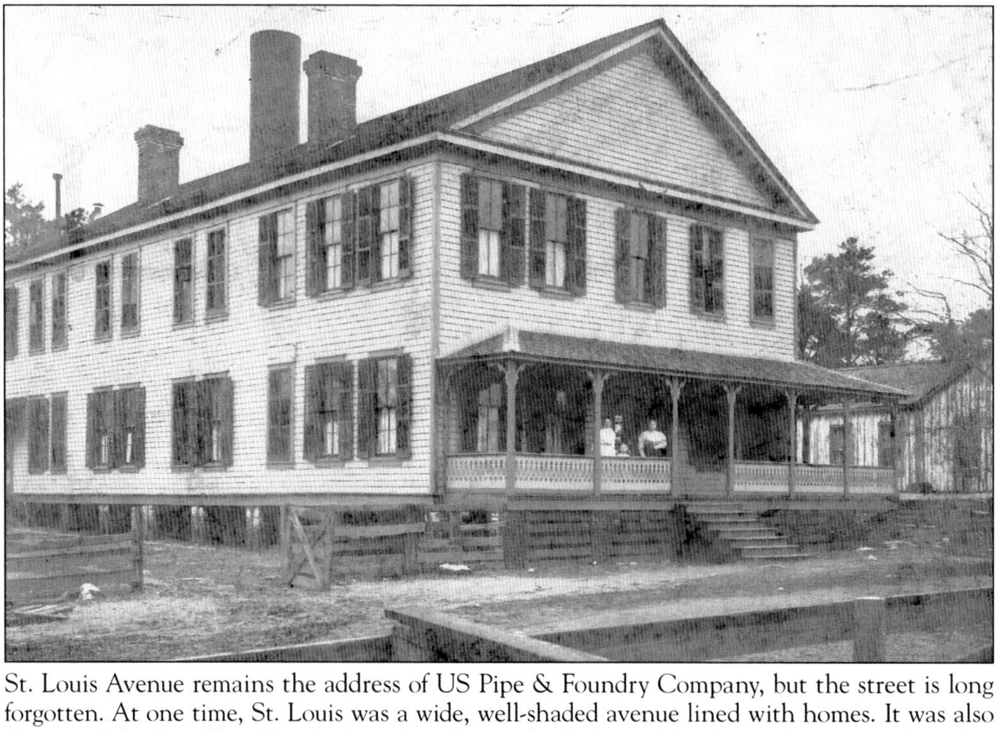

St. Louis Avenue remains the address of US Pipe & Foundry Company, but the street is long forgotten. At one time, St. Louis was a wide, well-shaded avenue lined with homes. It was also the site of the Pipe Shop Hotel, also referred to as the St. Louis Hotel, seen here in 1906. Today, the avenue, houses, and hotel are gone. St. Louis Avenue has become a ghost street.

Five

Government and Public Institutions

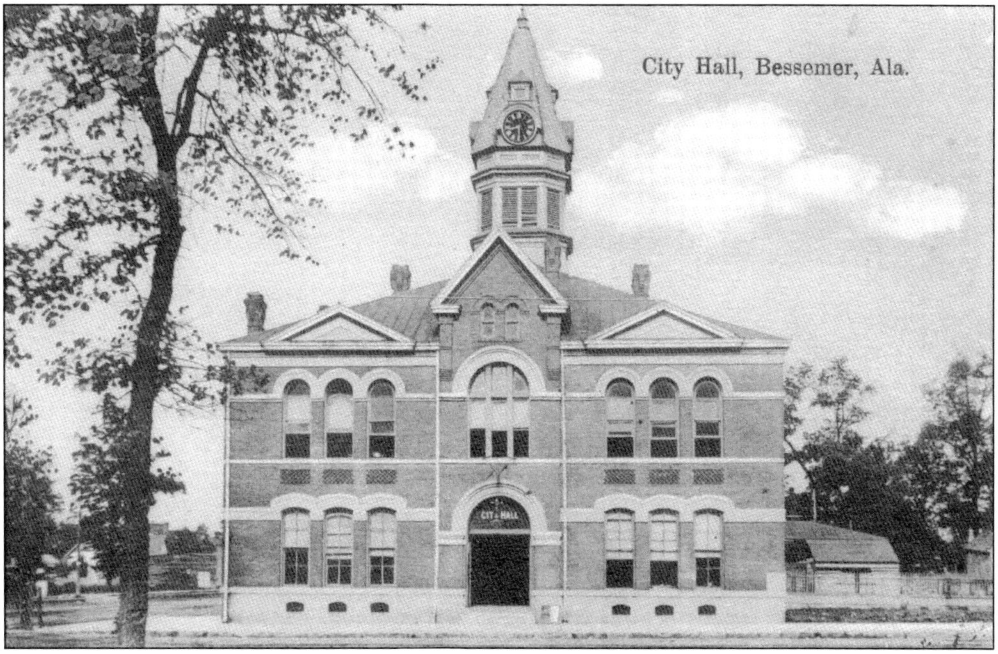

The Bessemer Land & Improvement Company laid out the streets, installed sidewalks, brought in businesses, and even built a school, but the new town still needed municipal government and other services. On September 9, 1887, Bessemer's citizens elected R.M. McAdory as the first mayor along with five aldermen, and the first city council meeting was held that evening. G.M. Torgerson, architect of the New Orleans Worlds Fair and Bessemer's Berney Block, designed Bessemer City Hall. P.J. Gillen was hired as contractor.

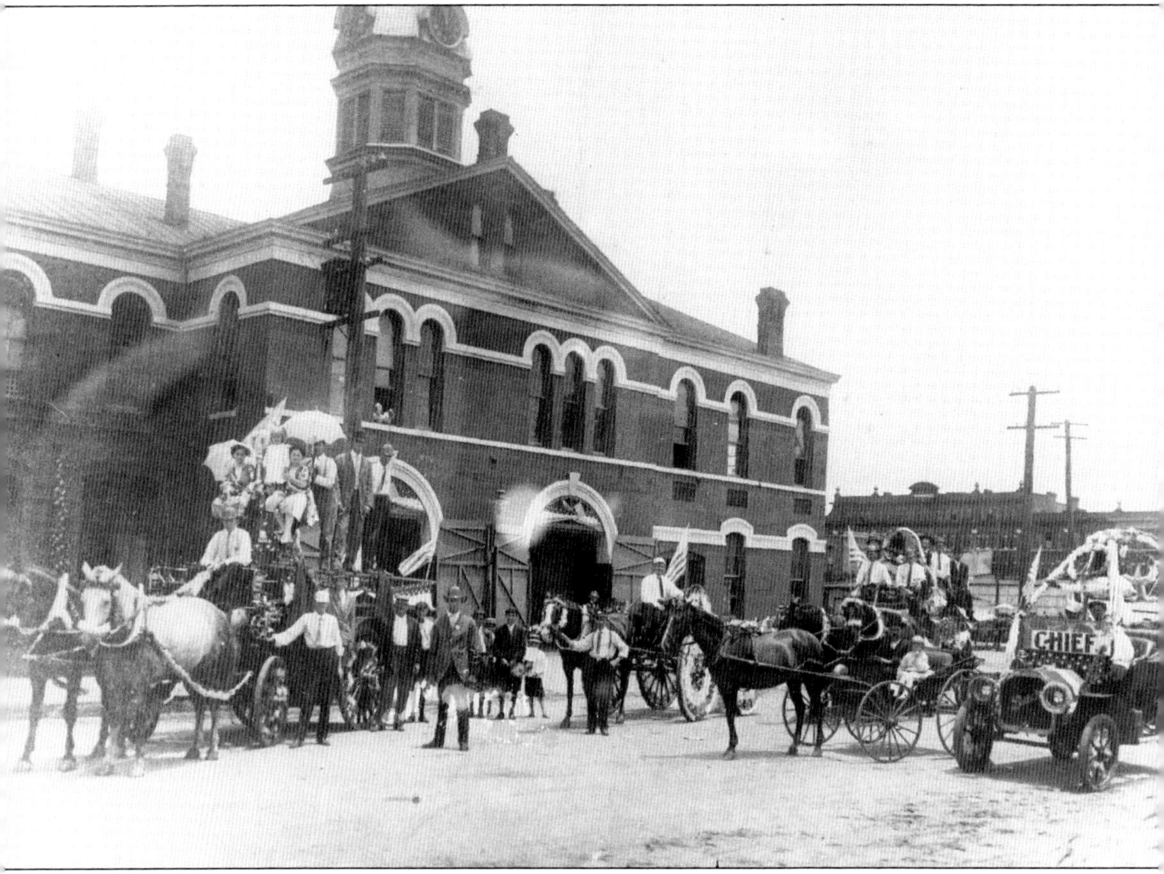

The finished city hall opened at the corner of Third Avenue and Eighteenth Street in 1889. The building had a large courtroom, offices, jail, fire engine house, and bell tower housing a 1,040-pound fire bell. In this photograph from around 1915, the Bessemer Fire Department with their families line up for a May Day parade. In addition to the department's latest engine (left), they also paraded their 1896 fire hose wagon and an older engine. The chief rode in a decorated 1910 Buick Model 17 (right). This view also shows the fire engine bays on the Eighteenth Street side of city hall and the Charleston Block along Second Avenue in the background. This original city hall building was destroyed by fire around 1933, and the Works Progress Administration constructed a new city hall later in the decade.

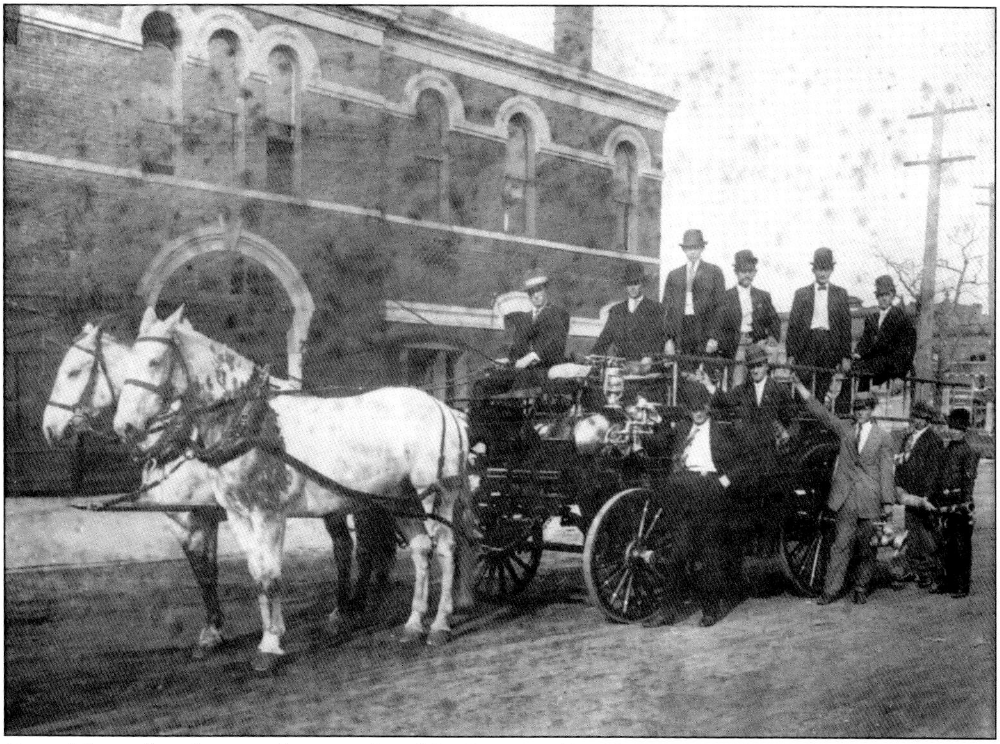

One of the earliest known photographs of the Bessemer Fire Department shows the 1909 firefighters with a new horse-drawn engine. In front of the engine are, from left to right, Joe Leonard, Tom Donahue, Leonard Marbert, Tom Calura, and Teddy Hewett. The men on the top of the engine are Frank Young, Norman Caldwell, Leo B. Hill, Joe Spisak, Sam Johnson, and unidentified. Young Leo Hill, who stands taller than the rest of the group, would later become fire chief.

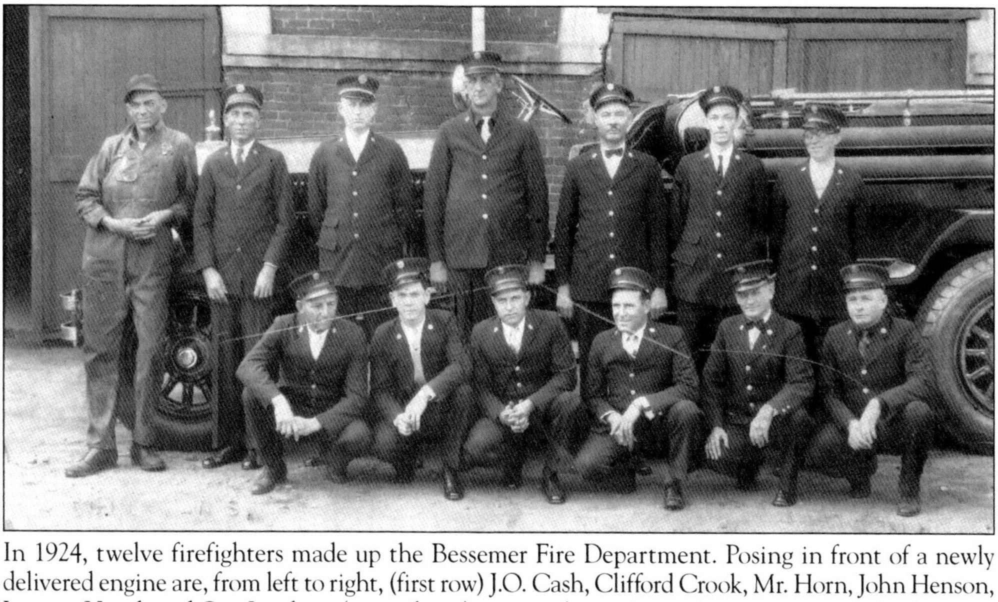

In 1924, twelve firefighters made up the Bessemer Fire Department. Posing in front of a newly delivered engine are, from left to right, (first row) J.O. Cash, Clifford Crook, Mr. Horn, John Henson, Lonnie Hood, and Coy Lindsay; (second row) city mechanic Bert Morton, assistant chief Claude Egger, chief Leo B. Hill, Shorty Williams, Jack Curren, Charles Borum, and Macon Horne.

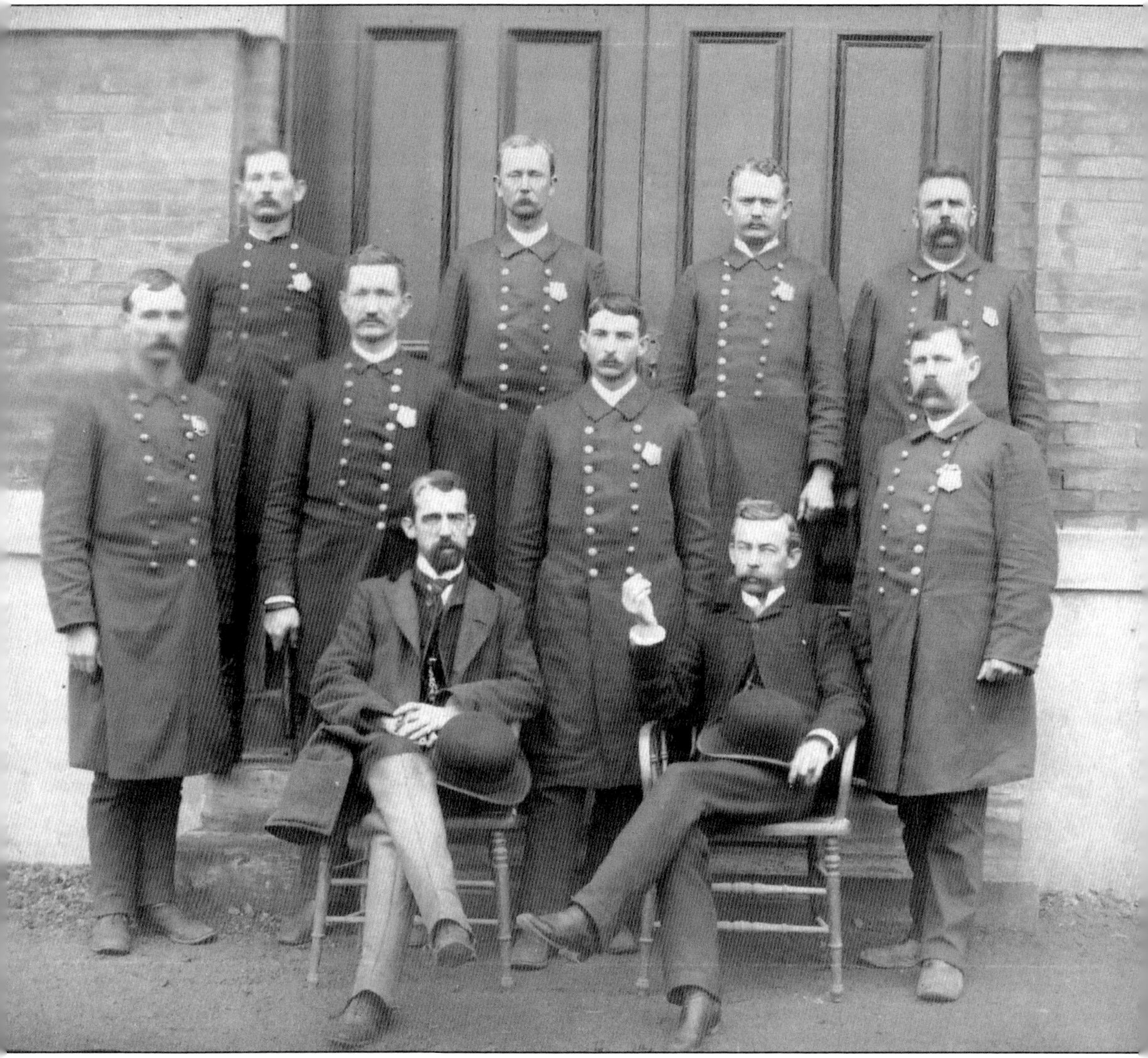

Bessemer's first police force was town marshal D.B. Sapp and three deputies—A.A. Hanes, T.F. Thomas, and L.A. Wilson. Due to the growing pains and politics that come with building a new city, there was rapid turnover in the force. Bessemer saw four police chiefs in its first year. In 1889, Robert Franklin Mims was named chief, and he served for seven years. This photograph of an early Bessemer police department includes Thomas Benjamin Wallace (seated, right), who became chief in February 1897. Wallace joined the Bessemer police when he was 26 years old. He came to Bessemer from Tuscaloosa, where he had been assistant supervisor of Bryce Hospital for three years. Wallace was killed on duty in 1916 while trying to help two detectives who were struggling with a prisoner.

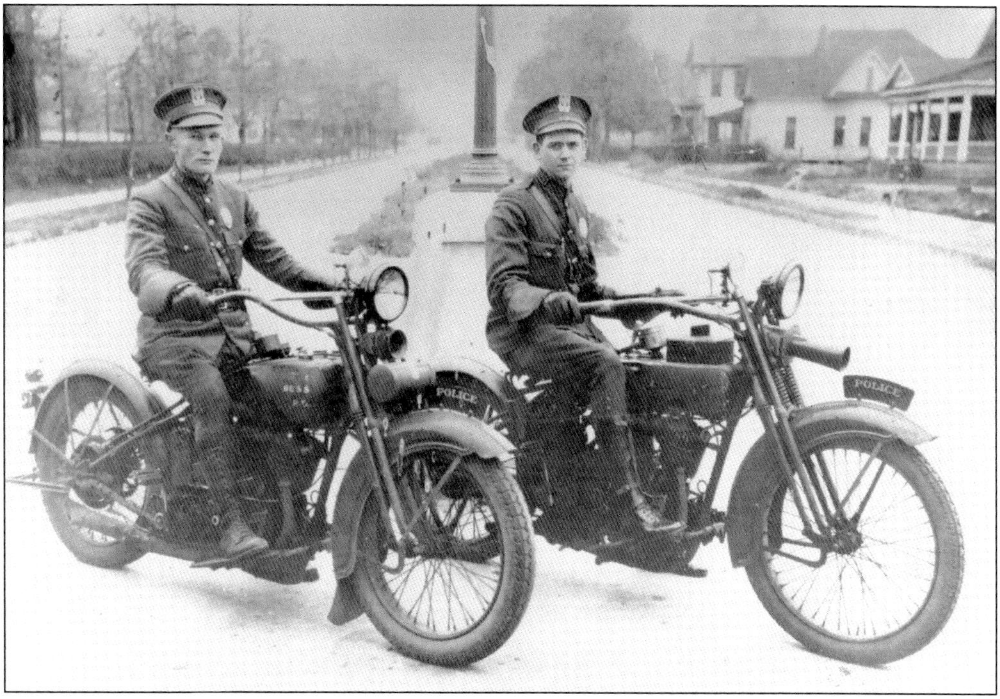

For many years Bessemer's police officers had three options for transportation: foot, horseback, and bicycle. As more residents purchased automobiles, traffic problems required more and more police attention and the police acquired motorcycles to use for enforcing traffic violations. Officers assigned to the motorcycles were referred to as "speed cops." Above, Officer Lipscomb (right) and another speed cop pause for this snapshot taken at a Clarendon Avenue intersection in 1924. Below, a Bessemer Police Department parade float was part of the city campaign to raise awareness and improve traffic safety. The man third from the left is chief J.G. Thomas.

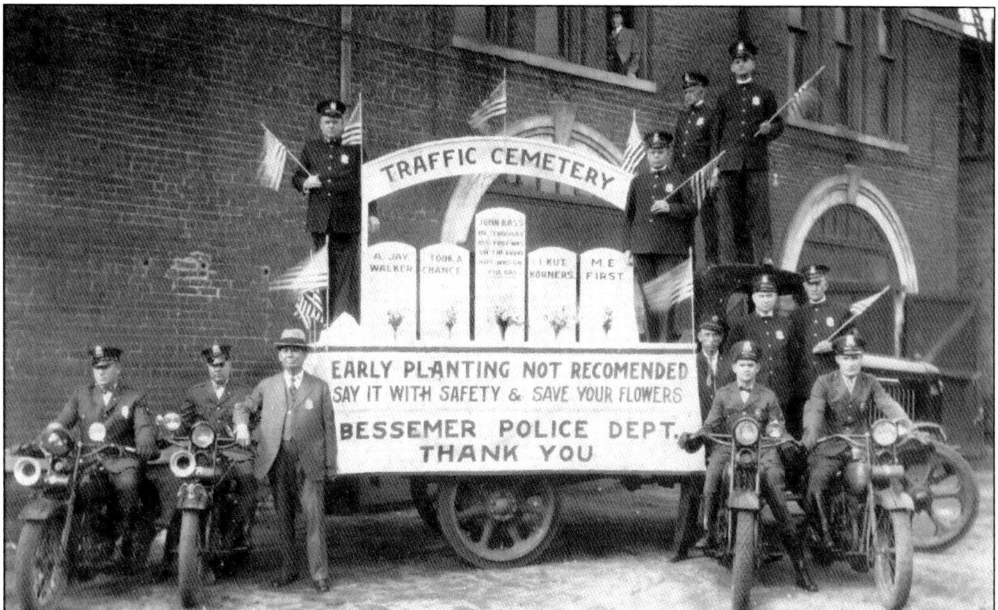

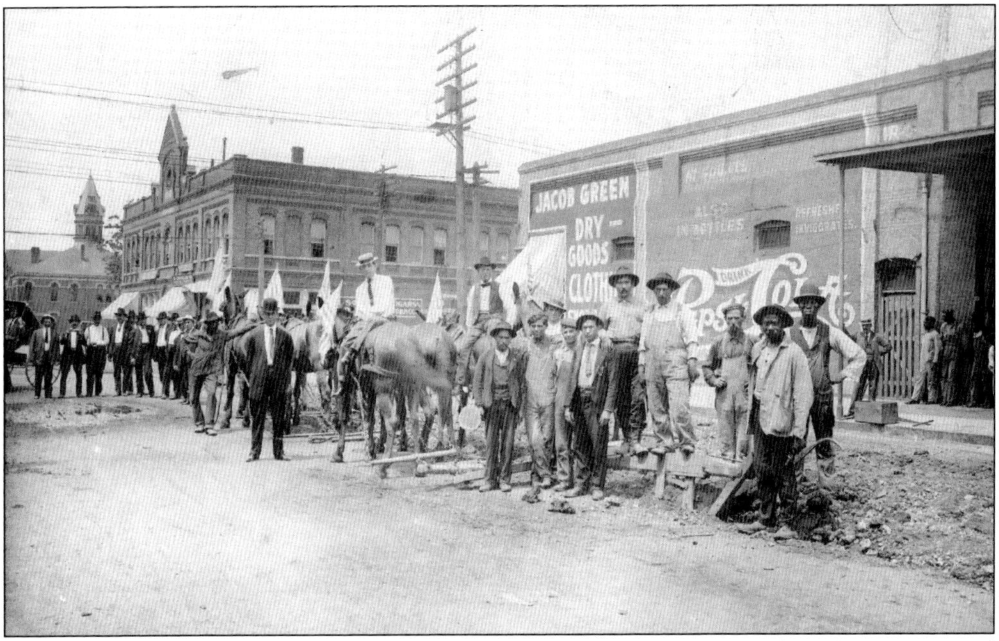

An editorial in the January 2, 1909, *Bessemer Weekly* expressed "hope that the city council will take vigorous hold of the paving of our streets." The council listened, presenting a paving ordinance the following week with only one hitch. They insisted that the streets be paved with brick even though most towns had abandoned cobbles for bitulithic pavement. Above, contractor P.H. O'Brien and workers on Third Avenue near the corner of Nineteenth Street prepare to install a concrete bed for brick pavement. The buildings, from left to right, are city hall, Rebie Hall, and Jacob Green Dry Goods. Below, workers are installing brick pavers on Third Avenue. The McAdory Building, home of E.L. Huey Furniture Company, is on the left. Note the streetcar passing on Nineteenth Street in the background.

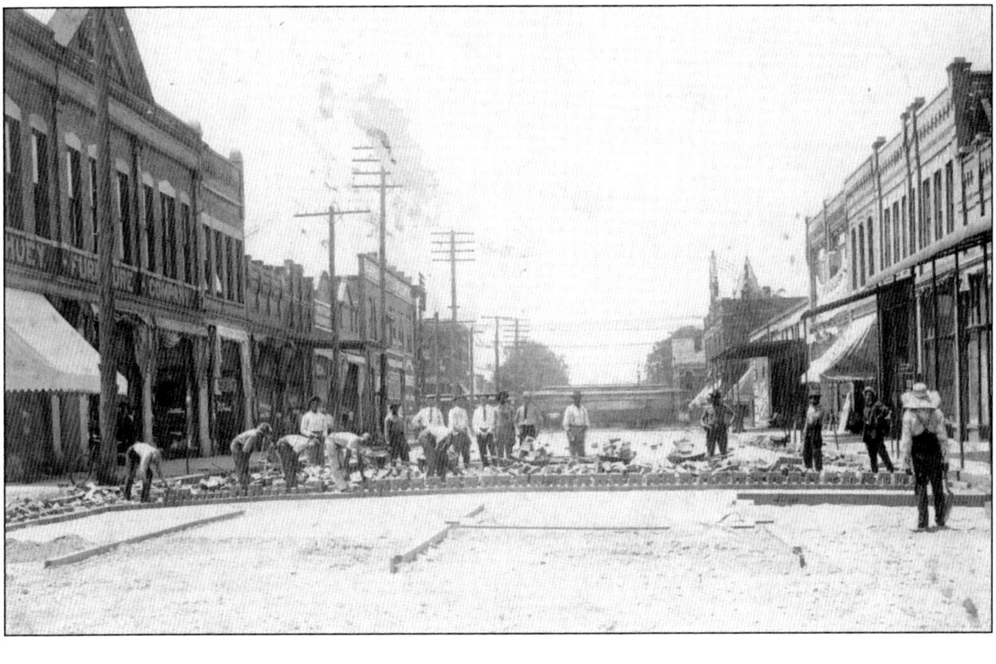

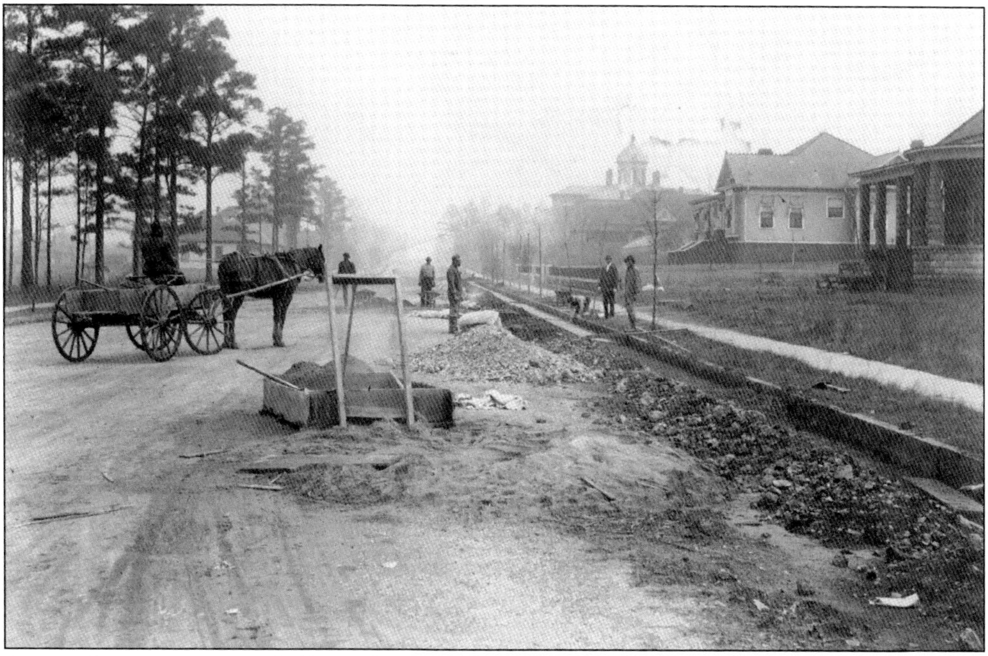

A man drives a cart past Sullivan, Long, and Haggerty workers installing granite curbs along Clarendon Avenue (looking west from Eighteenth Street). The first house on the right is the Rarden home, then the George Rutledge house, Brown house, and Clarendon School. The steeple beyond the school is the tower of the Jeff Clay home.

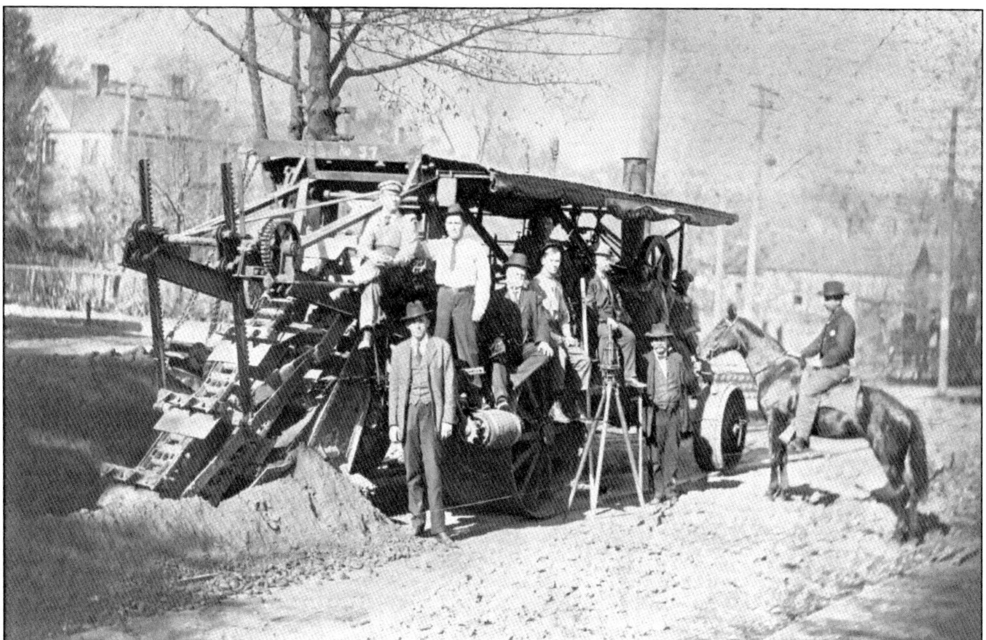

The Sullivan, Long, and Haggerty crew poses for a portrait in front of the company's steam powered trencher on Clarendon Avenue. This machine was used to dig a bed for the granite curbs that still line the streets on Bessemer's south side. In 1905 and 1906, Bessemer installed 40,000 feet of five-inch granite curb in the neighborhood.

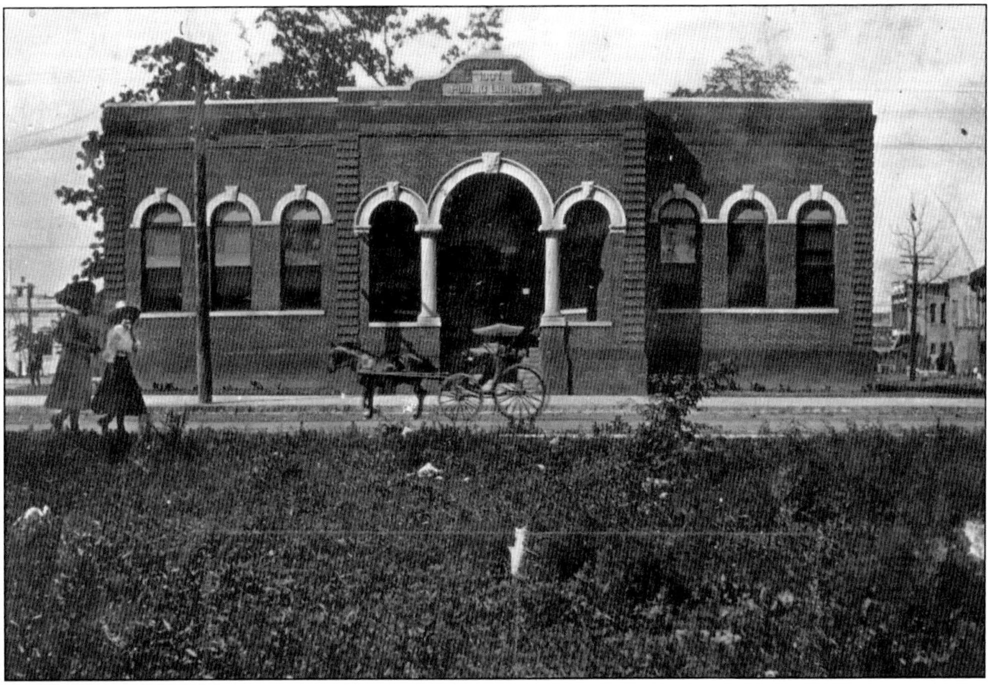

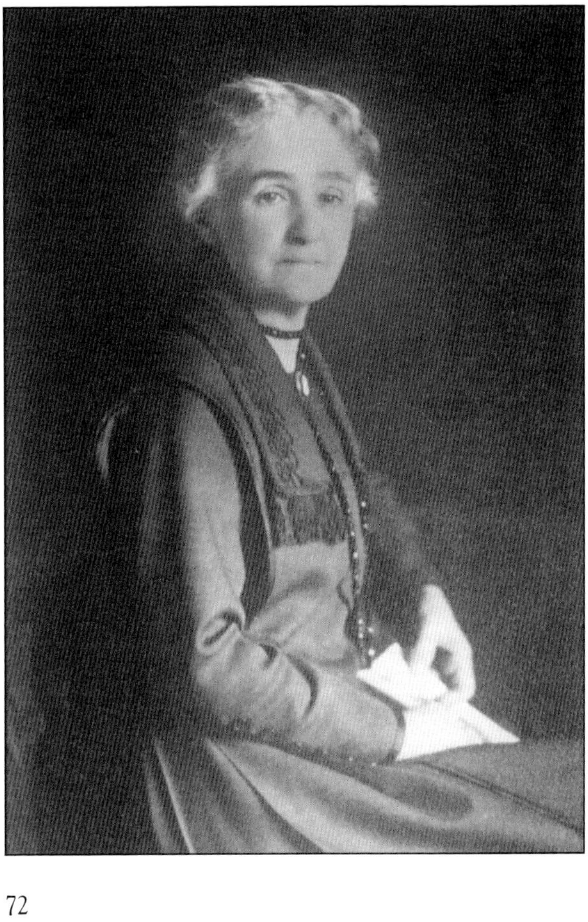

Bessemer's second public library building, above, was opened on Eighteenth Street in September 1907. Designed by William Benns and built with grant assistance from the Andrew Carnegie Foundation, the building was one of 1,679 Carnegie Libraries. In order to get a $10,000 grant, the city had to appropriate $1,000 per year for library maintenance. Librarian Annie Mingea and the local library committee raised funds for the furnishings, books, and cataloging. The old public library donated its entire collection to the new institution. Within two months of opening, the library had more than 500 members. The library building is now home to the Bessemer Area Chamber of Commerce. At left, Nora Golson was one of Bessemer's first librarians and the mother of real estate and insurance business owner W.P. Golson.

Dr. Thomas Franklin Robinson started his first medical practice in Jonesboro after receiving his medical degree from Vanderbilt University in 1885. In 1886, he married Arabella Prince, seen in this portrait of the couple. Bella died in 1895, and in 1900, Robinson married Caro Brown Marsden. Robinson served on Bessemer's first city council, and founded the city's first hospital, the Robinson-Hanby Infirmary (later, Robinson's Hospital) in 1906.

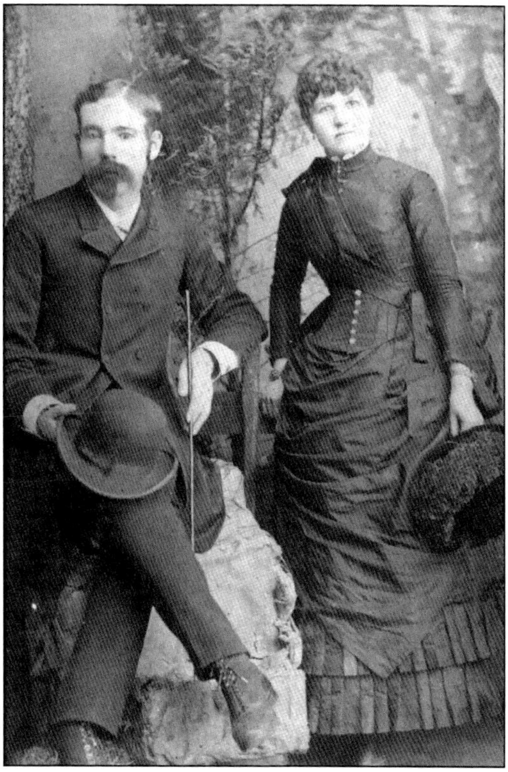

Bessemer's need for the hospital was so great that within three months of its 1906 opening, Dr. Robinson had to purchase the first library building and expand to 25 beds. In 1909, Robinson donated the hospital to United Charities. Again, the city quickly outgrew its hospital and the 40-room Elizabeth Duncan Hospital (below) was opened in January 1913. This was later known as Bessemer General Hospital.

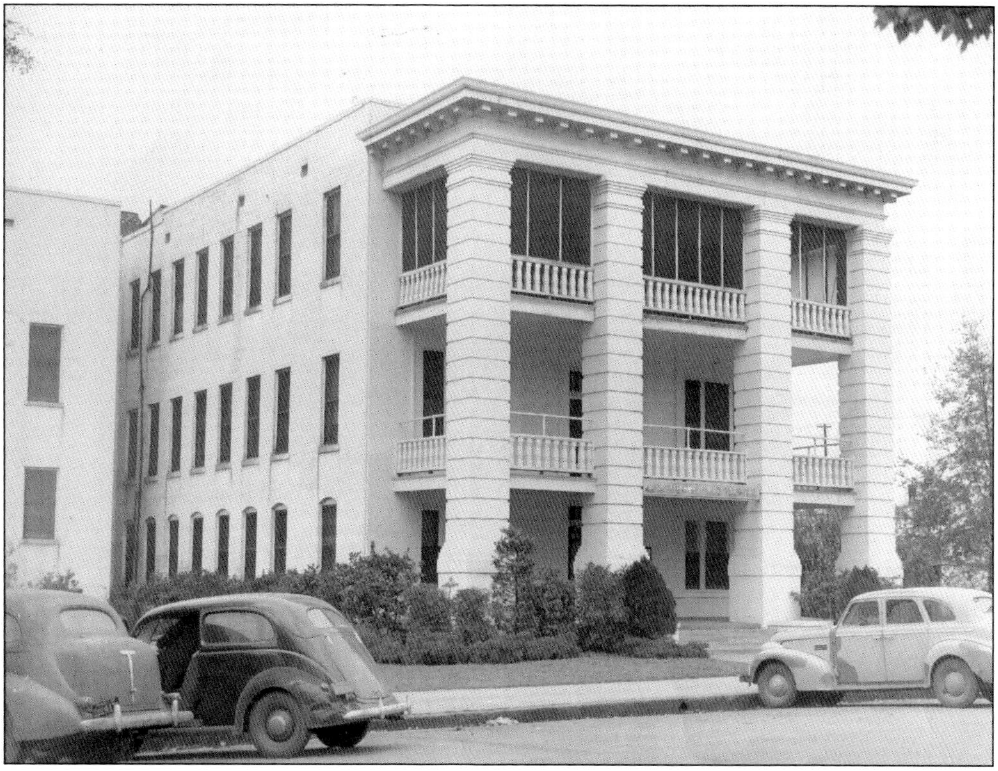

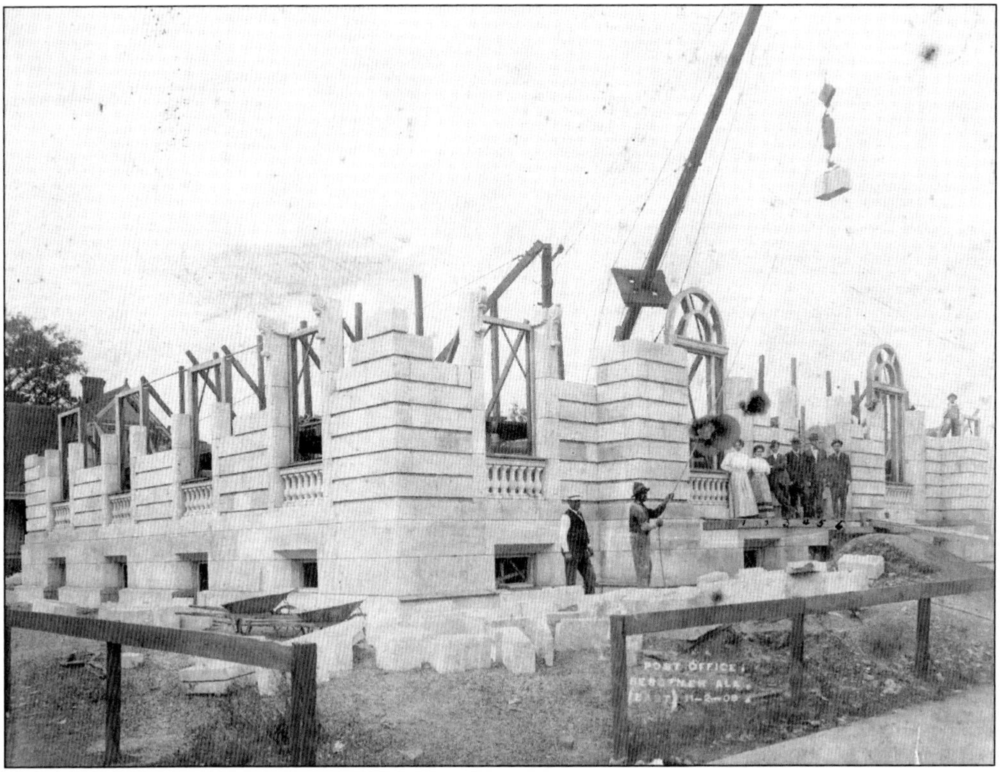

Bessemer's United States Post Office branch was located in the Charleston Block almost from the city's founding. Above, in 1908, construction was started on the Bessemer Post Office building on the corner of Nineteenth Street and Fourth Avenue. C. Ackenhauser, Mrs. C.P. Grigsby, Leo Marcus, Dave Smith, unidentified, and Lewis Milton pose on a ledge at the building's future main entrance. Below, a postcard view shows the completed building's Nineteenth Street facade about 1910. The building was purchased by the city in 1965 for use as a library. In 2008, the building was beautifully restored and expanded and is still home to the Bessemer Public Library.

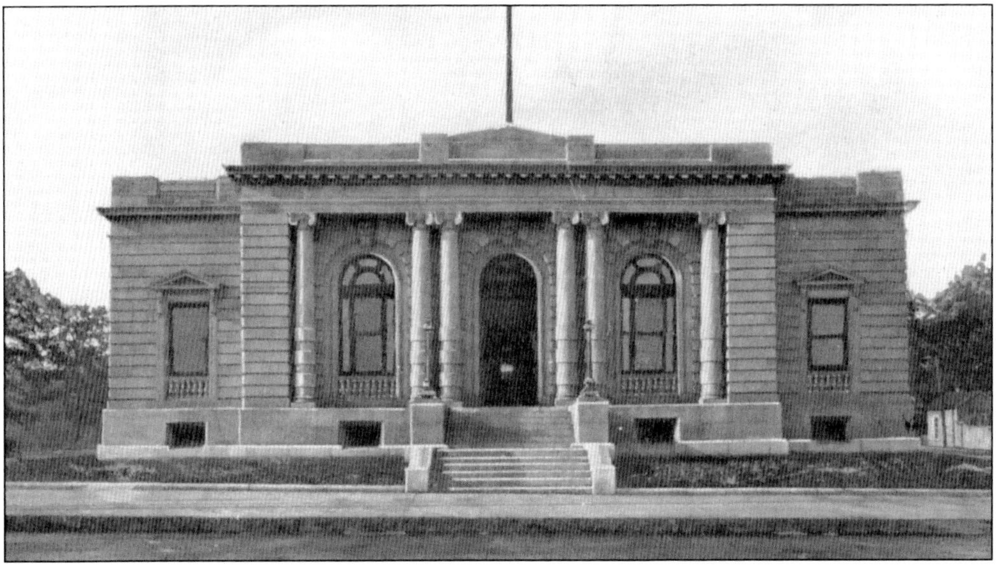

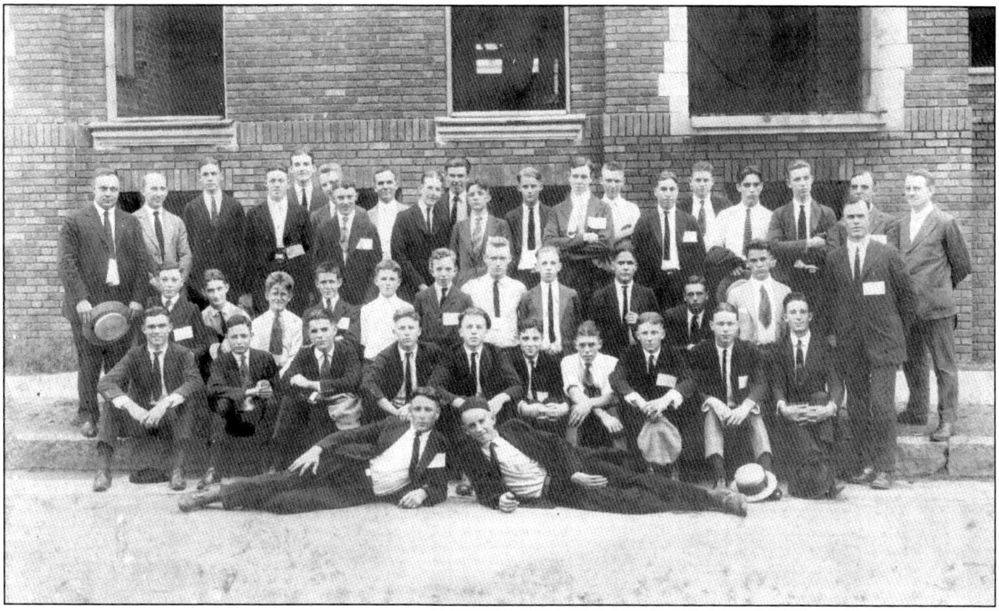

As early as 1912, the *Bessemer Weekly* was reporting citizens' desire for a Young Men's Christian Association building. Above, the Y's founding members pose for a portrait in front of the unfinished building on Eighteenth Street and Fourth Avenue. Bessemer's YMCA finally opened in 1926. Local contractor W.L. Coston & Sons constructed the building (below). Coston's construction company erected many of Bessemer's best-known landmarks including Arlington School, Elizabeth Duncan Hospital, Bessemer High School on Fourteenth Street, the Presbyterian Church (1909), the Orleans Apartments and Dr. Stover's residence.

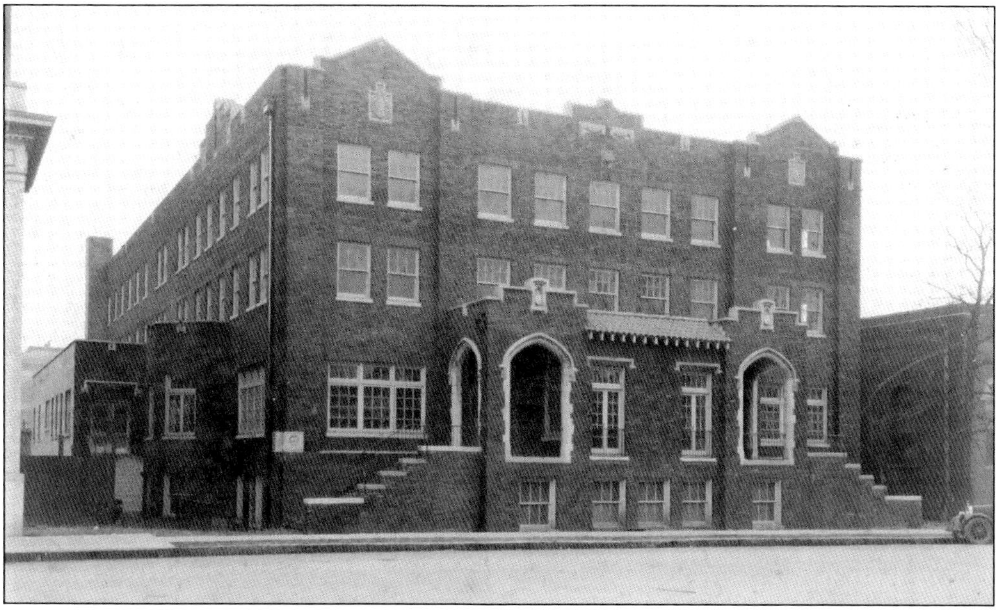

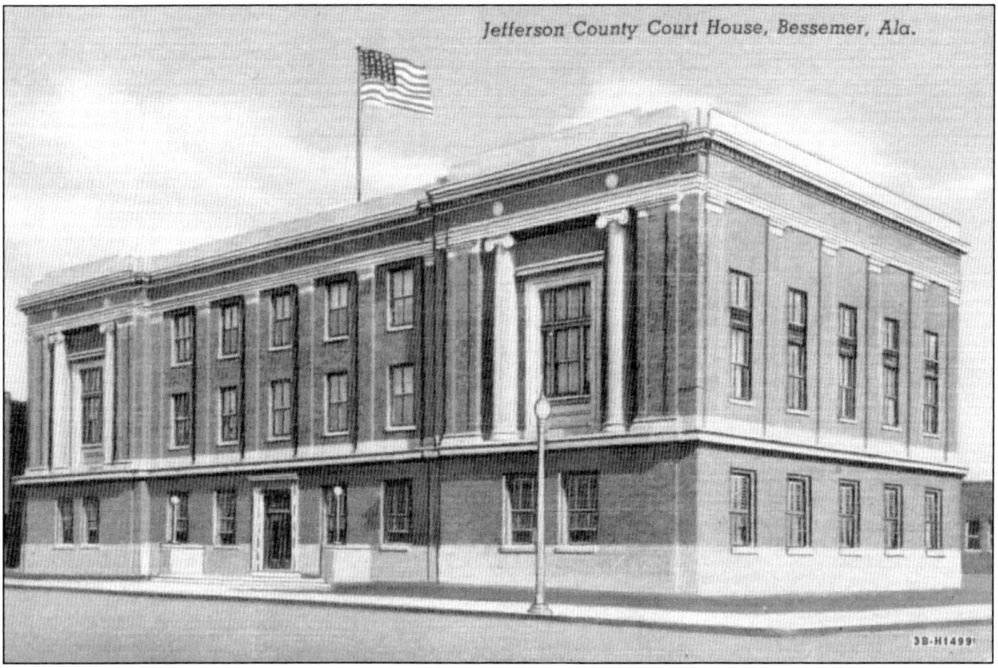

As early as 1898, city attorney J.K. Trotter had proposed a Jefferson County court of inferior jurisdiction for Bessemer, similar to the county's inferior court in Birmingham. Nearly 17 years later, in 1915, the county constructed a courthouse with full facilities to meet the needs of people in the Bessemer Cut-off. The courthouse stands directly across Third Avenue from city hall. The three-story, buff brick structure is built in the enframed block design, a popular style for public buildings of the era. (Author's collection.)

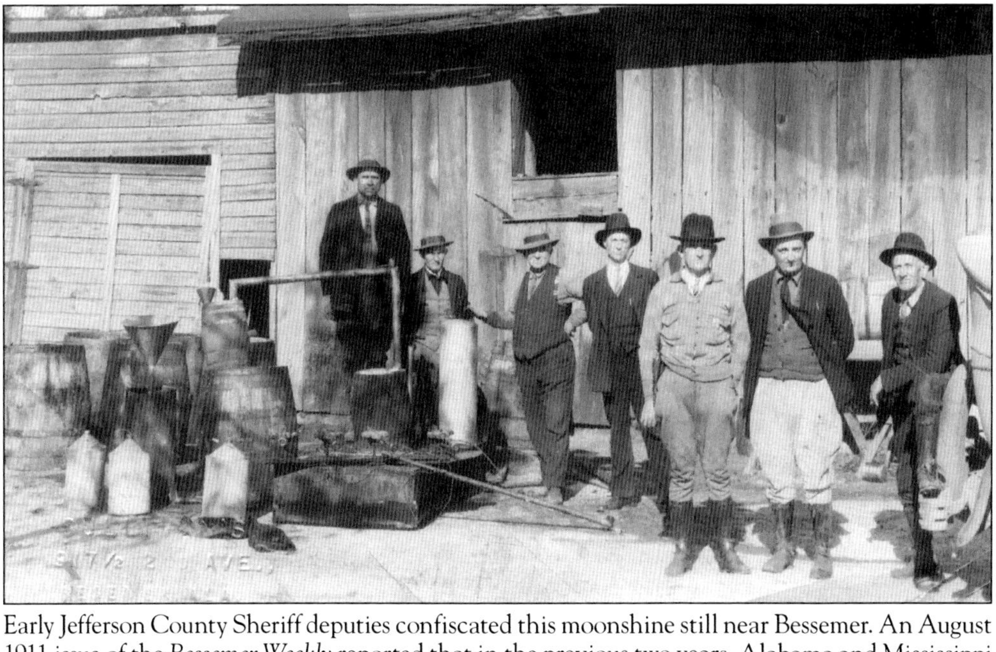

Early Jefferson County Sheriff deputies confiscated this moonshine still near Bessemer. An August 1911 issue of the *Bessemer Weekly* reported that in the previous two years, Alabama and Mississippi deputies made over 400 moonshining arrests and destroyed nearly 1,000 stills.

Six

SCHOOLS

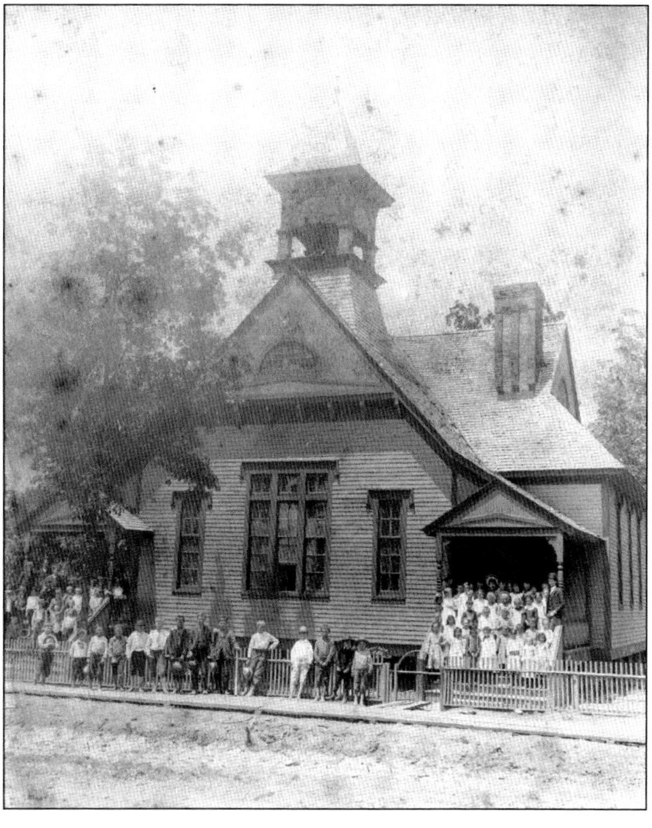

In 1888, the Bessemer Land and Improvement Company erected the city's first public graded school building on the corner of Nineteenth Street and Seventh Avenue (right). The city hired professor A.N. Hendon as principal along with two teachers, Miss Hickman and Miss Weaver. By the start of the fall 1889 session, there were nearly 100 students in attendance. Before this building was completed, the public school, known as Red Mountain Academy, met in a one-room frame building near Thompson Town. (Birmingham Public Library Archives, File No. 1556.22.64.)

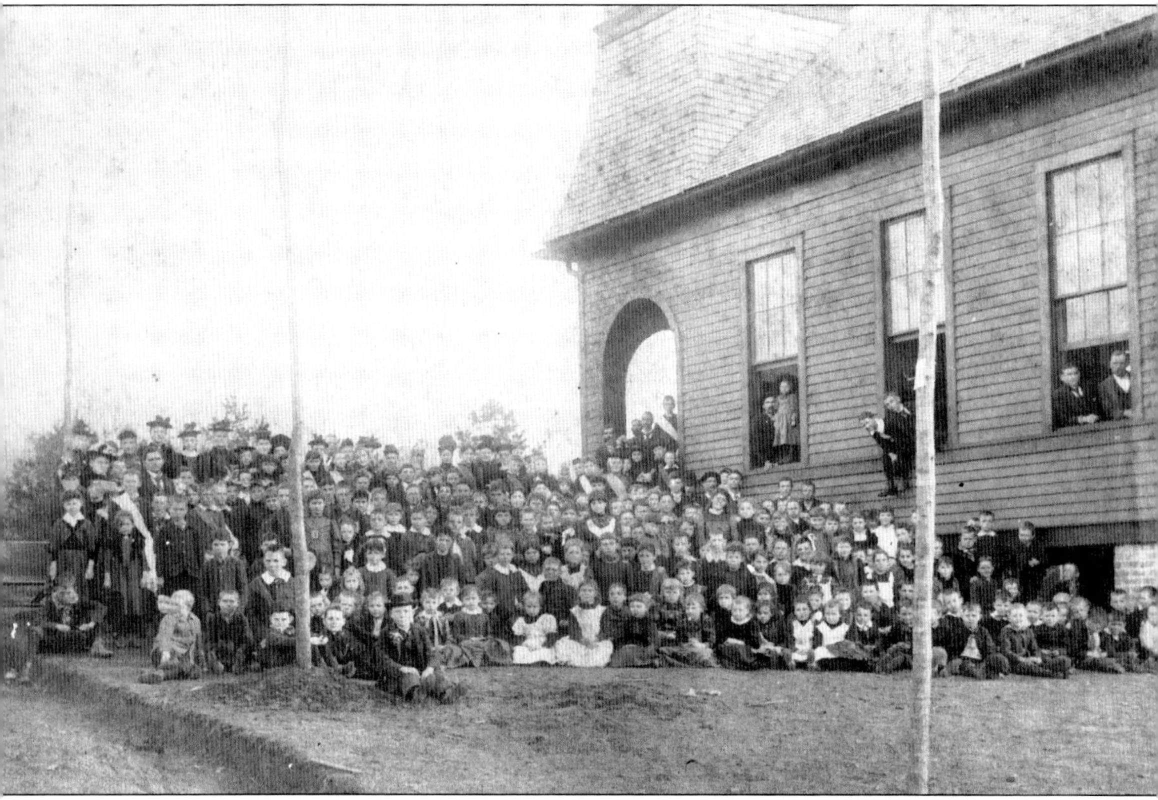

In October 1890, the Hilliker-Krebs Building Company was putting the finishing touches on the new, two-room, 40-by-60-foot Howell School building on the corner of Dartmouth Avenue and Nineteenth Street. When the building opened in November, there were 83 students enrolled. In 1900, grades one through three were taught at Howell and 172 students were enrolled. In this February 1892 photograph, the students, along with principal Mrs. Harthan and fourth-grade teacher Helen Douglas, celebrate George Washington's birthday.

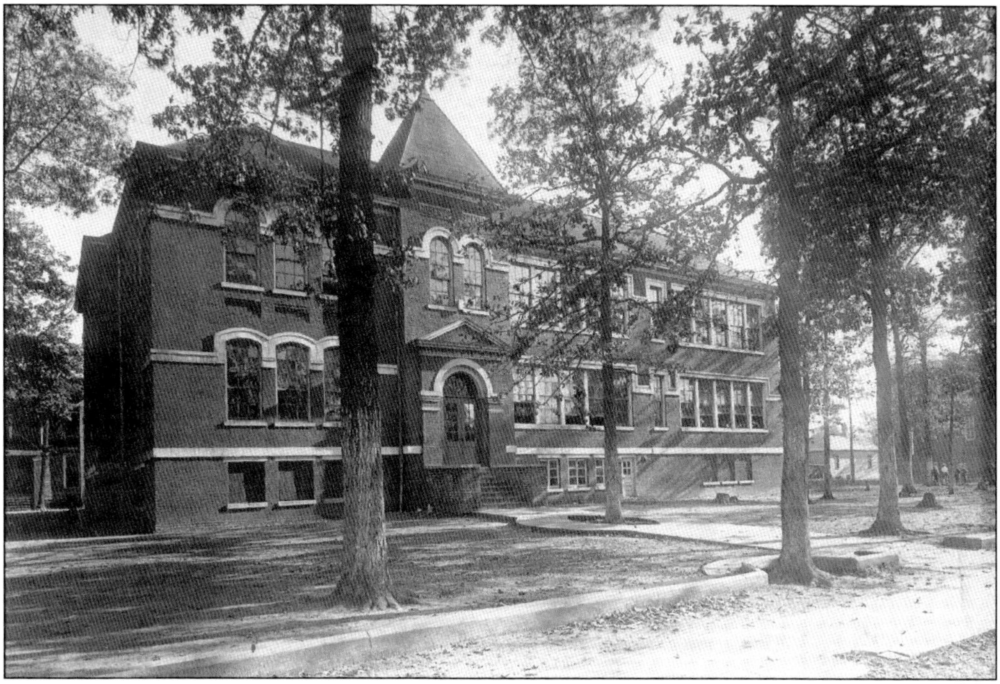

Bessemer's first "modern" brick schoolhouse, the Roberts School, was built in 1892 on the corner of Seventeenth Street and Fifth Avenue. By 1901, there were 435 students enrolled at Roberts School. The first class to graduate from Roberts in 1894 had three students—Pearl Griffin, Sadie Cockrell, and Alice Glenn.

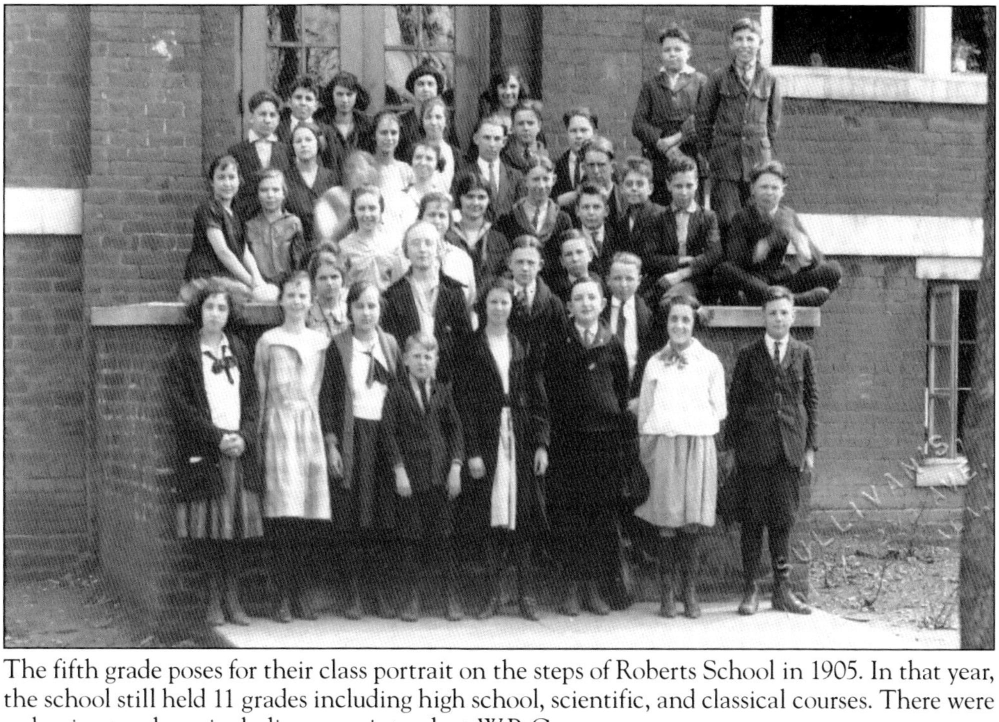

The fifth grade poses for their class portrait on the steps of Roberts School in 1905. In that year, the school still held 11 grades including high school, scientific, and classical courses. There were only nine teachers, including superintendent W.P. Gunn.

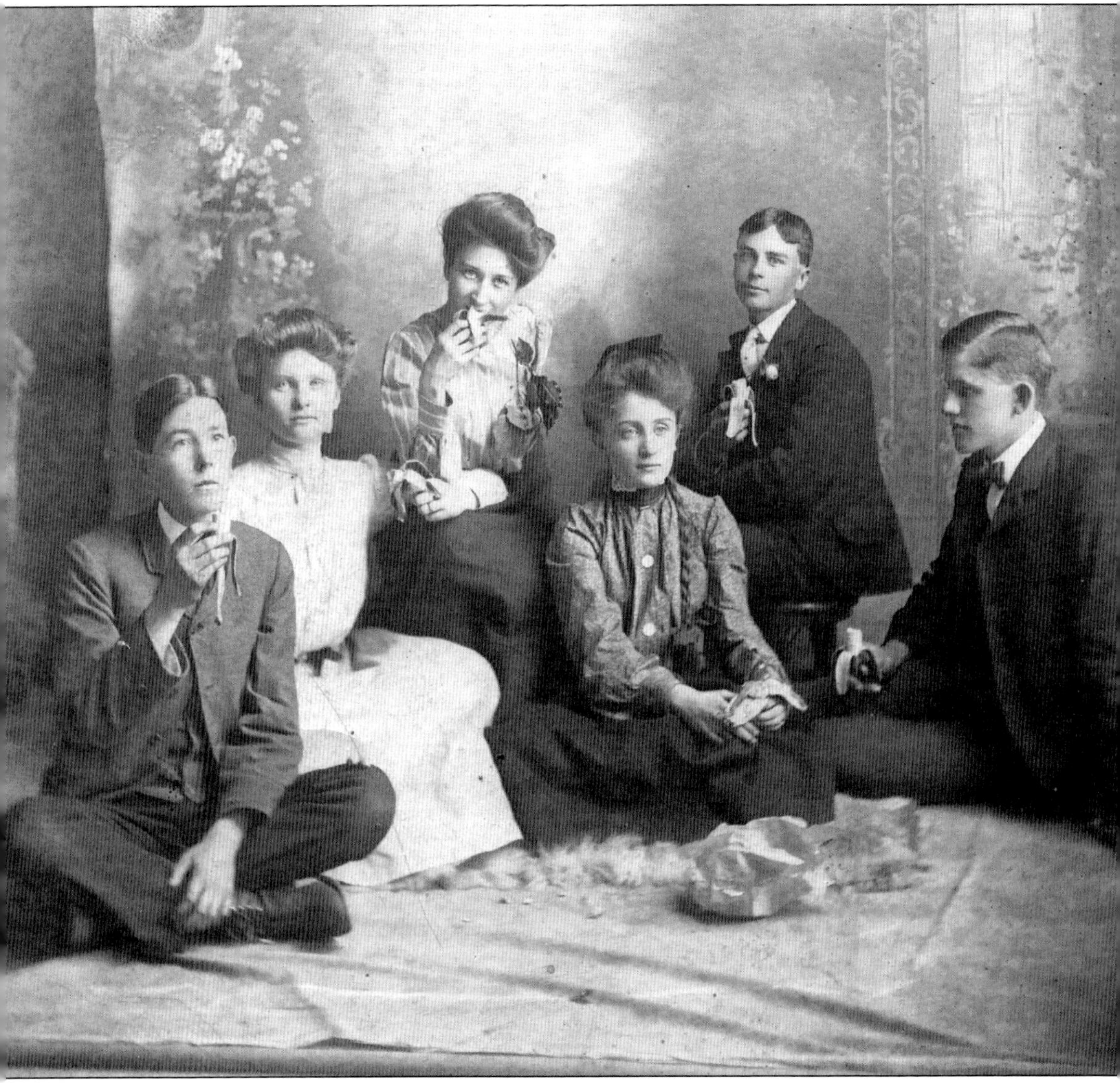

The Bessemer High School seniors of 1903 add an element of fun to their class portrait by all eating bananas. From left to right, they are Chester Tubb, Matura Benton, Stella Grace Spencer, Carmelite Pilcher, Lawrence Barnette, and Percy Benton.

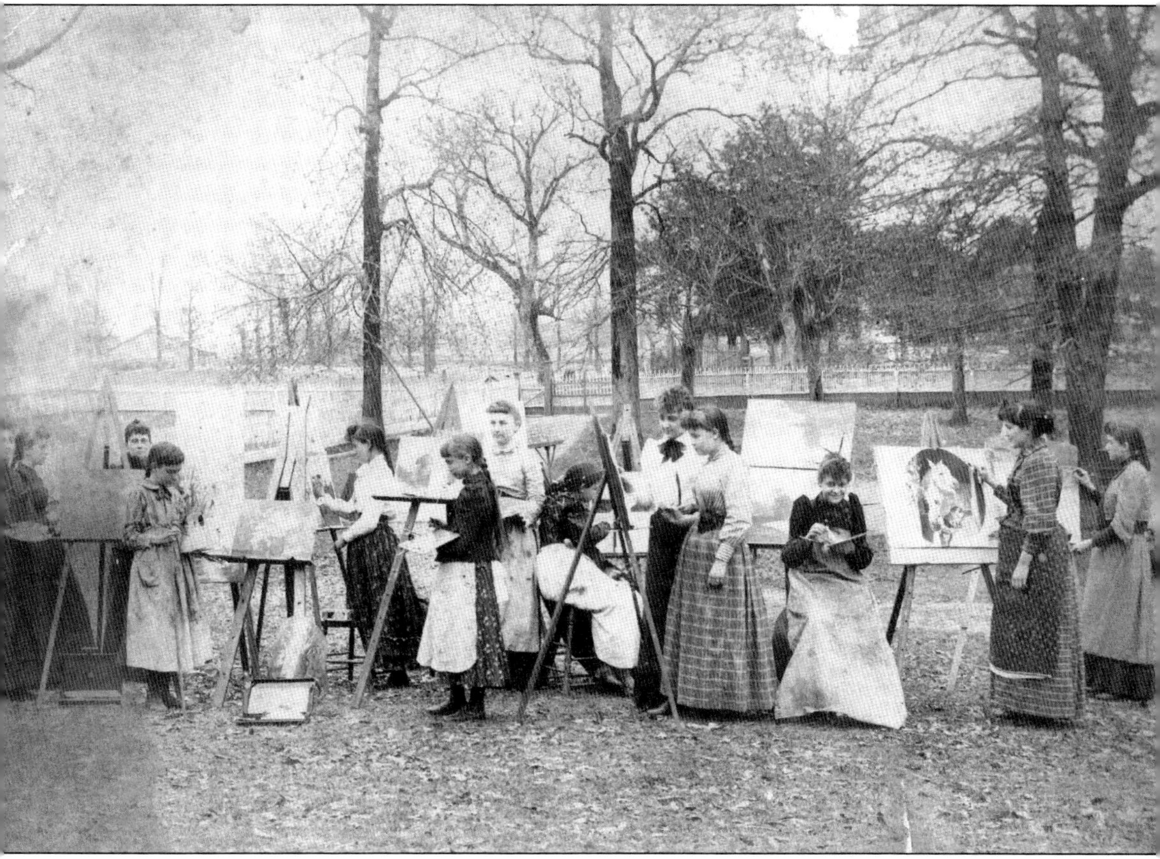

In addition to the public school system, Bessemer had several private academies and a parochial school at St. Aloysius. In the fall of 1889, Miss L. Henderson opened a private school at the corner of Nineteenth Street and Tenth Avenue. Henderson taught in Charleston, South Carolina, before coming to Bessemer. This 1892 painting class, believed to be Miss Henderson's, met in a downtown park.

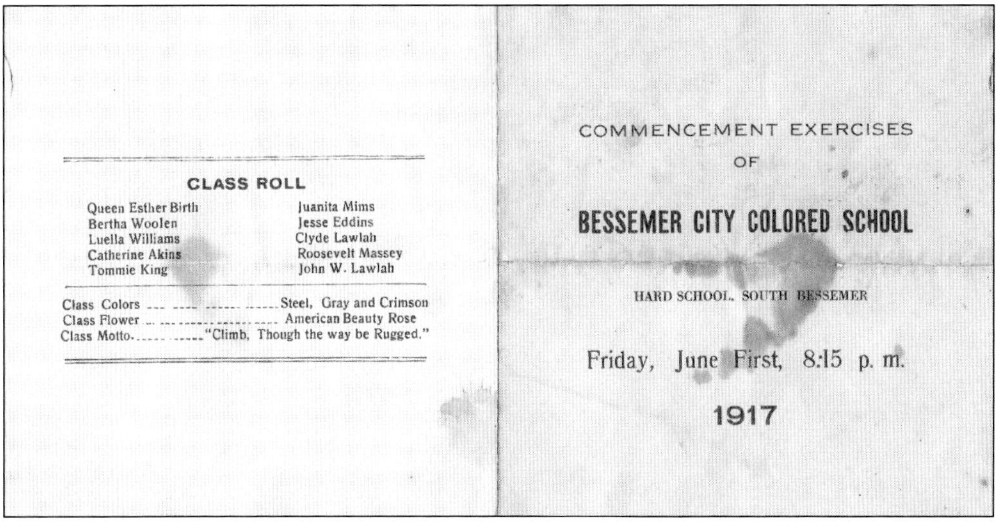

CLASS ROLL

Queen Esther Birth
Bertha Woolen
Luella Williams
Catherine Akins
Tommie King
Juanita Mims
Jesse Eddins
Clyde Lawlah
Roosevelt Massey
John W. Lawlah

Class Colors .... Steel, Gray and Crimson
Class Flower .... American Beauty Rose
Class Motto............ "Climb, Though the way be Rugged."

COMMENCEMENT EXERCISES
OF
BESSEMER CITY COLORED SCHOOL

HARD SCHOOL, SOUTH BESSEMER

Friday, June First, 8:15 p. m.

1917

In 1894, a new school for African American students was built at Arlington Avenue and Twenty-fourth Street. The school was named for Bessemer's second mayor, Charles F. Hard. The Hard school's original buildings stood until they were destroyed by fire in 1958. This 1917 graduation program shows a graduating class of 10.

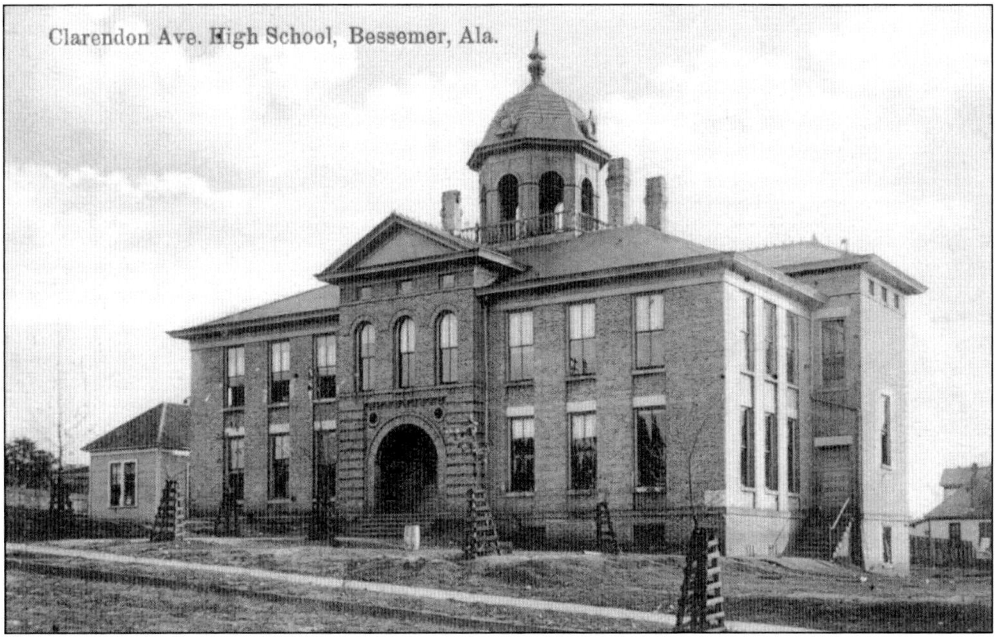

Early Bessemer's population explosion required ever-larger schools. In 1907, the Clarendon School (corner of Clarendon Avenue and Nineteenth Street) replaced the Howell School, opening to 42 high school students. Professor Stevenson was the first principal at Clarendon, followed by Prof. John B. Chapman in 1908.

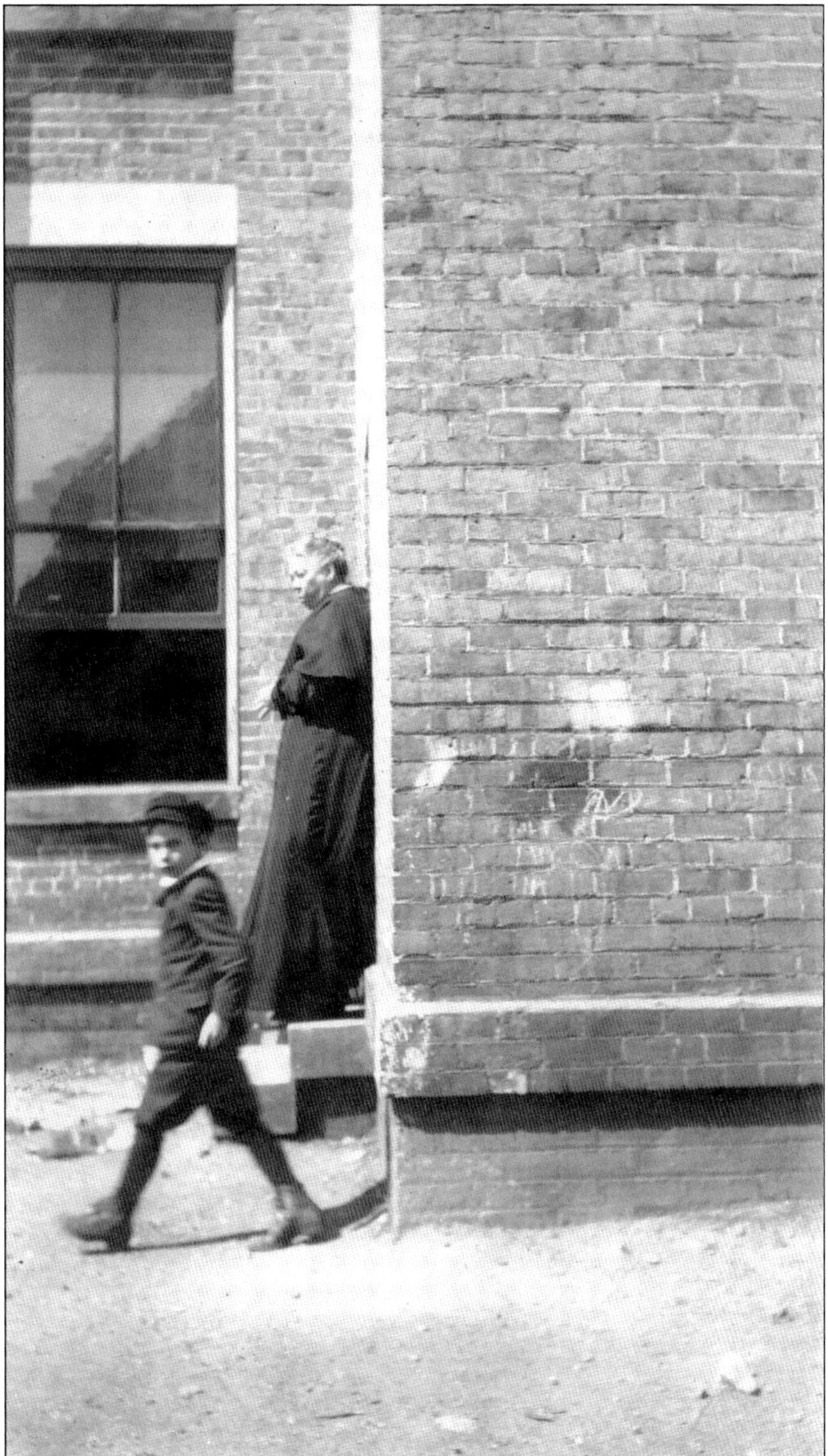

Ella Leaper originally taught at Roberts School, but transferred to Clarendon School when it opened. In this 1910 photograph, she keeps an eye on a young student at Clarendon.

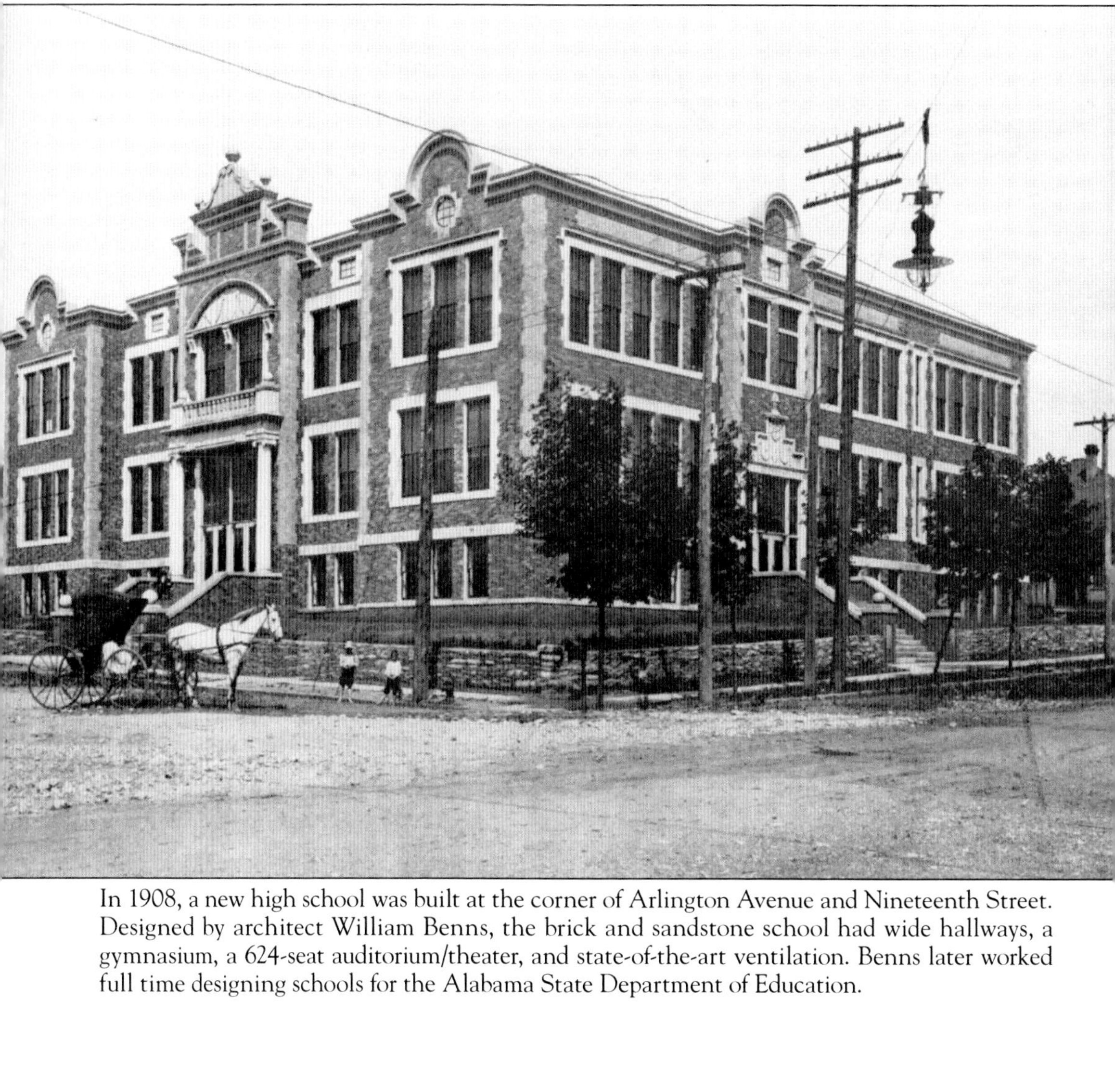

In 1908, a new high school was built at the corner of Arlington Avenue and Nineteenth Street. Designed by architect William Benns, the brick and sandstone school had wide hallways, a gymnasium, a 624-seat auditorium/theater, and state-of-the-art ventilation. Benns later worked full time designing schools for the Alabama State Department of Education.

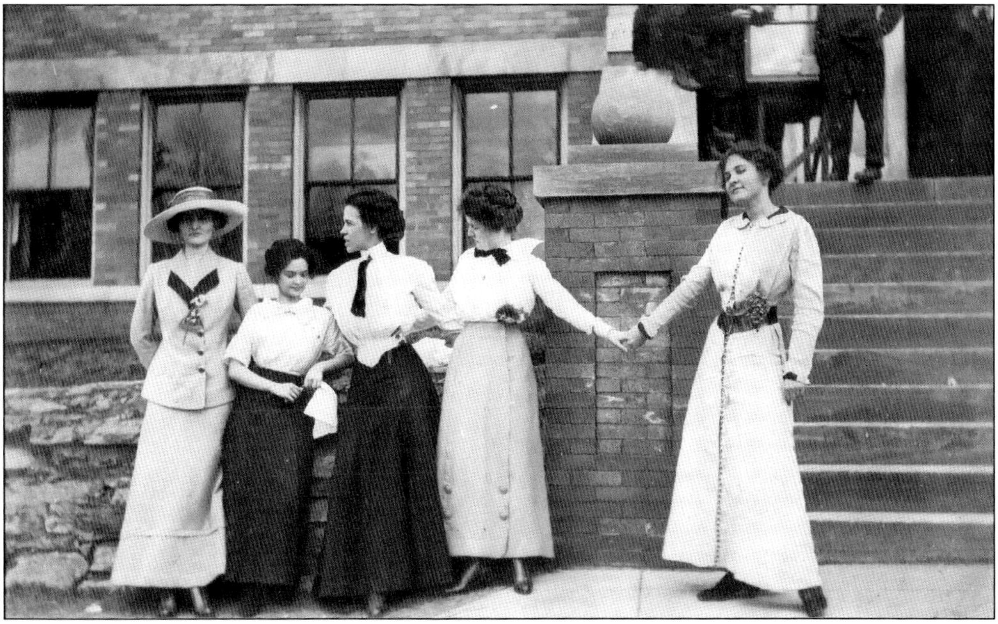

Five young Arlington teachers, Matura Benton, Inez Lopez, Ella Sapp, Bessie Parker, and Ellen Davis, are photographed for a yearbook. The Bessemer High class of 1911 published the school's first yearbook, *Kalista*. The name was suggested by R.A. Mickle, the principal and classics scholar. In the production of iron, dross (slag) is skimmed from the top of the molten metal. The class liked his idea and chose "Kalista," the Greek word for dross, to represent the skimming of their high school experience.

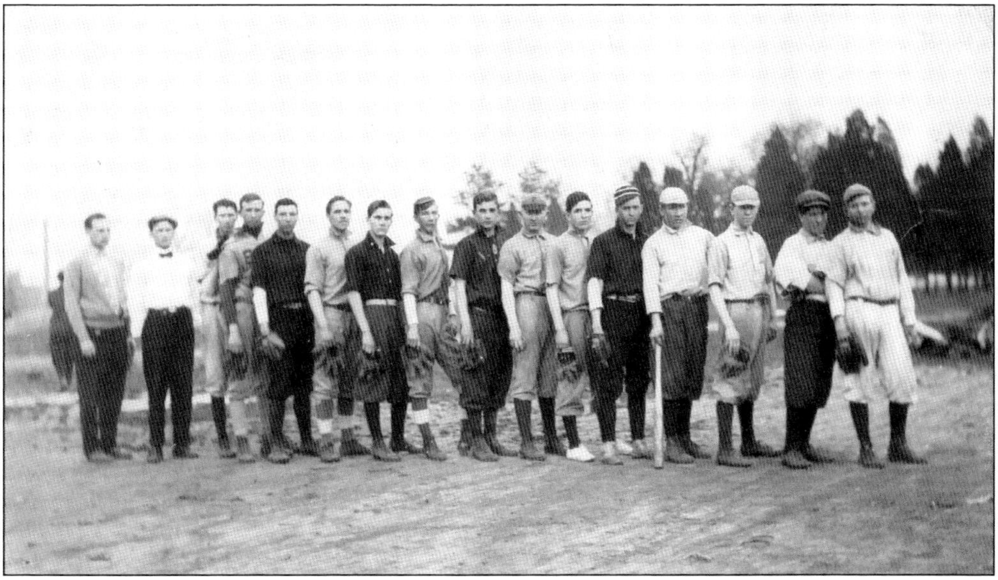

Professors Kuchinski and Kyzer (left) coached the 1912 Bessemer High School baseball team. The team practiced against other local schools during the preseason. The first game of the season was played against Massey Business College. Bessemer was victorious with a score of 7-2.

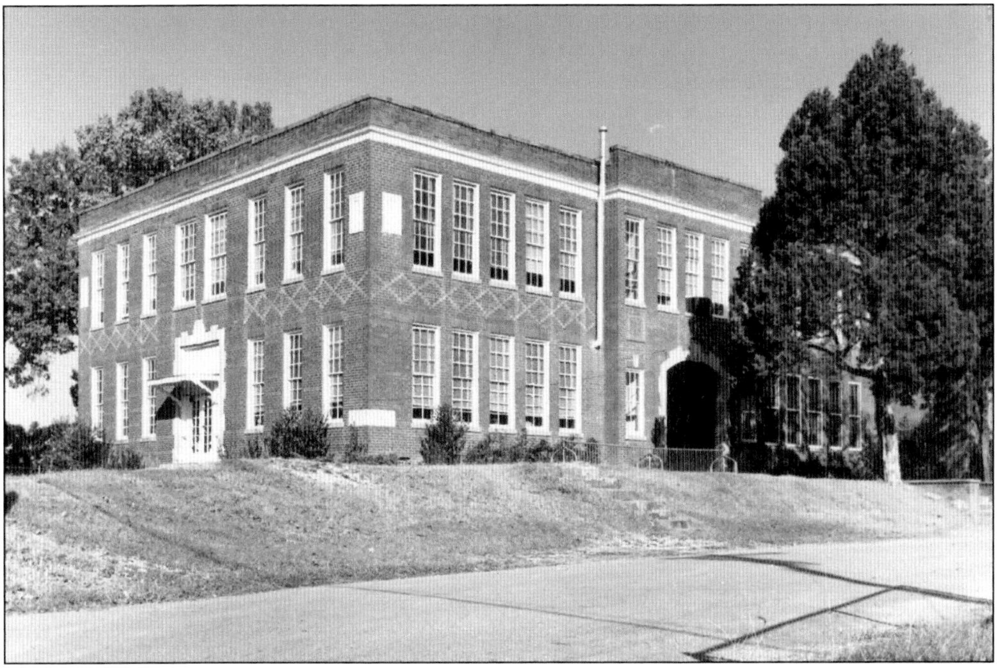

Bessemer continued building schools at a remarkable pace, opening nine new schools between 1902 and 1933. The first Jonesboro Elementary School, above, was located at Owen Avenue; it opened in 1909 and remained in operation until 1952. The site of the school is now the Jonesboro Community Garden. Vance Grammar School, below, opened in 1920 at Fifth Avenue and Sixteenth Street. Other schools from this period include Ninth Avenue School, Arlington, Fourth Avenue School, Dunbar High, Bessemer High School, and Carver School.

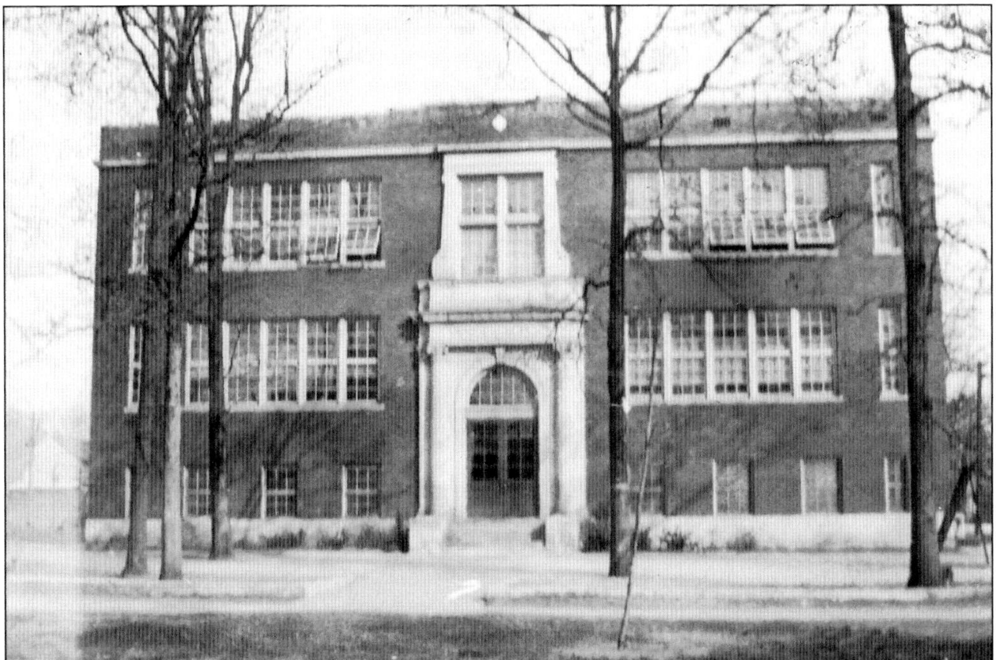

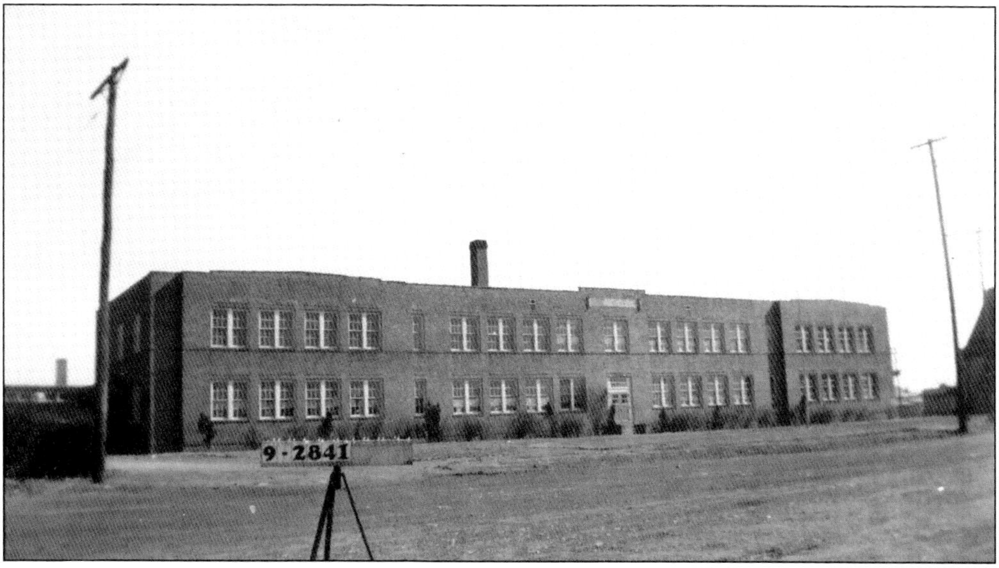

In 1923, Bessemer Colored High School opened on Sixth Avenue and Twenty-seventh Street. The school's first principal, J.B. Bickerstaff, had the school's name changed to Dunbar High School in 1928 to honor African American poet Paul Laurence Dunbar. Dunbar High School was listed in the National Register of Historic Places in 2011. (Birmingham Public Library archives, File No. 38-3-3-2-2.)

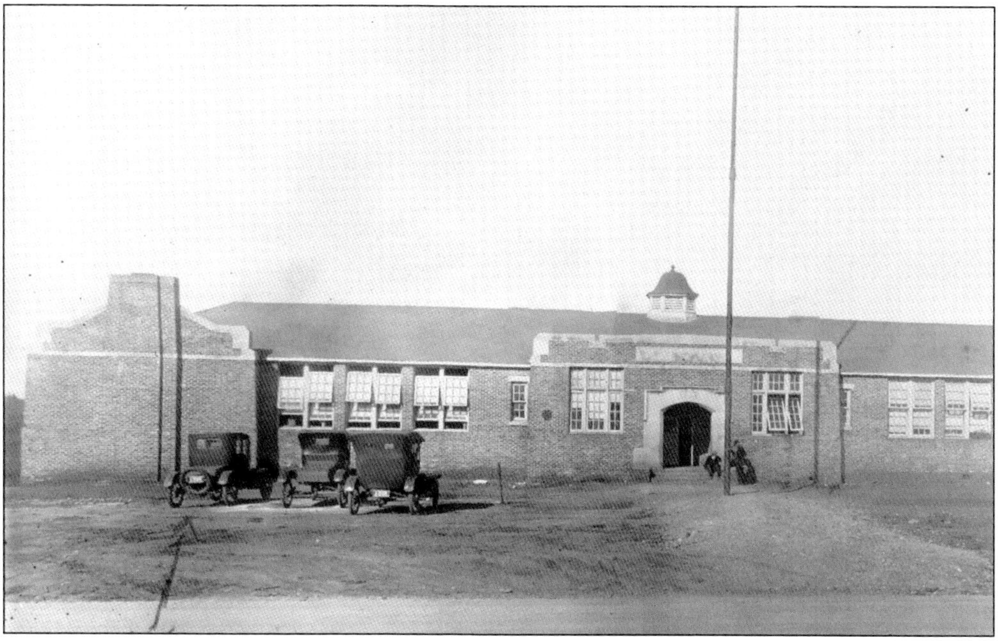

The McNeil School was formed in 1923 and met in shotgun houses near Westlake, until this building with 10 classrooms opened in November 1926 with 468 students enrolled in grades one through nine. B.E. Lee was McNeil's first principal, and the first teachers were Elma Thomas, Elizabeth Mayes, Mildred Glidewell, Ruby Lee, Lucy Gwen, and Lelia Sturdivant.

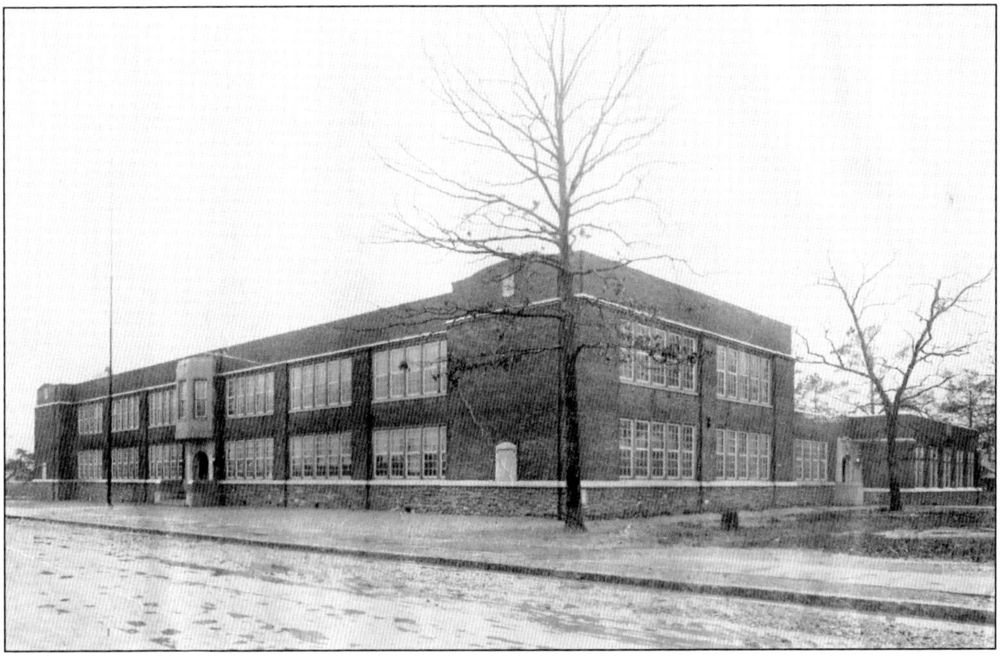

In 1923, Bessemer built a school that was large enough to serve it for many years. Bessemer Senior High School opened on Fourteenth Street and Second Avenue. The new school had room to grow its student body and a site that allowed for expansion. Over the next 15 years, additional classrooms and a gymnasium were added. Bessemer High remained at the Fourteenth Street campus until 1970. For many years, it was recognized as one of the best schools in the state.

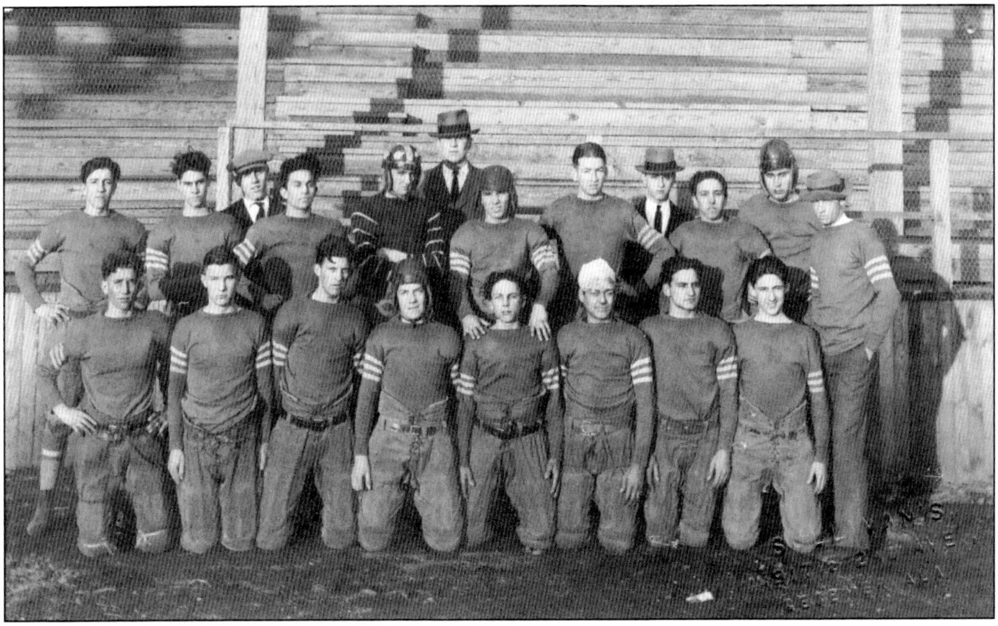

Bessemer High School's 1925 football team did not win a state championship for the Purple Tigers, but they did crush rival Ensley High, the 1924 champions, with a 19-0 victory. Longtime football coach "Red" Harris and Bill Thomas led the team. Much of the football team was also in the Pershing Literary Society and won the literary society championship.

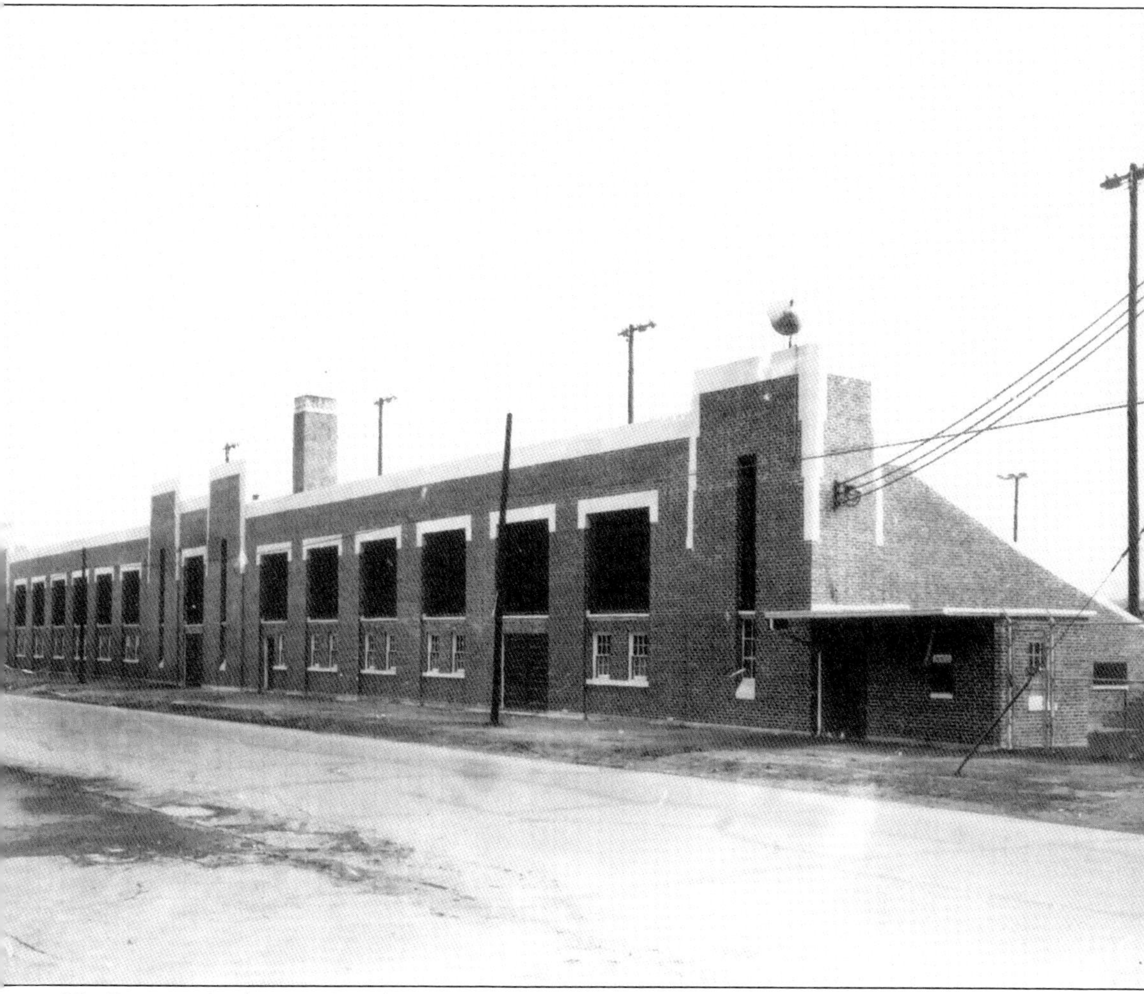

The Bessemer Stadium, on Fourth Avenue and Ninth Street, saw its first football game on November 11, 1935. In 1972, it was named Snitz Snider Memorial Stadium in honor of Bessemer's beloved coach, who led Bessemer to seven state football championships between 1933 and 1963.

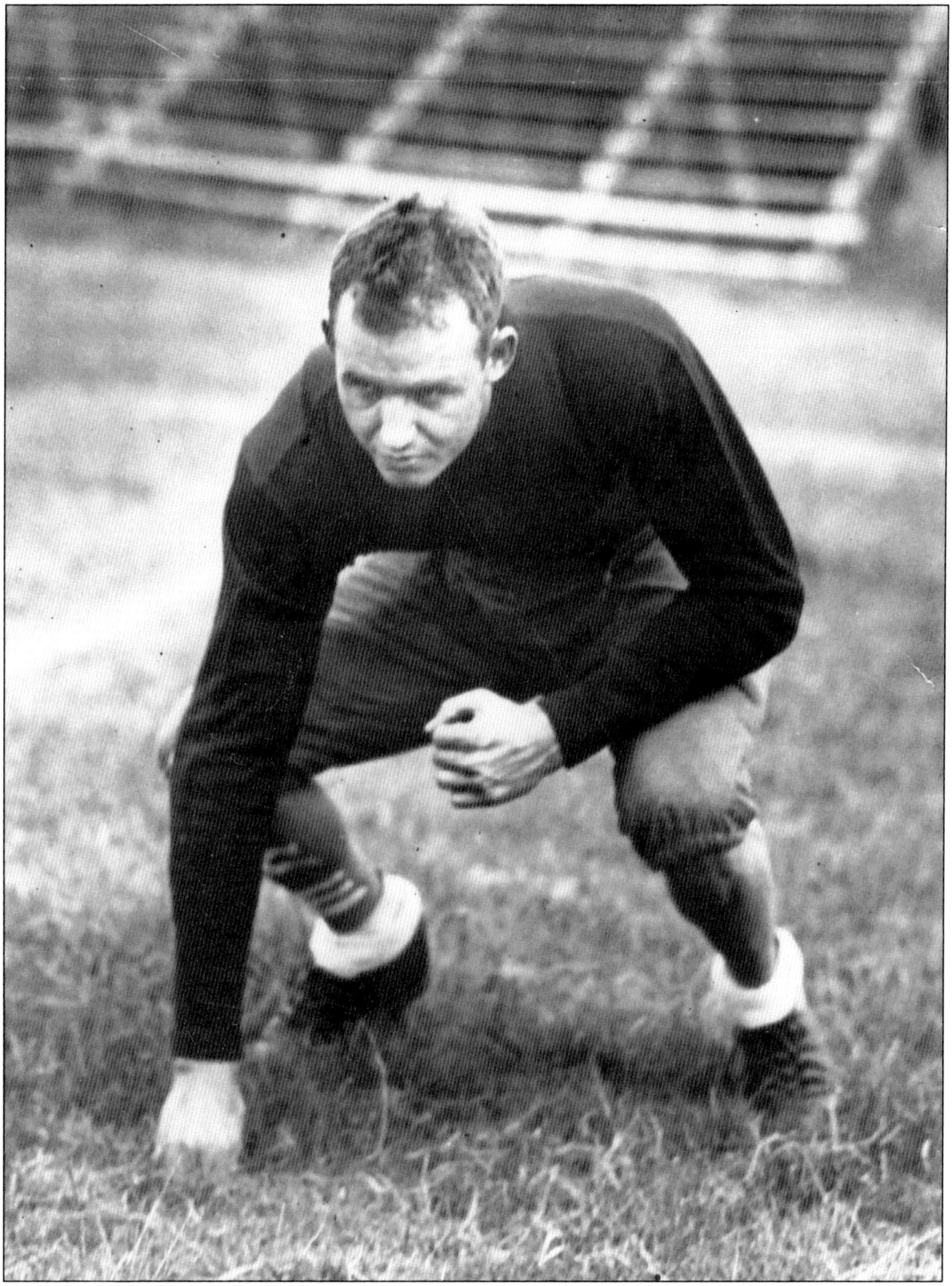

Before coaching at Bessemer, Euil Snitz Snider earned eight varsity letters as a member of Auburn University's football, basketball, and track teams. He competed on the 1928 American Olympic track team in Amsterdam and won a bronze medal in the 1928 NCAA Track and Field Championships.

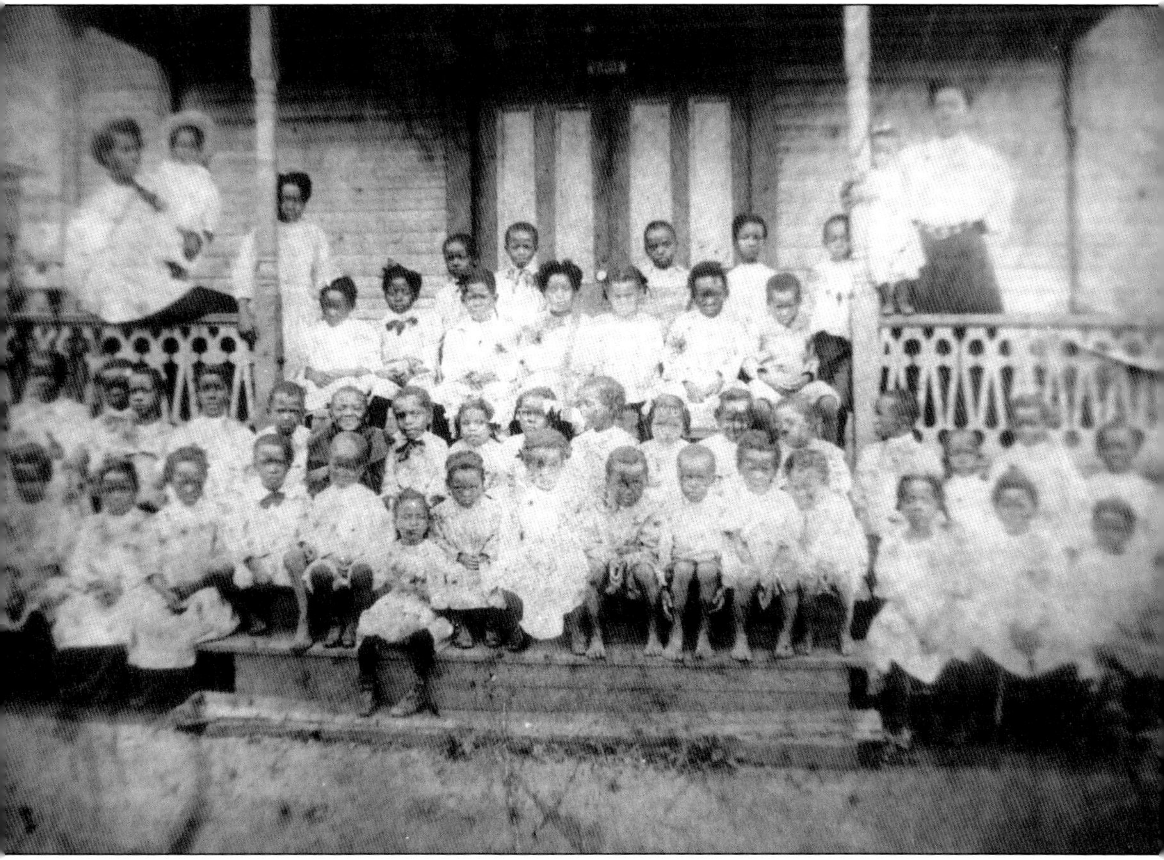

In addition to public and parochial schools, the Bessemer area had a number of company schools. The Nelson Pipe and Foundry community kindergarten was located at 2301 Eighth Avenue North. Some of the children in this c. 1907 photograph include Hortense B. Henderson (inducted into the Alabama Jazz Hall of Fame in 1986), Augustus Chambers Sr., and Louise Pitts. (Henderson family pictures, Bessemer Hall of History.)

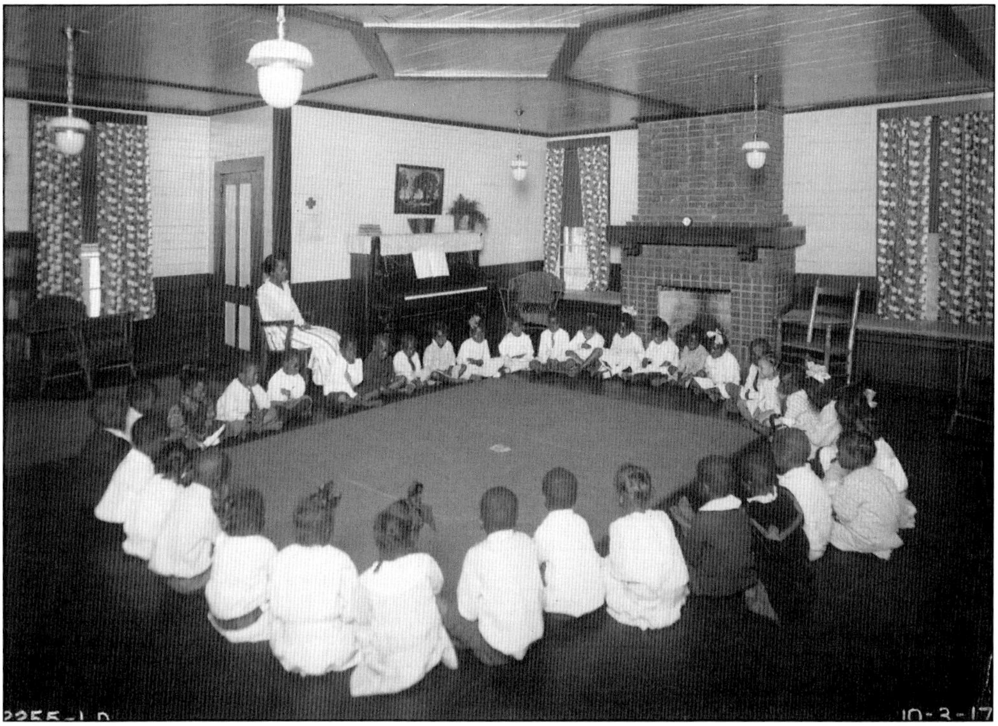

Tennessee Coal, Iron & Railroad Company provided schools for its employees' children. Above, a kindergarten class meets in the Muscoda Iron Ore Mines Colored School. Muscoda Ore Mines White School—below, photographed in 1916—still stands beside Highway 150 near Fairfax Avenue. The Muscoda Red Ore Mining community is noted for having the finest concentration of worker housing and company-built community facilities in the Birmingham District. In addition to the schools, there was a clinic, church, and housing for teachers and a doctor. (Both, W.S. Hoole Special Collections Library, the University of Alabama.)

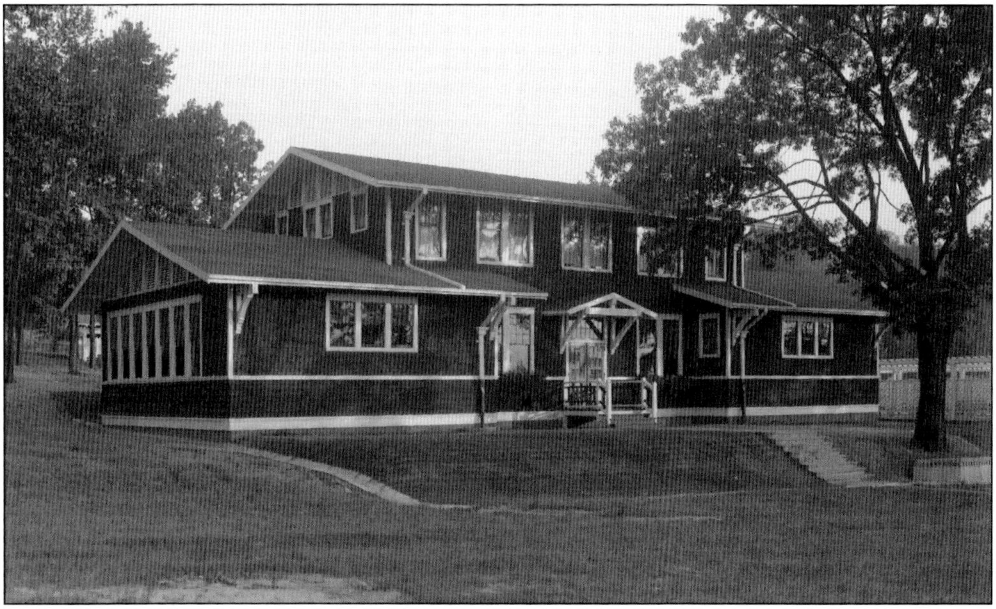

Seven

CHURCHES

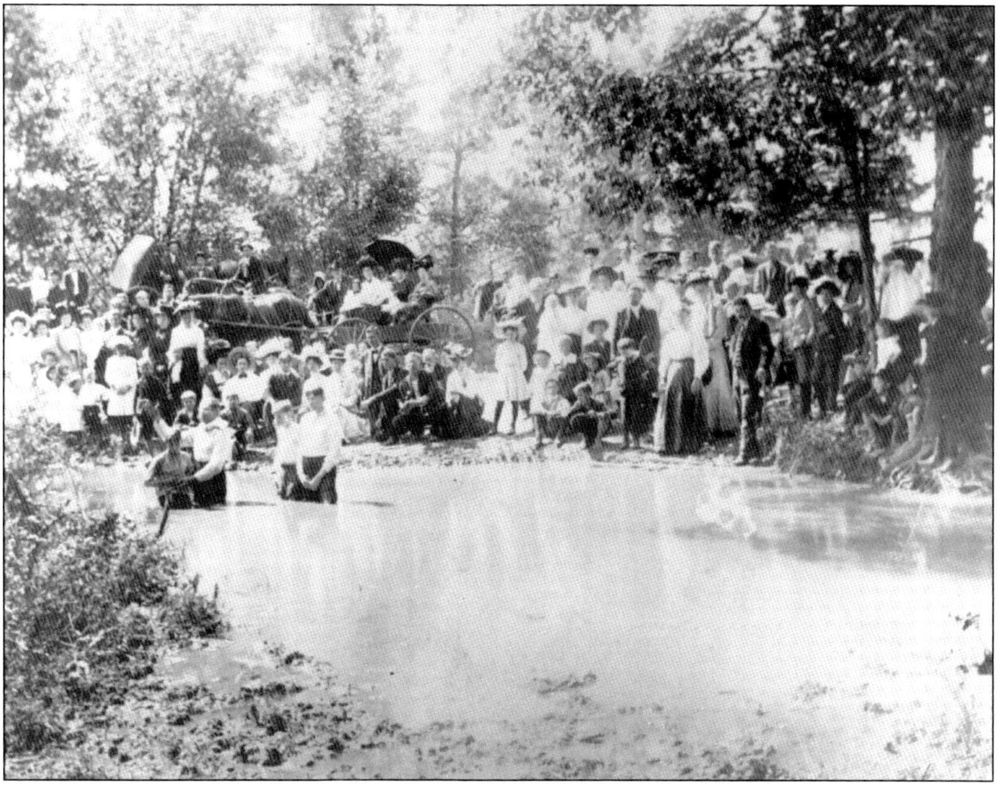

The church history of Bessemer is as rich as its minerals. Bessemer's Canaan Baptist, the oldest church in Jefferson County, was organized in 1818 (a year before Alabama gained statehood). Hosea Holcombe, frontier church organizer and author of *A History of the Rise and Progress of the Baptists in Alabama*, was pastor at Canaan until his death in 1841. Holcombe would have found this 1906 view of a baptism in McCalla Creek familiar. The back of the photograph notes that the Carter family, Jim Moore's family, and Lisha Kendrick's family are in attendance.

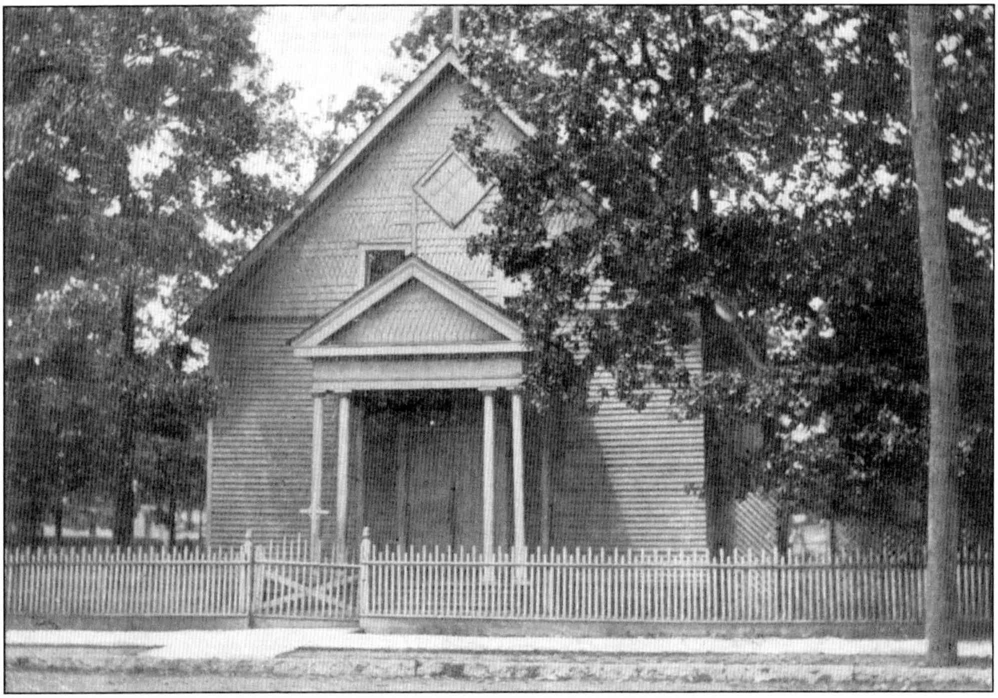

Recognizing the importance of religious life to local communities, the Bessemer Land & Improvement Company reserved city lots for churches of every denomination. One of the first five groups to build in the new town was the Catholic Union. Catholic men from the Rolling Mills erected St. Aloysius (above), a wood-frame building on the corner of Fifth Avenue and Seventeenth Street, in 1888. Below, Rev. Joseph A. Wright, who was appointed the first resident pastor in 1899, stands on the porch of the rectory that was built next door to the church. In 1912, the church built a modern brick school building, and in 1924, a beautiful brick church next door. Fire destroyed the church in 1989, but the school building is still standing.

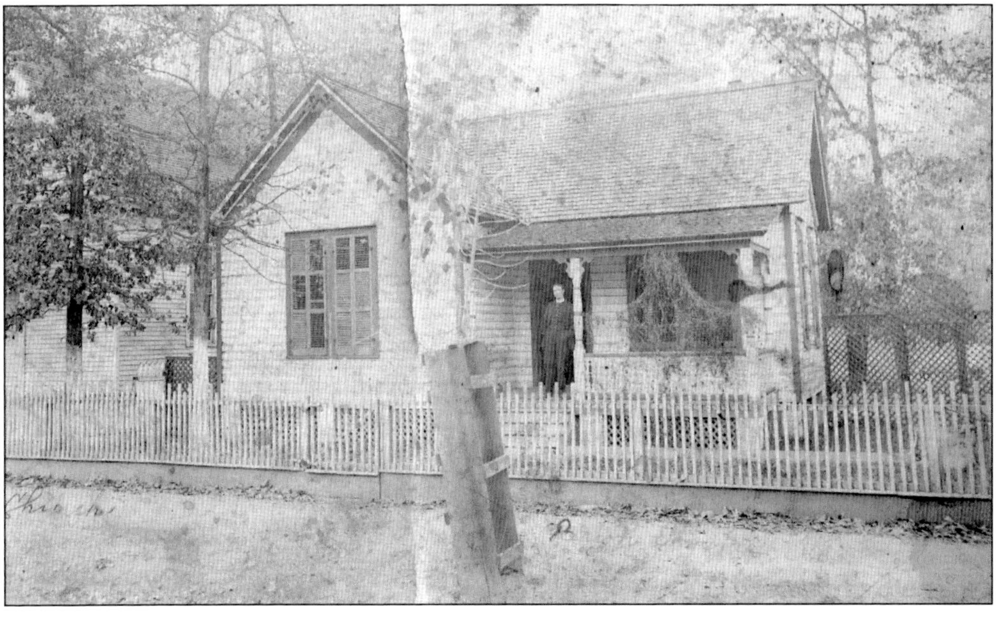

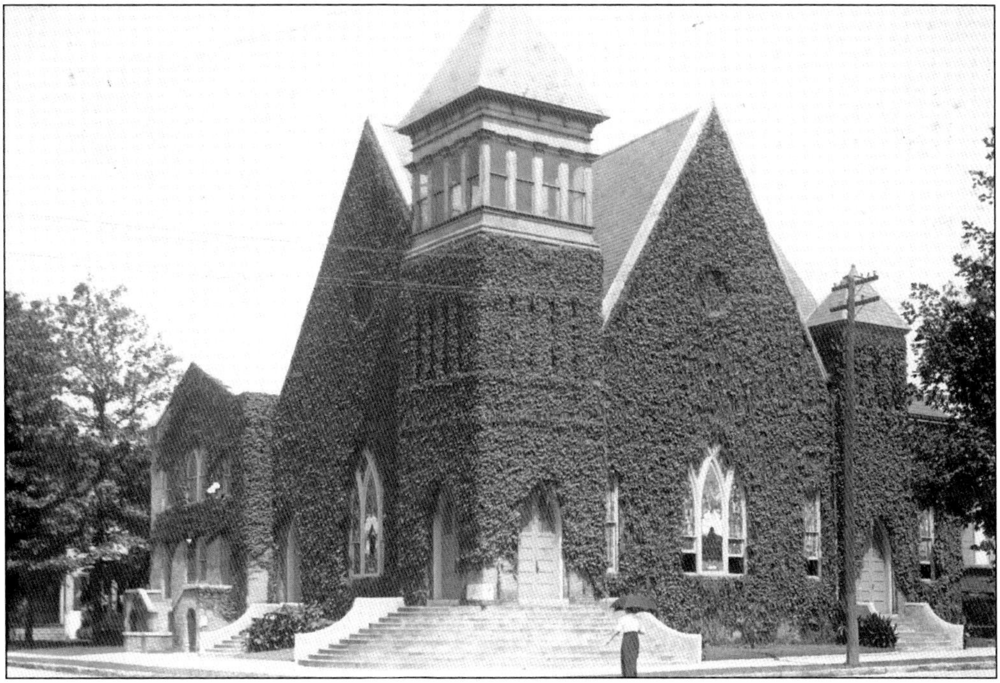

In August 1887, a group met at the Red Mountain School and organized the First Baptist Church of Bessemer. The church's first building was located on Nineteenth Street between Seventh and Eighth Avenues. The building seen here was designed by Wallace A. Rayfield and built in 1907 at the corner of Fifth Avenue and Eighteenth Street.

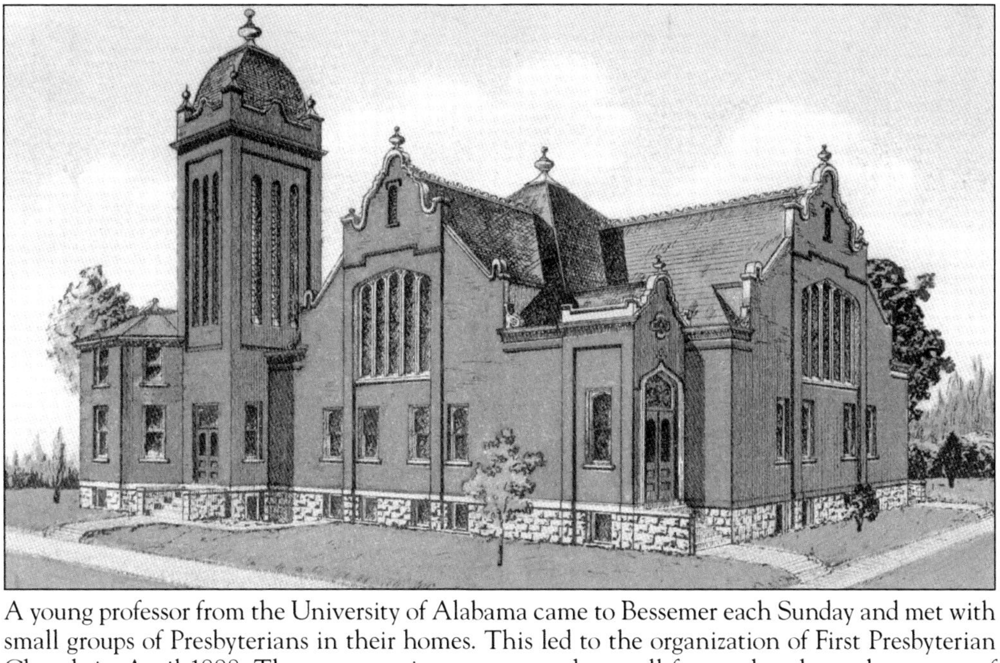

A young professor from the University of Alabama came to Bessemer each Sunday and met with small groups of Presbyterians in their homes. This led to the organization of First Presbyterian Church in April 1888. The congregation constructed a small frame church on the corner of Nineteenth Street and Sixth Avenue. First Presbyterian's second church, the red brick Gothic-style building seen here, was built at the corner of Eighteenth Street and Third Avenue in 1909.

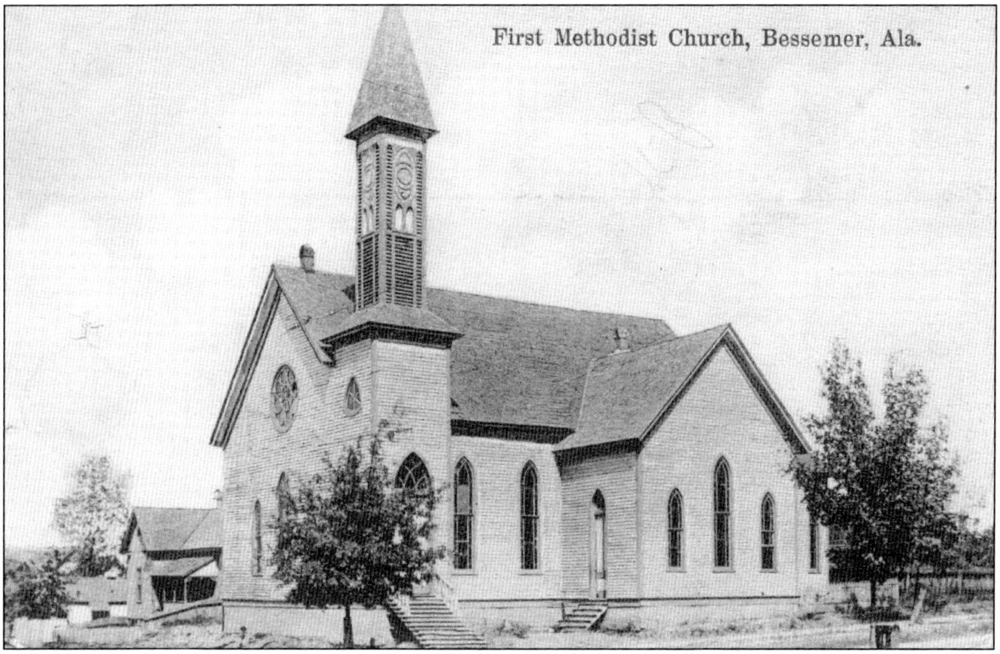

The First Methodist Episcopal Church South was built on Clarendon Avenue and Twenty-third Street in 1889. By 1892, most of the church members were living on the west side of Nineteenth Street and closer to downtown. After considering building a new church, the congregation decided to move its existing building to the corner of Arlington Avenue and Nineteenth Street. On June 4, 1892, the *Bessemer Weekly* reported that the wings of the church being moved had reached Arlington Avenue, and by July 30, the congregation was meeting in its new location, above. When the wood-frame structure burned, the congregation built a church on the opposite corner. The 1916 building, below, was faced in white Franklin County limestone and had a colossal portico supported by massive Corinthian columns.

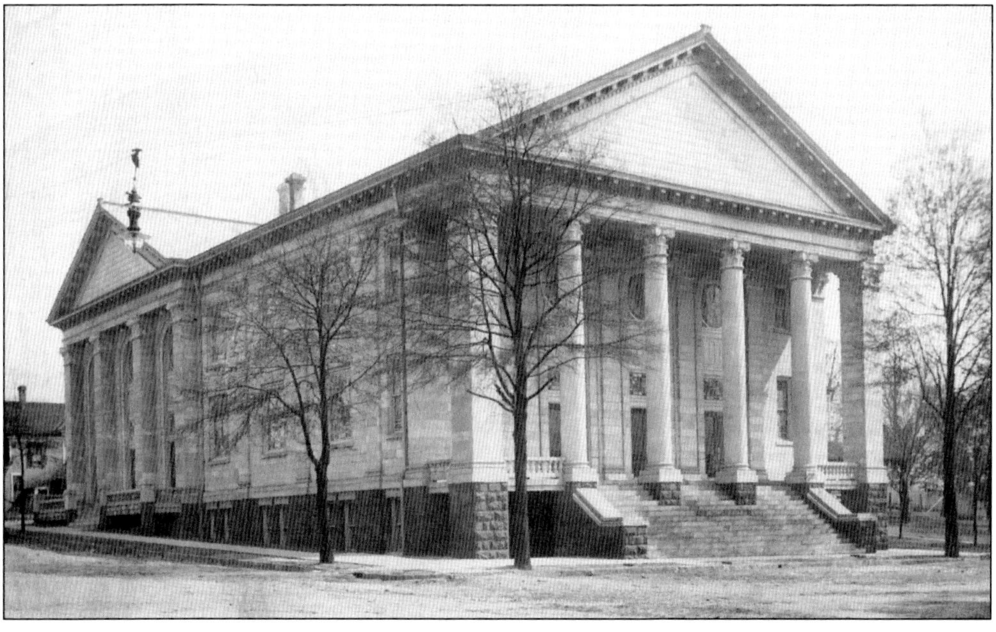

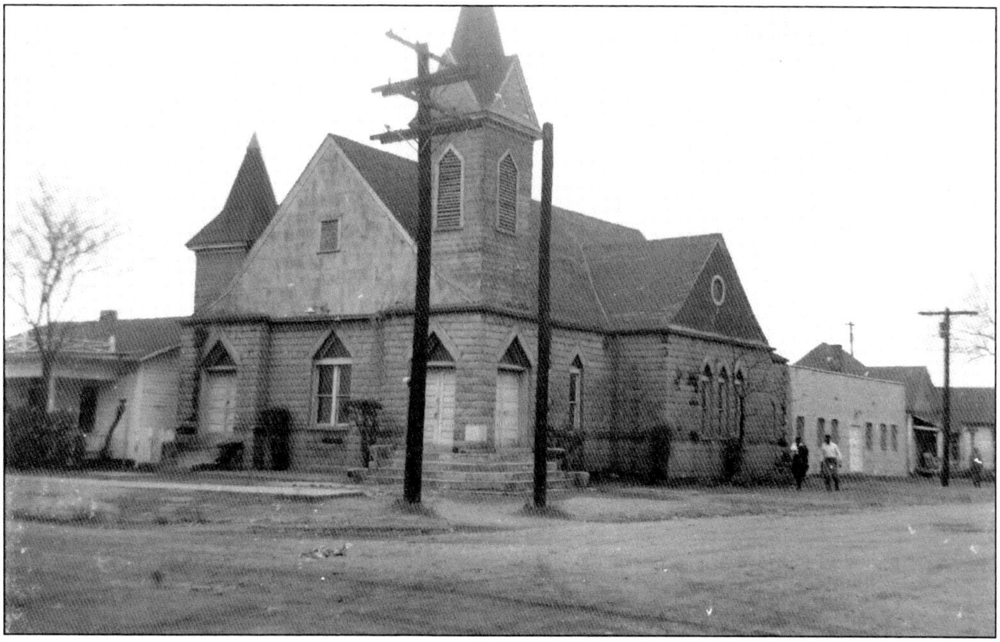

Baptists living to the north of downtown Bessemer wanted to establish a community church and organized Jerusalem Baptist in 1889. The church building stands on the corner of Tenth Avenue North and Twenty-fifth Street. When the church was incorporated in 1934, its name was changed to New Jerusalem Baptist. The building seen here stood until 1979, when the congregation built a new church and education building. (Courtesy of New Jerusalem Baptist Church.)

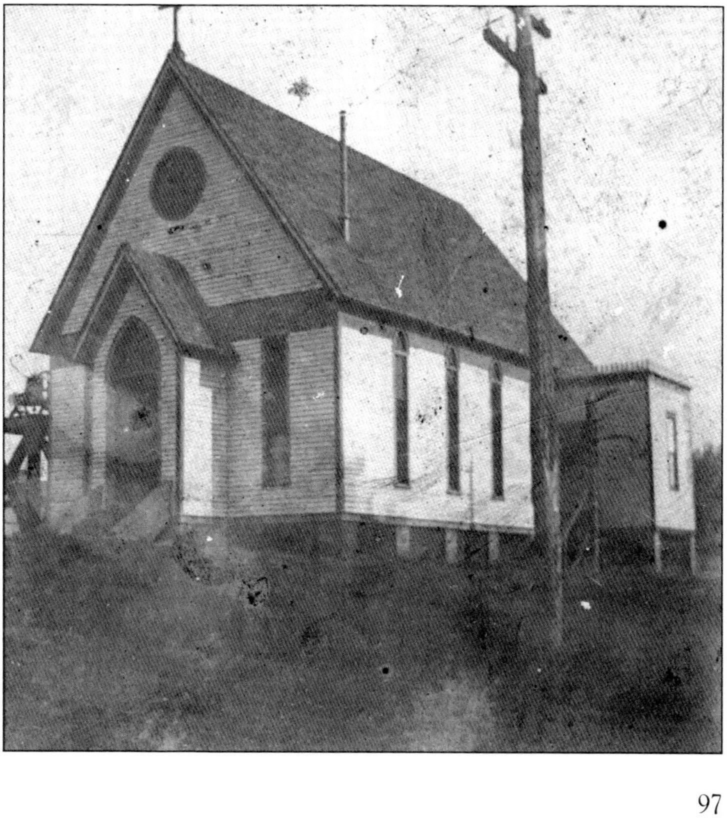

Trinity Episcopal Church was organized in the winter of 1886, and met in the Charleston Block until 1889, when their building was completed on Twentieth Street and Berkeley Avenue. The new church seated about 100 parishioners and was led by Rev. J.A. Van Hoose. Other early ministers who served at Trinity included Rev. Noble C. Powell, who became dean of the Cathedral in Washington, DC, and Edgar R. Neff, director of St. Johns' Episcopal in Montgomery.

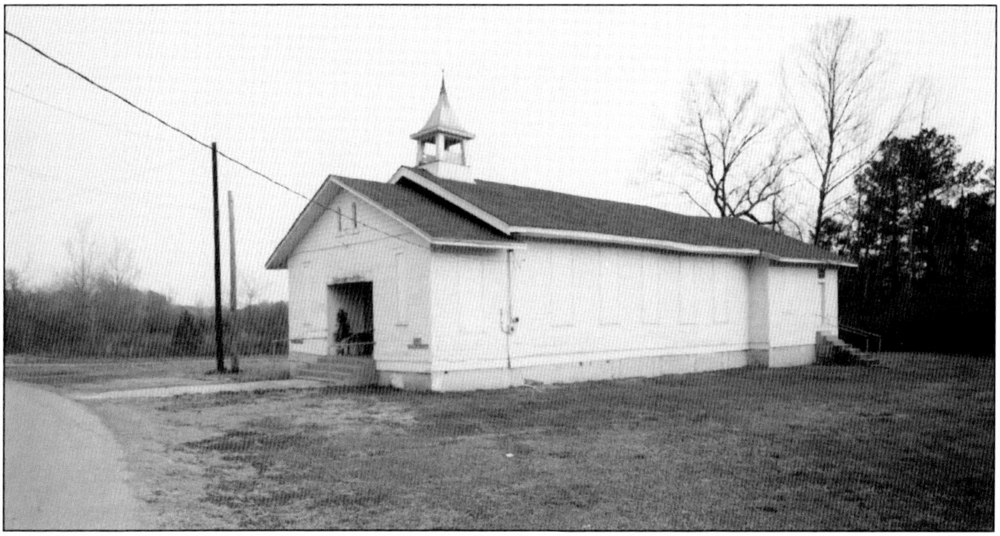

Mining companies not only built homes, schools, and community centers for their employees, but on some occasions church buildings as well. This was often the case in African American quarters of company villages. Congregations sometimes referred to these as "union churches" because Baptists and Methodists used the same building. In the case of the 1901 union church built by TCI at Muscoda, four churches worshiped on rotating Sundays. According to Fallin's *The African American Church in Birmingham, Alabama 1815–1963*, the New Salem Baptist Church, Magnolia AME Church, Mason Chapel United Methodist Church, and Starlight Baptist Church all shared the building (above). Red Mountain Baptist, another of the earliest African American churches in the area (1886) was organized in a church built for them at Sloss Village. (Library of Congress, Prints & Photographs Division, HAER ALA, 37-BES.V, 12.)

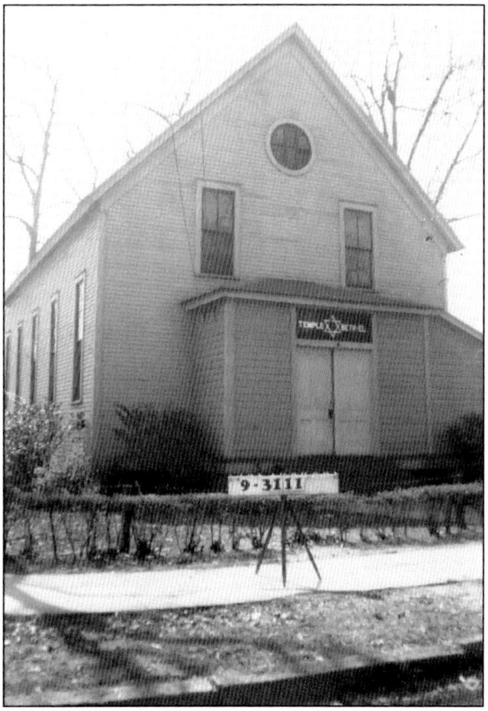

When the city was founded, Bessemer Land & Improvement Company set aside land for a synagogue. In 1889, a small Jewish community began meeting and in 1892, established Congregation Beth El. They built Temple Beth El on the corner of Fifteenth Street and Sixth Avenue. The first service was held on Rosh Hashanah 1906. Lay services were held until Beth El hired their first rabbi in 1917. (Birmingham Public Library archives, File No. 38-9-1-31-19.)

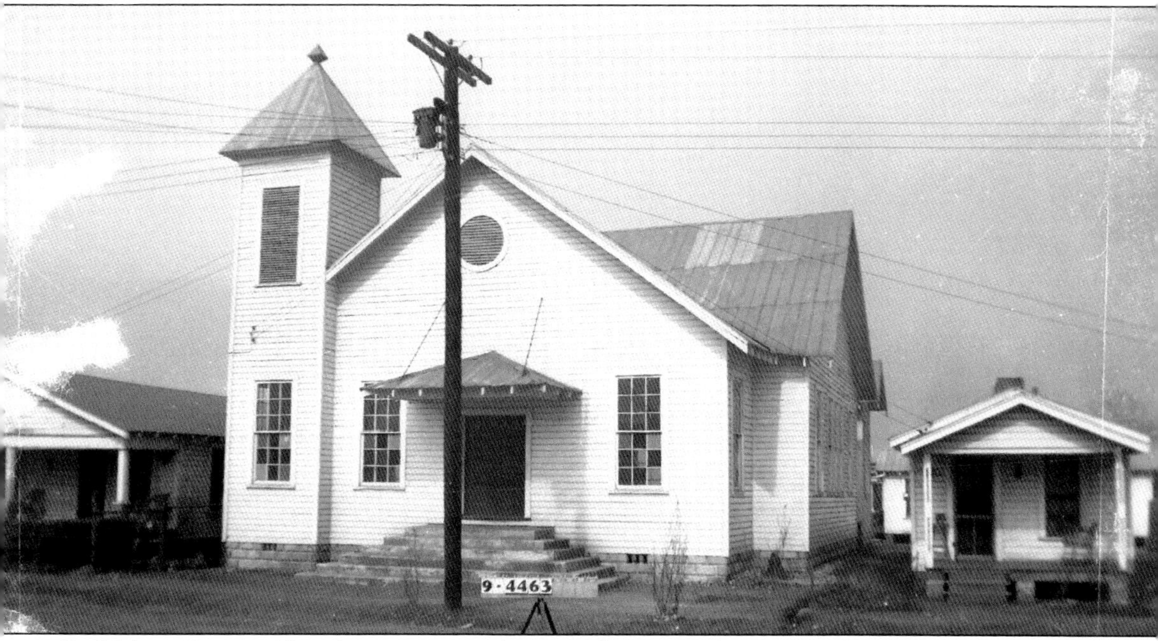

Bethlehem Baptist Church was organized in March 1901 with Rev. Joseph Bowden as pastor. The church's first building, at Eighteenth Street and Eleventh Alley, burned in 1918. Until the structure seen here was built, the congregation met in their homes and a tent. While members were meeting in the tent, Rev. A.C. Burkes became pastor and the church name was changed to New Bethlehem Baptist. (Birmingham Public Library archives, File No. 38-4-3-18-11.)

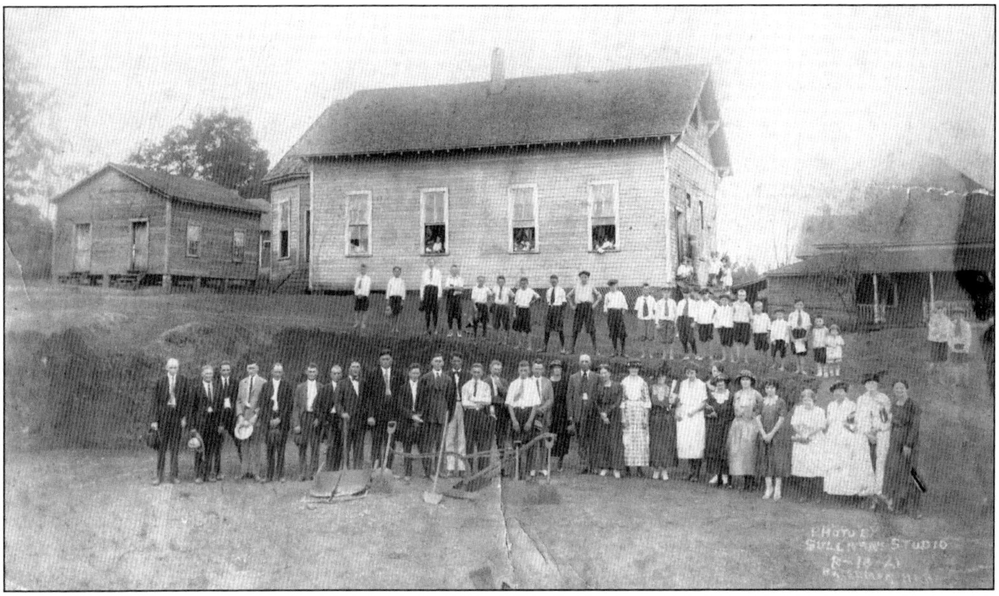

Above, the congregation of Second Baptist Church in Jonesboro gathers to break ground for their second building in August 1921. Below, the Second Baptist Church choir was 35 members strong in 1934. Some of Bessemer's oldest families are represented in the choir's roster. They are, from left to right, (first row) Mrs. Cecil Ward, Mrs. J. Smith, Eloise Lee, Ella Ruth Hallman, Edith Ellis, Marie Hall, Tiny Gunnels, Willie Mae Kendrix, Margaret Steward, Mrs. Luther, two unidentified, and Mrs. Lee Hallman; (second row) Rev. Cecil Ward, Mrs. George Newsome, Lula Hosey, Flora Kendrix, Pearl Jenkins, Christean Hicks, Gladys Franklin, Ethel Hallman, Lois Hallman, Carry Lou Ray, Pauline Edwards, Mable Hosey Self, Jessie Smitherman, Edna Hallman, and choir director Sam Davis; (third row) Vincent Graydon, W.L. Barner, Erice Langston, Howard Langston, T.M. Benson, Mr. Luther, and unidentified.

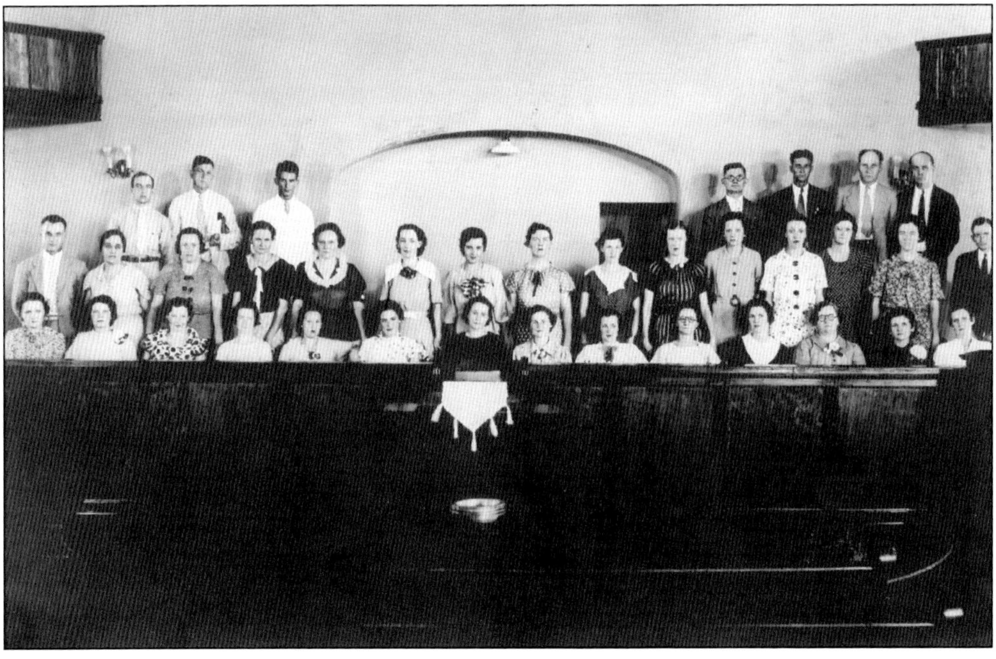

Eight

HOMES

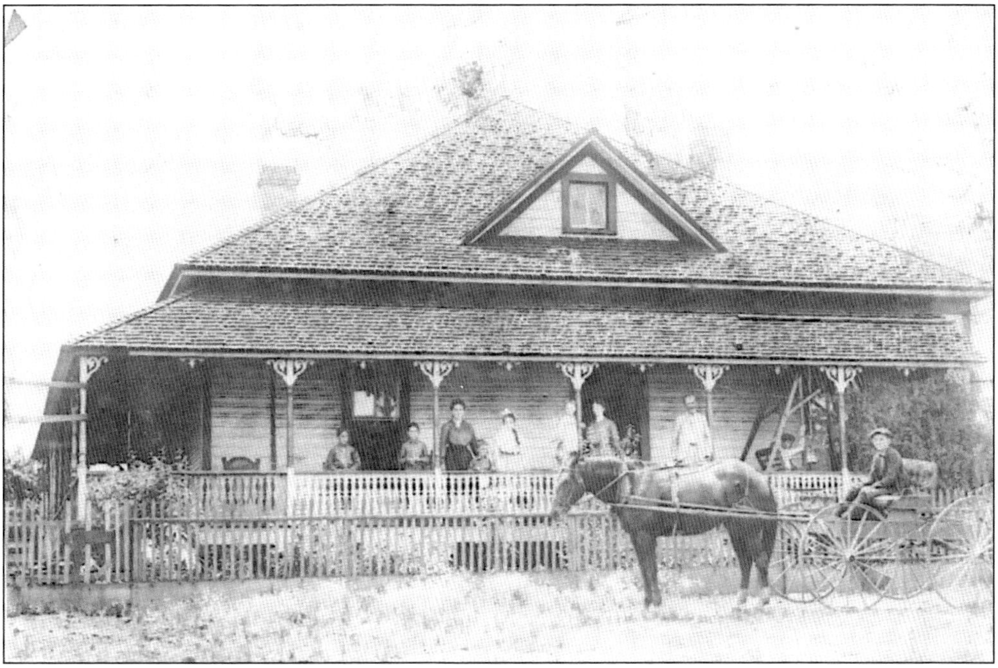

Bessemer's neighborhoods boast a remarkable collection of late Victorian and early-20th-century residential architecture ranging from simple company houses to elaborate showplaces. Early photographs of these homes and the people who lived in them illustrate wonderful pride. The Ross family gathers on the porch for a portrait of their home on Exeter Avenue and Thirtieth Street about 1900. The home was on the far side of the South Bessemer Addition. Located just south and east of the Montezuma Hotel, it was one of the city's earliest residential neighborhoods.

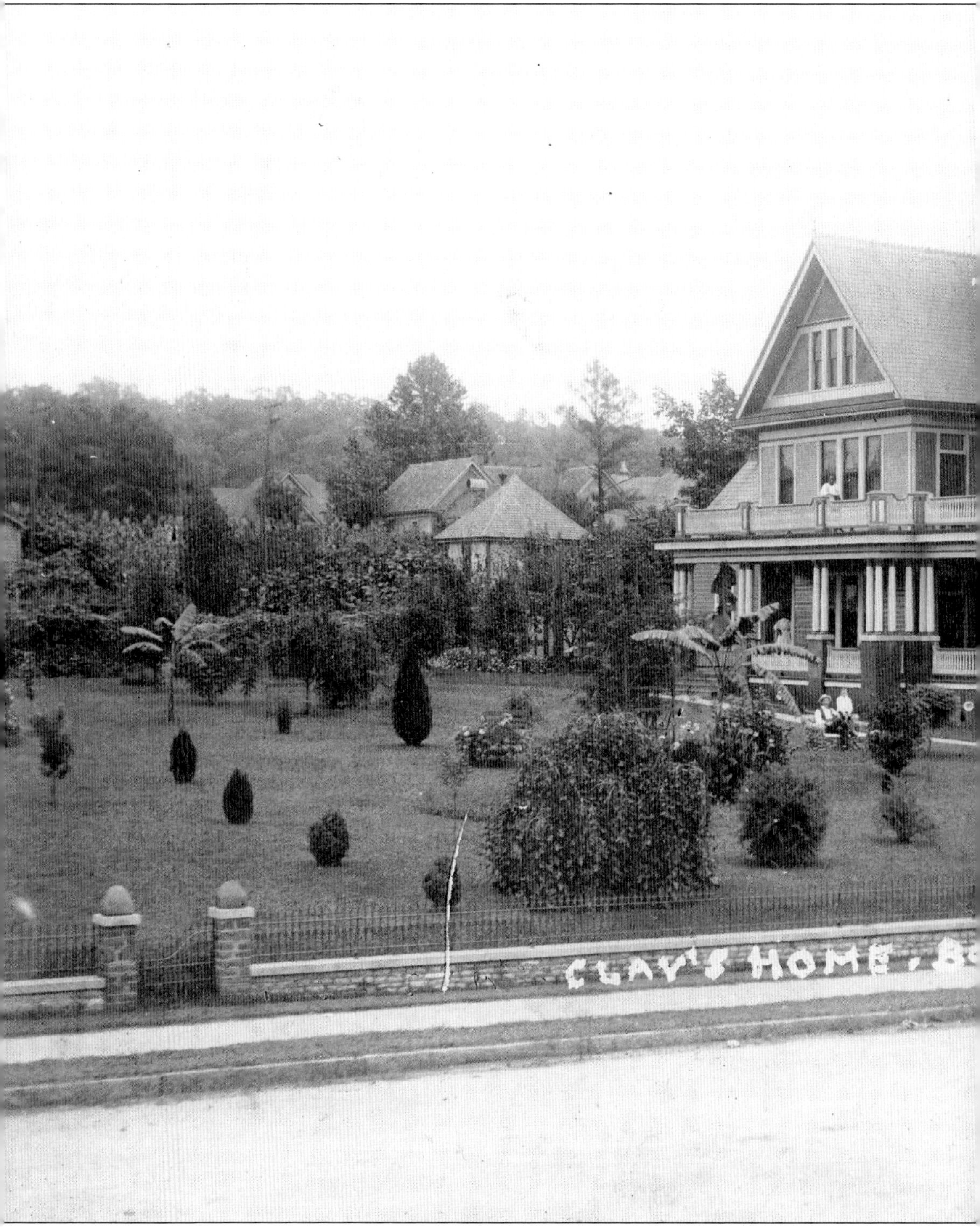

Jeff Clay's home, Four Oaks, was completed in 1906. Clay, president of the Citizens Bank on Twentieth Street, hired architect William Benns to design his dream home on Clarendon Avenue. Contractor M.A. "Bones" Sanford was hired in 1903 and worked on the house, dependencies,

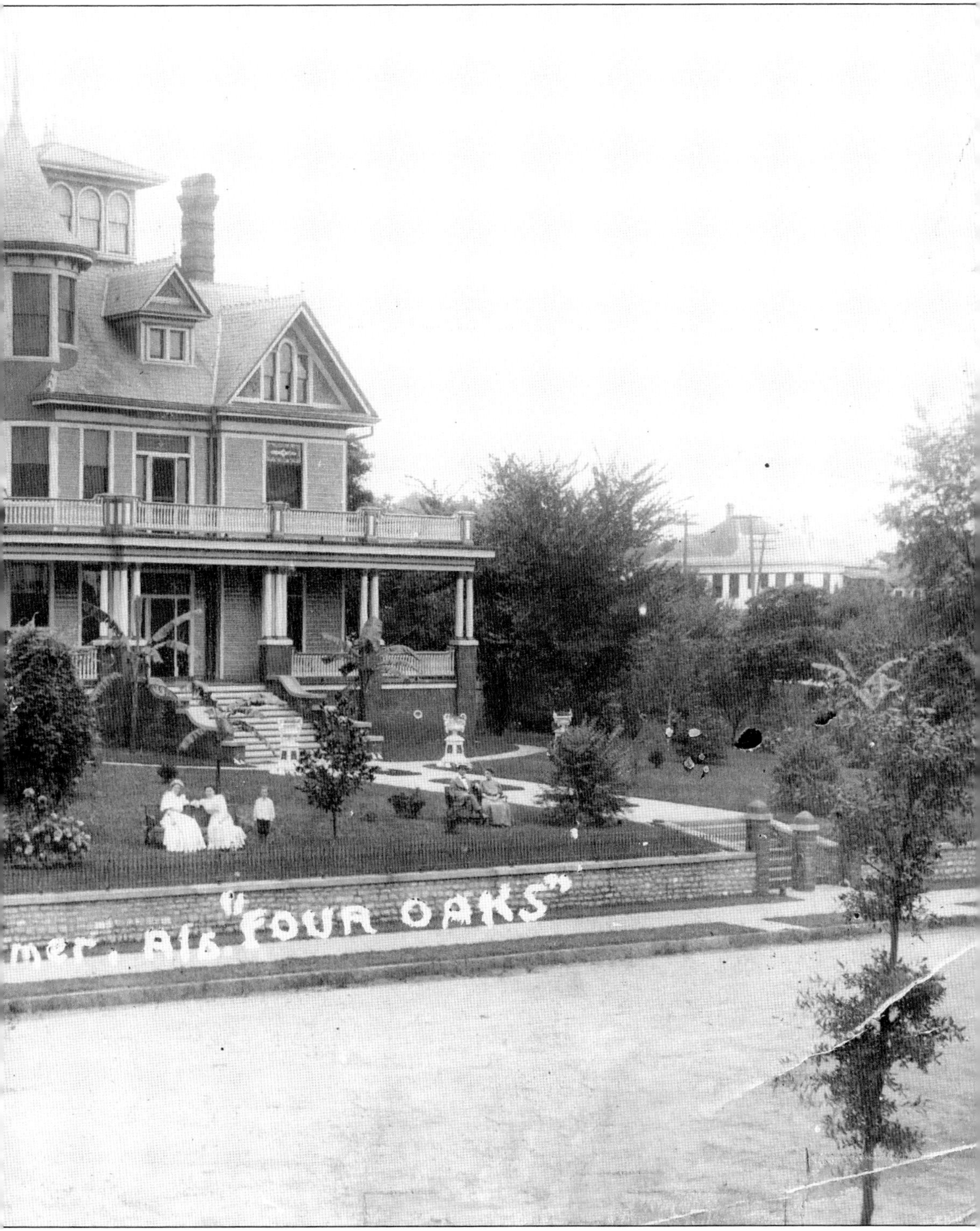

and grounds for three years. The property included buildings for an office, laundry, and carriages. This 1908 view of Four Oaks shows the scale of the house and garden. Mac Clay's home can be seen to the right.

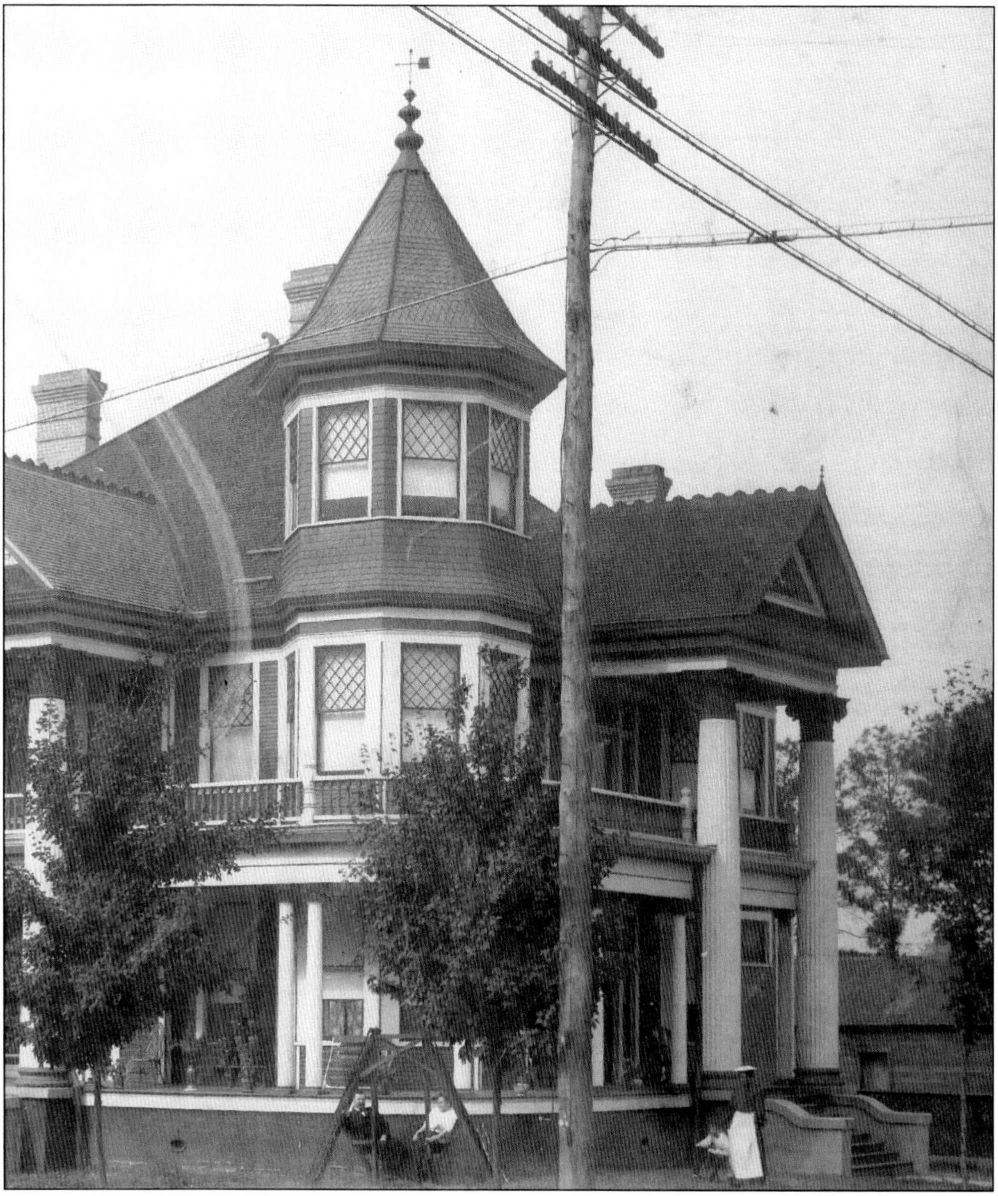

Henry Sweet and his family enjoy the front yard of their new home. Designed by architect William E. Benns, the Sweet House is one of Bessemer's most substantial residential properties. Located on Arlington Avenue, the Queen Ann Neoclassical structure features two colossal porticoes and an octagonal corner turret. Situated on a corner lot, the building is two stories with two street facades (one facing Arlington, the other facing Nineteenth Street). The Sweet House was completed in 1906, the same year as the Clay house. Legend has it that Henry Sweet challenged his neighbor Jeff Clay in a race to build the tallest house. Clay's turret topped out higher than Sweet's, but Sweet's house was completed first. Sweet played vital roles in the local and state economy. He was Bessemer's first undertaker and a furniture merchant, helped to bring the University of Alabama Medical Center to Birmingham, and served as director of the Alabama and Georgia State Docks. The beautifully restored Sweet House and garden is now used for weddings and events. (Courtesy of the Sweet House.)

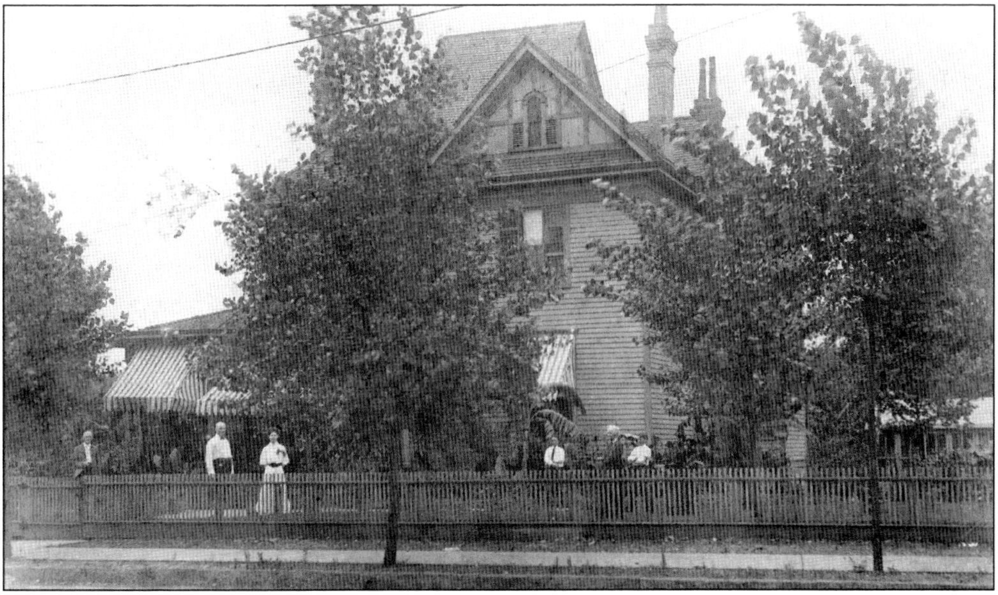

G.M. Lovejoy purchased this home on the corner of Dartmouth Avenue and Nineteenth Street in 1895. Originally known as the Moody Cottage, it was built in 1893. Lovejoy was the third superintendent of Bessemer city schools. From left to right, Darden Jones, G.M. Lovejoy, Mrs. Lovejoy, Howard Lovejoy, Mrs. W.P. Jones, and Jeff Lovejoy stand in the home's front yard. When Lovejoy sold the home in 1906, it was stripped of its Queen Anne details and given a neoclassical facade.

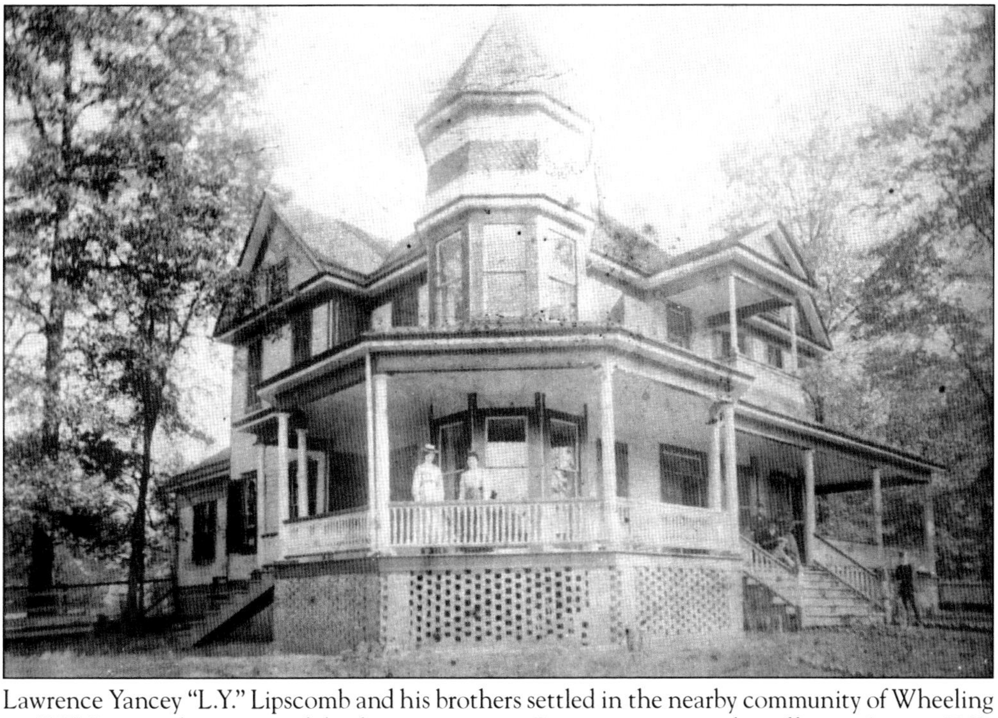

Lawrence Yancey "L.Y." Lipscomb and his brothers settled in the nearby community of Wheeling in 1885. Lipscomb was one of the first attorneys in Bessemer, opening his office in August 1887. Elmhurst, the Berkeley Avenue home of the Honorable L.Y. Lipscomb and Mary Grace Pharr Lipscomb, was built in 1889. The neighboring city of Lipscomb is named for him.

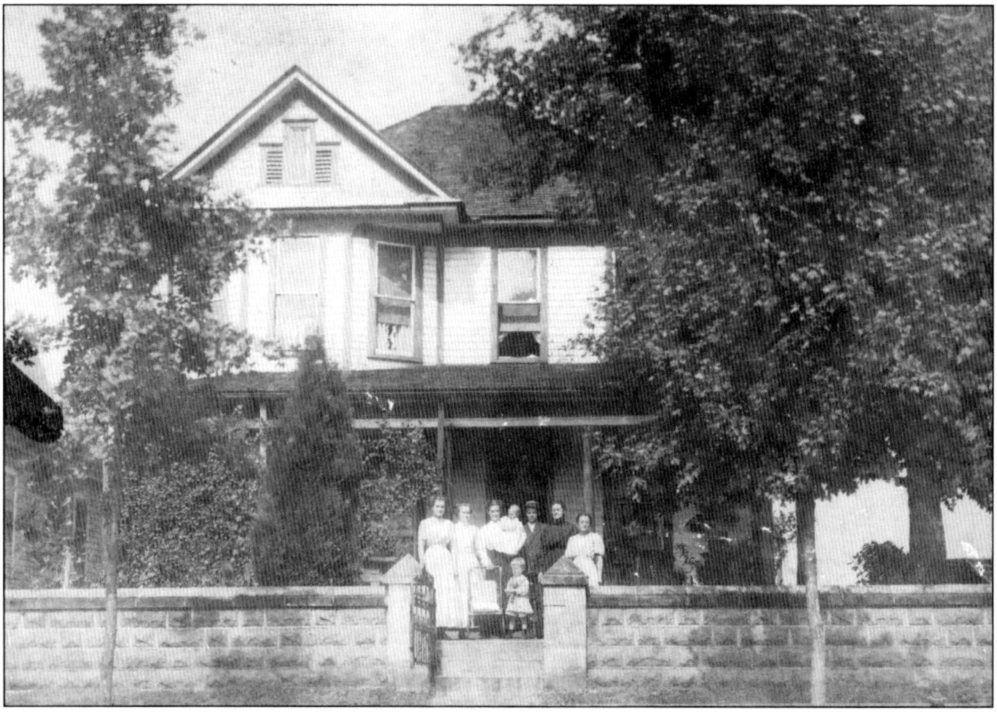

The Terry family moved to Bessemer from Harris County, Georgia, about 1900. Several Terry brothers operated a business that ultimately became Terry Realty Company. The Terry family stands at their front gate facing Berkeley Avenue in this 1909 photograph. They are, from left to right, Lena Terry, Lucille Murrah, Margaret (Terry) Phillips with children Catharine Elizabeth Phillips and Alford Byrd "A.B." Phillips Jr., George Terry Murrah, Mary Catherine "Katie" (Griffin) Terry, and Margaret Murrah. (From the collection of Catherine Reuther.)

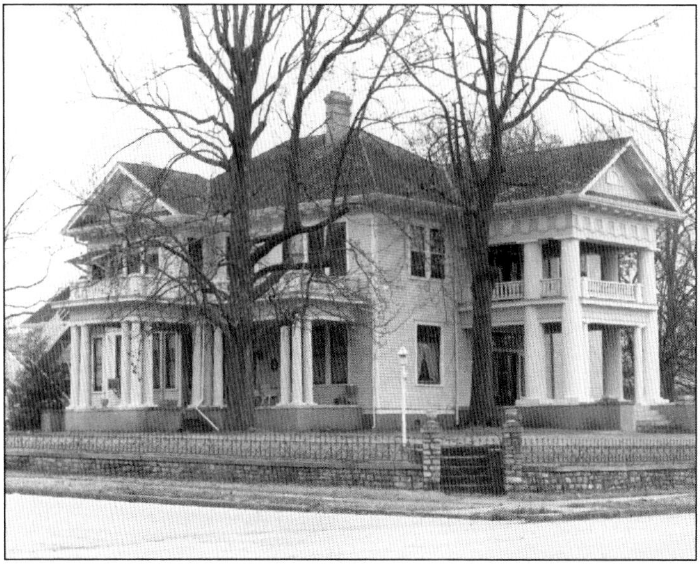

W.H. Porter was a business owner and civic leader in Bessemer. He was co-owner of Jefferson Real Estate Company and vice president of the Bessemer State Bank. The W.H. Porter home was built on Clarendon Avenue in 1914. Bessemer architect William Benns was hired to work with Sallie Porter on her designs for the structure. The house is a well-known landmark, with beautiful stained and beveled glass.

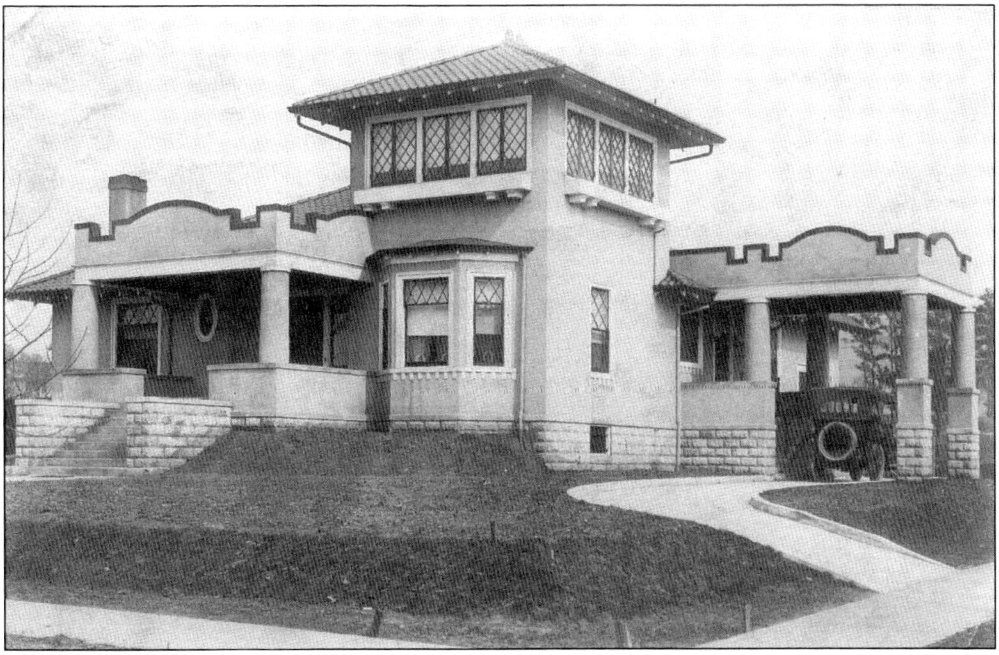

The distinctive Erlick home on Clarendon Avenue was built for department store owner Samuel Erlick in 1920. The Craftsman-era house is Mediterranean in style. The most notable features are the two-story square tower with a pyramidal roof and the parapets on the roof of the front porch and porte cochere to the side. The Erlick & Lefkovits store was established in 1889.

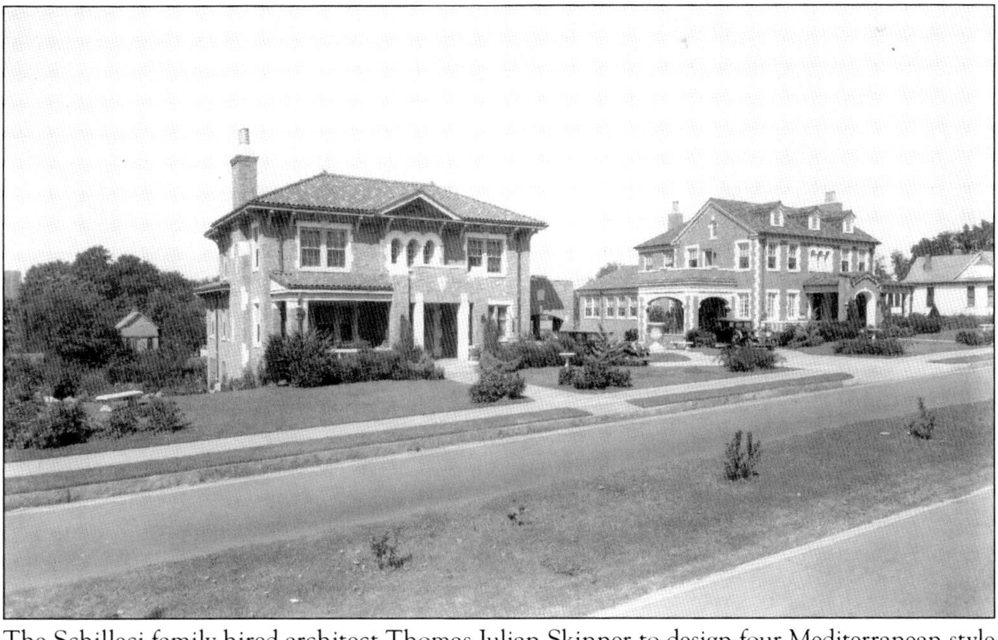

The Schilleci family hired architect Thomas Julian Skinner to design four Mediterranean style houses along Clarendon Avenue. The two seen here, between Twentieth and Twenty-first Streets, were built for Sam Schilleci and Charles Schilleci in 1930. The Schillecis owned Superior Ice Cream Company. Grocer and dry goods merchant W.A. Simmons built the white frame house to the right in 1898.

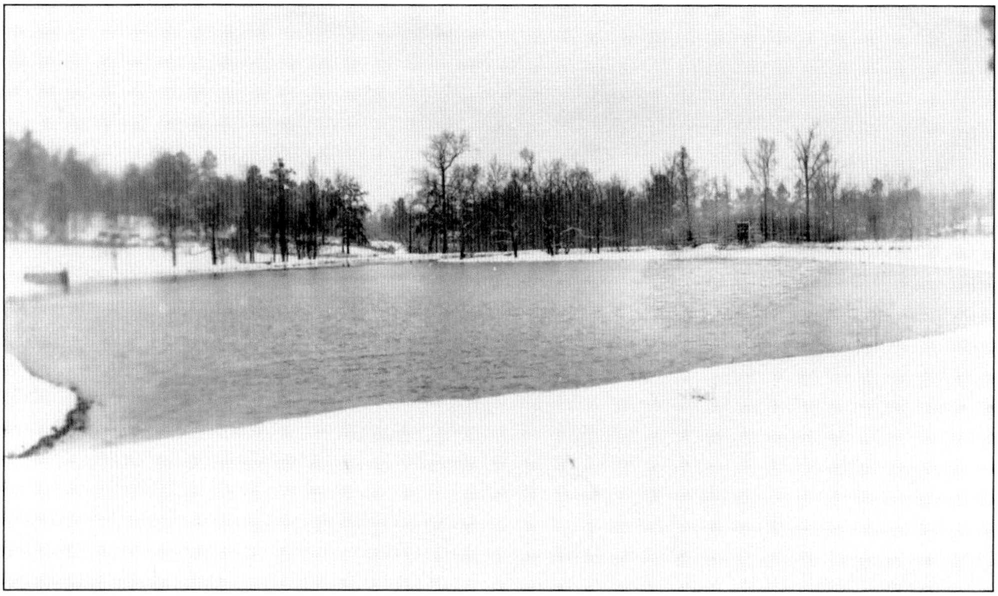

Bank president William Harper Lewis founded the Lakewood Estates community in August 1925. The neighborhood was beautifully situated in Glenn Hills, a popular destination for picnics and camping, overlooking the spring-fed lake. The first section of homes was built by Lewis and his friends and is known as the "Original Seven."

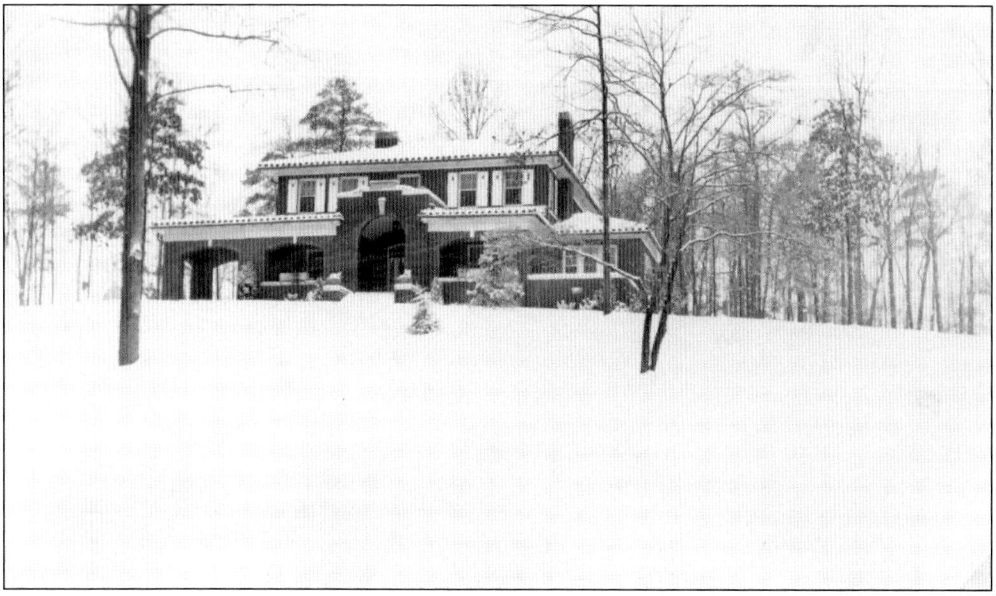

This 1927 Prairie-style house was the first home built in Lakewood Estates. Original owner W.H. Lewis was a civic leader, owner of Lewis Drug Company, president of the First National Bank of Bessemer, and founder of Lakewood Estates. The property overlooks the lake and has a breathtaking view. The house has approximately 6,400 square feet and has had two additions since it was built.

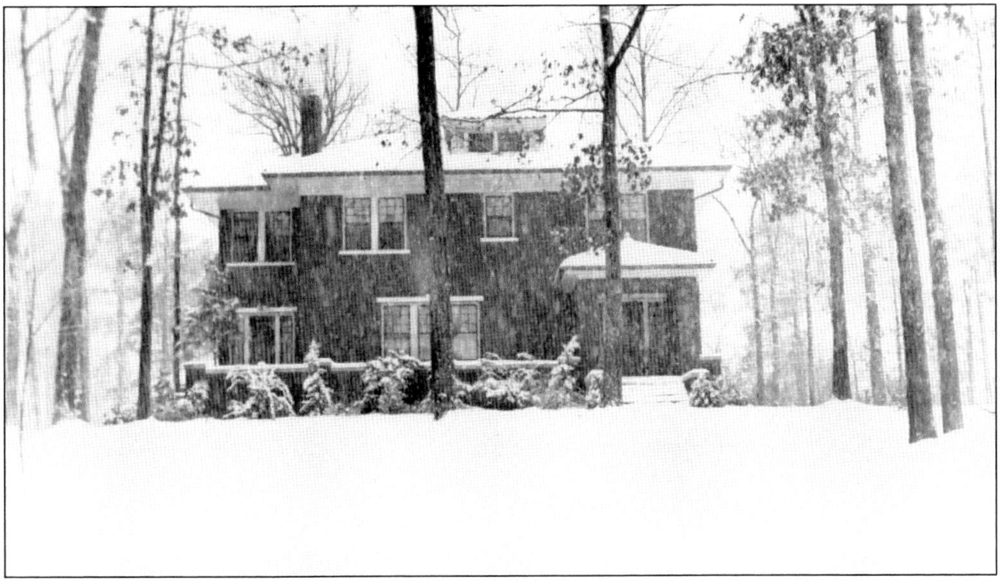

George Rutledge's 1928 high-style American Foursquare home retains outstanding vintage details including entrance doors with beveled glass sidelights, nine-over-one sash windows, beautiful interior woodwork, and the original bath fixtures and tile. Rutledge was a banker, civic leader, and former mayor of Bessemer (1912–1914). He lived in the home until 1942.

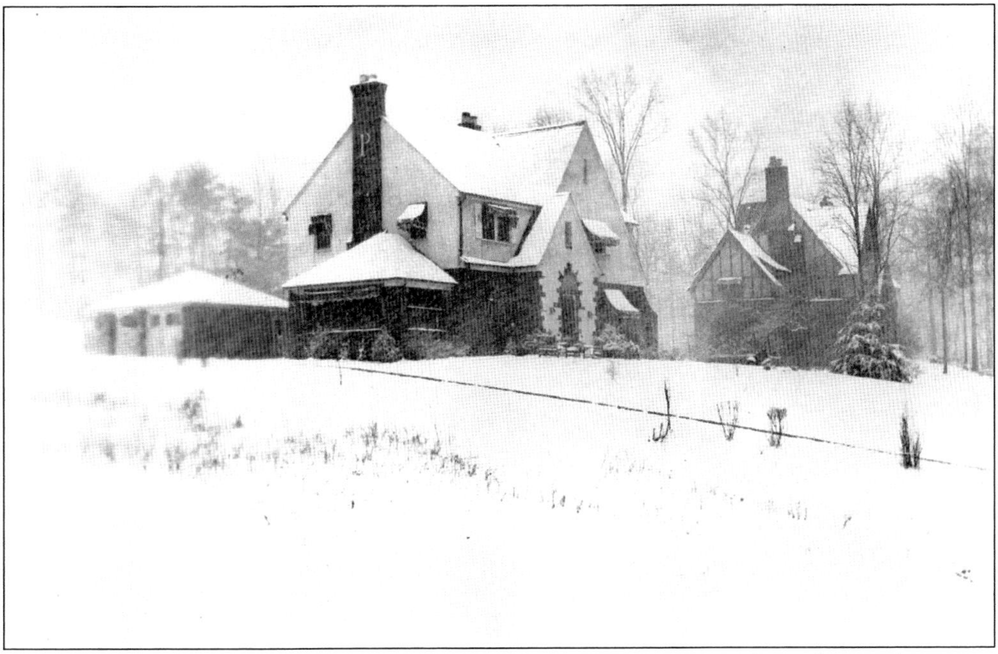

Built by Joseph C. Pope, owner of J.C. Pope Drug Company, the 1929 Tudor-style Pope home was another of Lakewood's "Original Seven" houses. Pope Drug Company was formerly Lewis Reed Drug Company. Dr. Pope purchased the company from W.H. Lewis in 1915 and operated in the Realty Building until 1941. (Courtesy of Allison Rainey.)

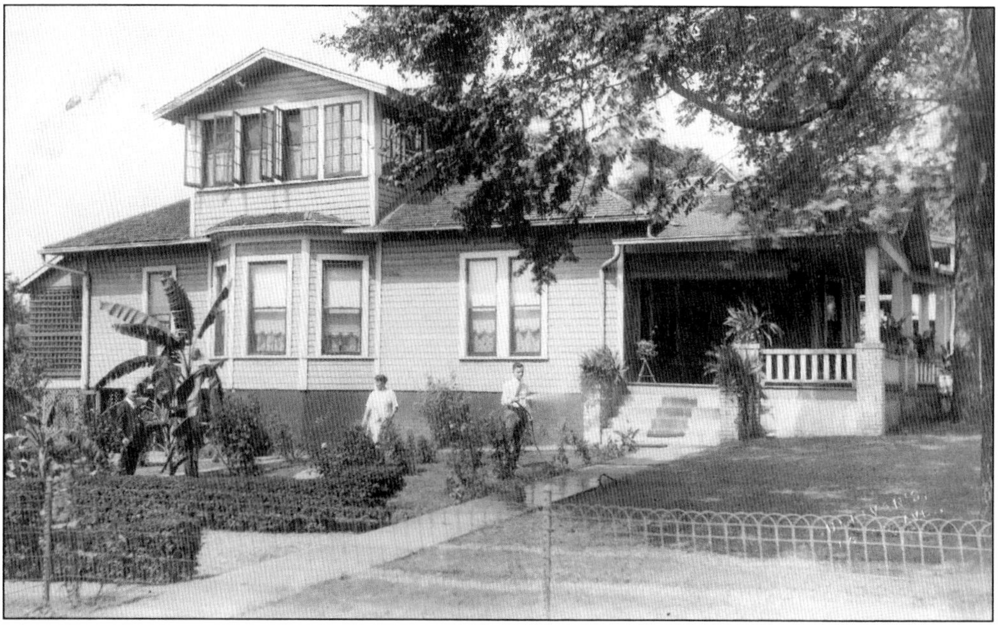

The Rosen home on Berkeley Avenue was known for its beautiful garden and the landscaping of its front and side yards. Above, Jeanette Rosen and son J.D. Rosen work in the garden in 1922. Below, from left to right, Rosen, J.D., and Mrs. Rosen sit on the front steps, facing Berkeley. The Rosens purchased the home in 1918, and it remained in the Bessemer merchant's family until the 1950s.

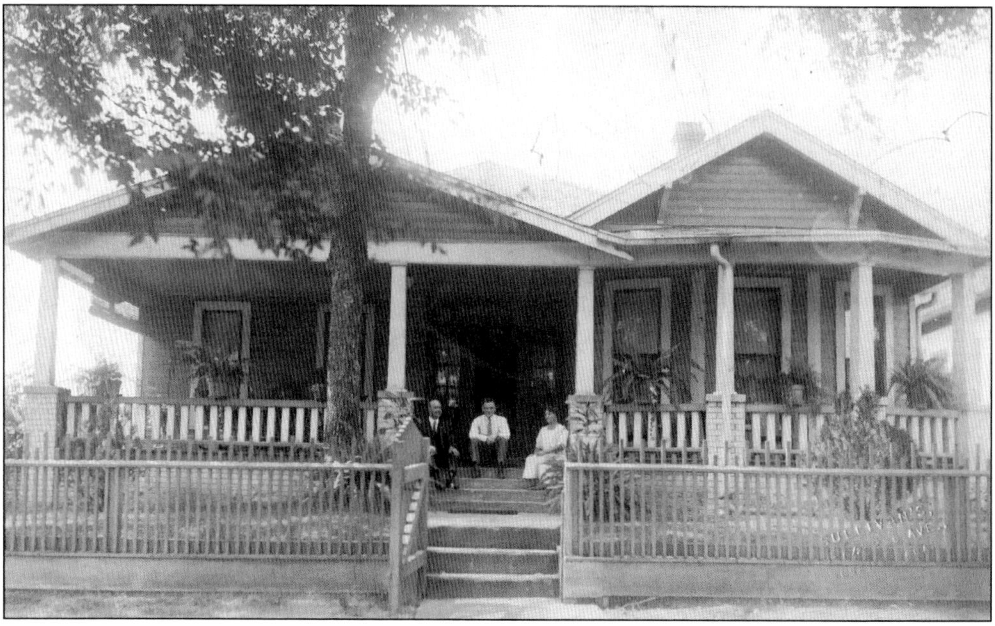

Nine

Recreation and Sports

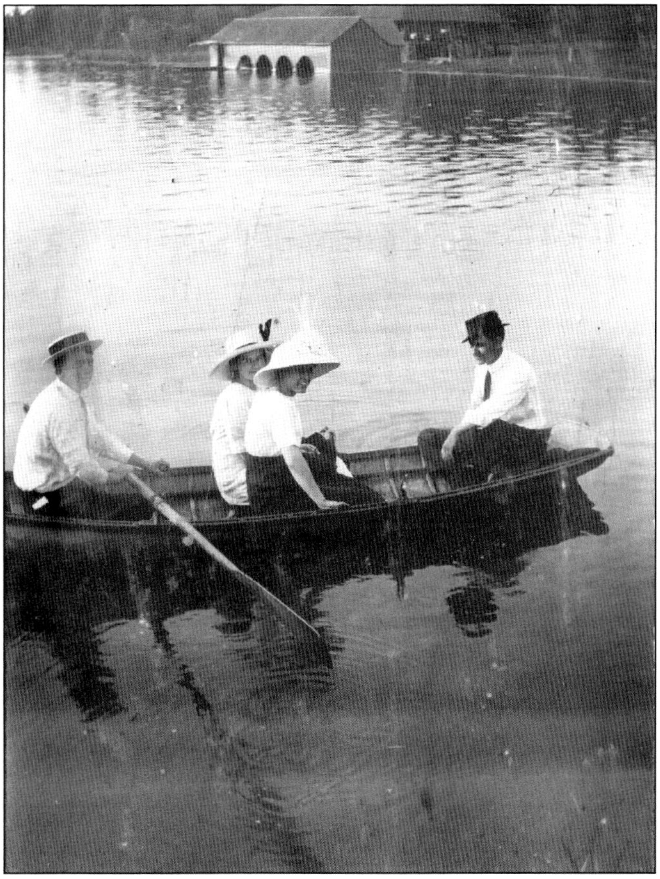

Bessemer offered its early residents a remarkable variety of recreations. Its location offered ready access to lakes, creeks, and springs for swimming and fishing. The Town Company laid out parks and public spaces for strolling and picnicking, and local organizations and residents planned parties, concerts, and sports. And with the Dummy Line and other rail options, excursions to Birmingham and other cities were easily planned. Here, two young couples relax on a boat at Westlake about 1915.

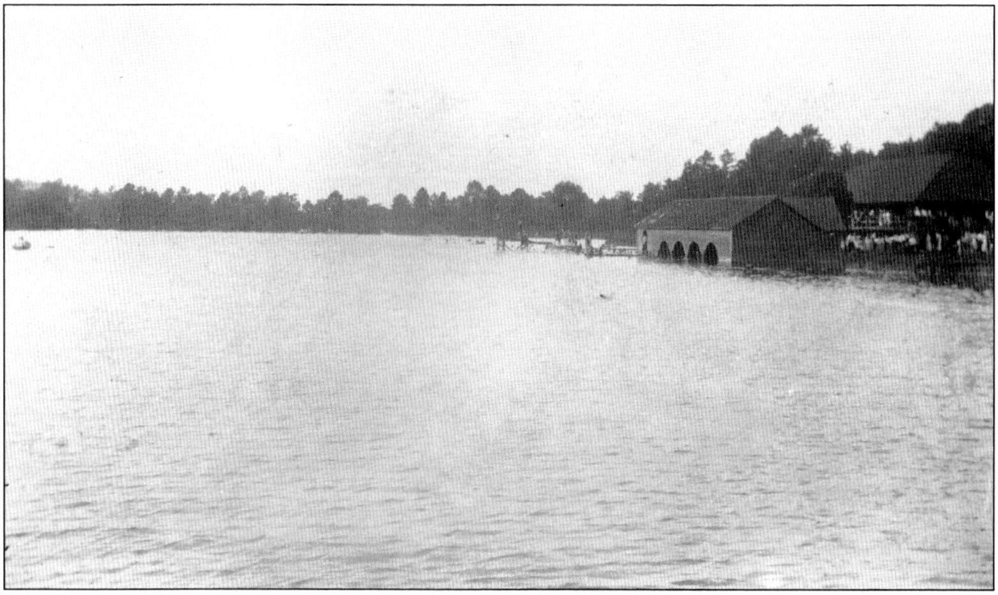

The city's first reservoir and waterworks was Westlake, just west of downtown at Tenth Street near Twelfth Avenue. The overflow of McAdory and Glenn Springs fed the reservoir. These springs, along with Mill Spring, flowed more than one million gallons of clean, fresh water each day. The lake was a popular attraction for decades. Above, a 1913 view of Westlake shows the pier, boathouse with arched openings on the water, and the pavilion behind the boathouse. Below, five young friends pose while swimming at Westlake on July 4, 1913. In addition to their swimming caps, these ladies were wearing wool or cotton swimming dresses and stockings.

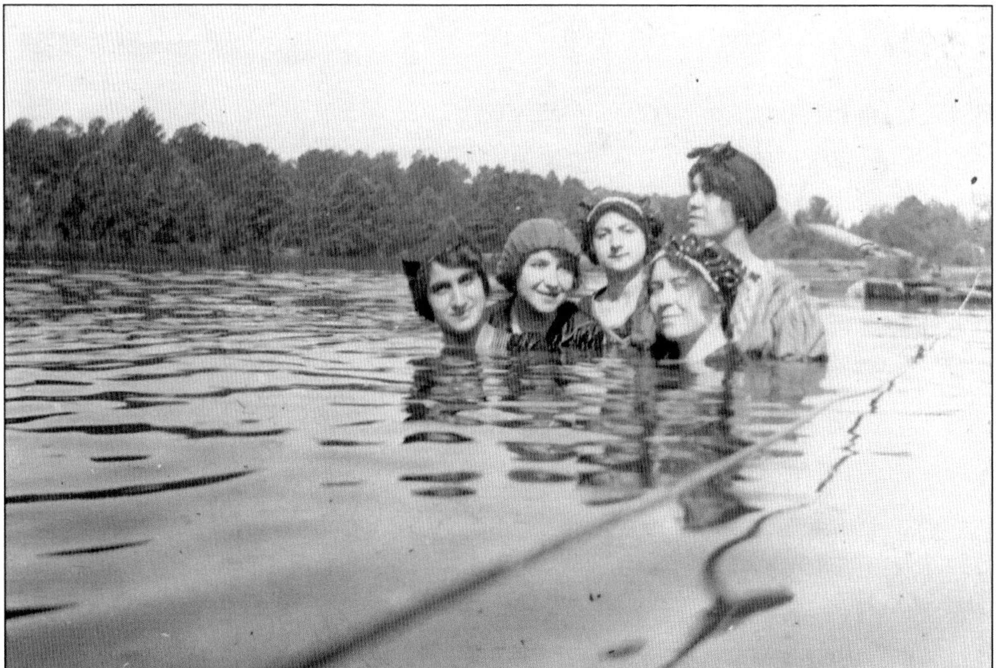

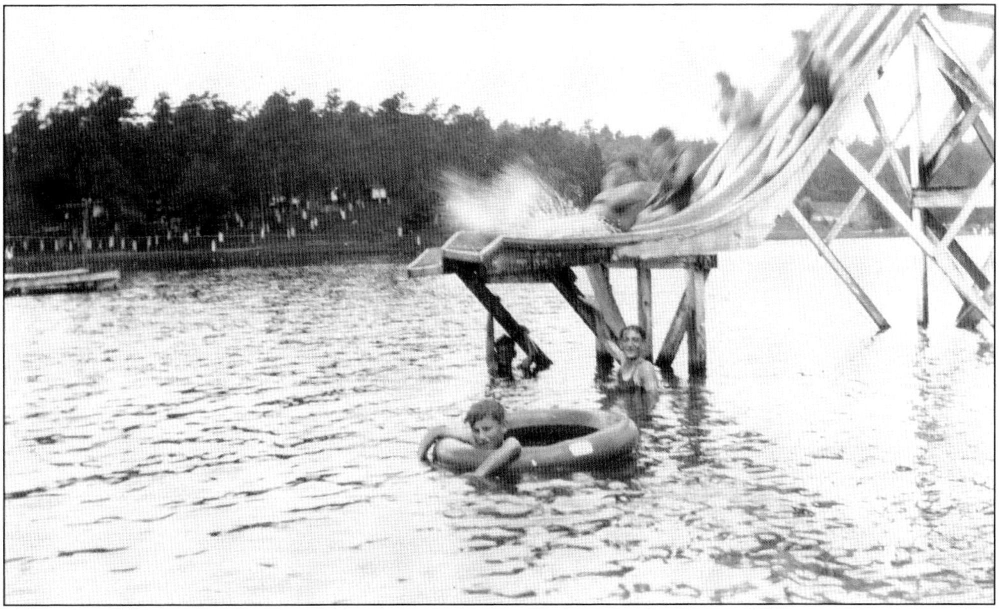

Johnny Ryan operated Westlake Park for many years. Ryan modestly referred to himself as "chief shoveler," but under his management, the park became an attraction for people beyond Bessemer. The *Birmingham Age-Herald* reported that the Birmingham Police Band performed for the Associated Business Men of Ensley's meeting at the lake in July 1928. Above, additional attractions such as the waterslides were added to the park in the 1920s. On the hillside behind the lake, note the cabins that were available for weekly rental. Below, a group of boys, ready to get back to horseplay in the lake, impatiently waits to have their picture taken.

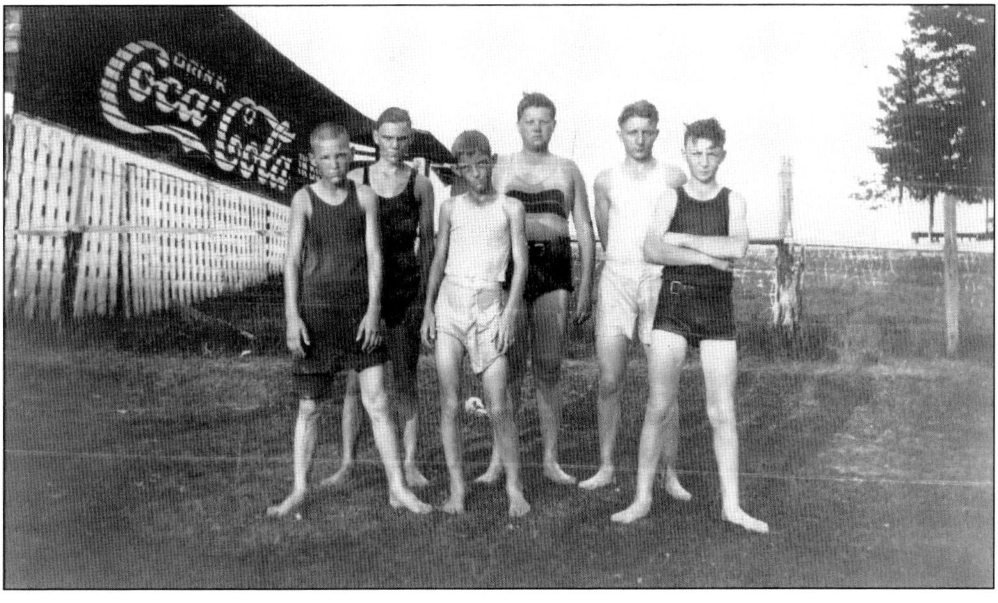

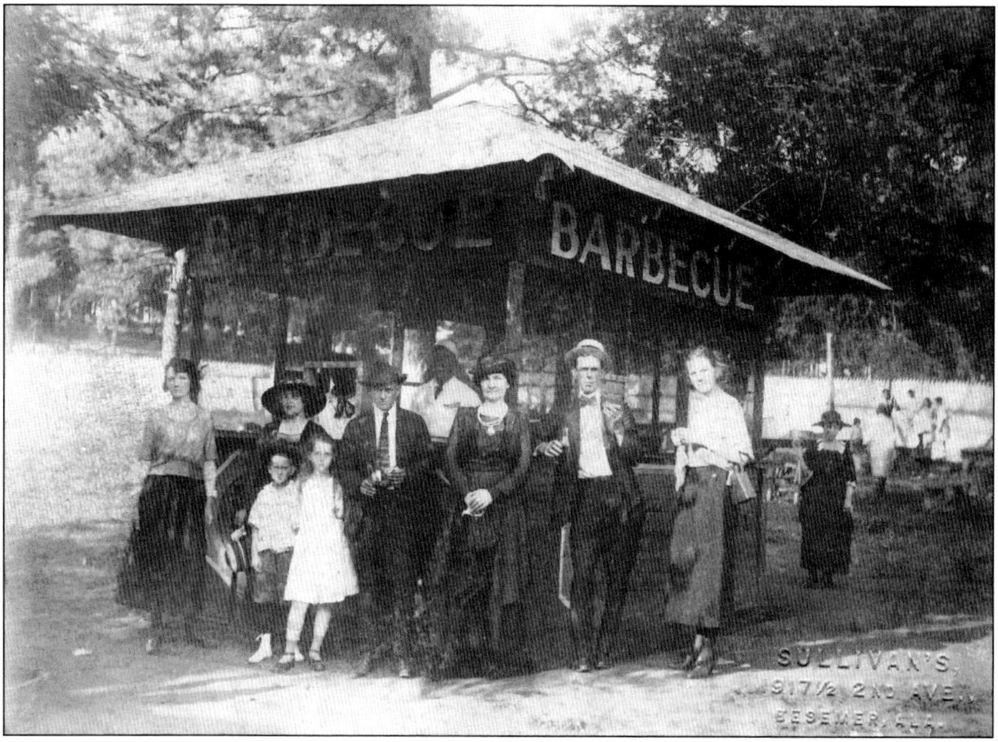

Not everyone who visited Westlake came to swim or boat. The lake was a pleasant and relatively quick walk or ride from downtown Bessemer. Some would visit just to enjoy the breeze or have a photograph made on the bridge. Others attended dances and concerts regularly hosted at the pavilion. Westlake also became a popular spot for weekend dining. Above, a young family and others pose at an early barbecue and refreshment stand. Below, the cooks at Westlake pavilion prepared fish caught fresh from the lake, along with fried chicken and barbecue.

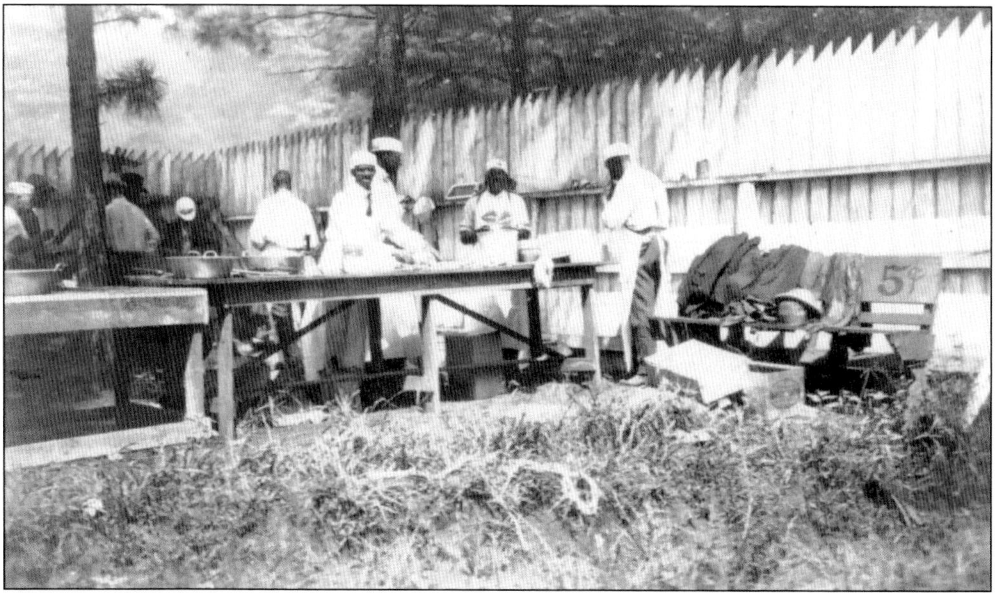

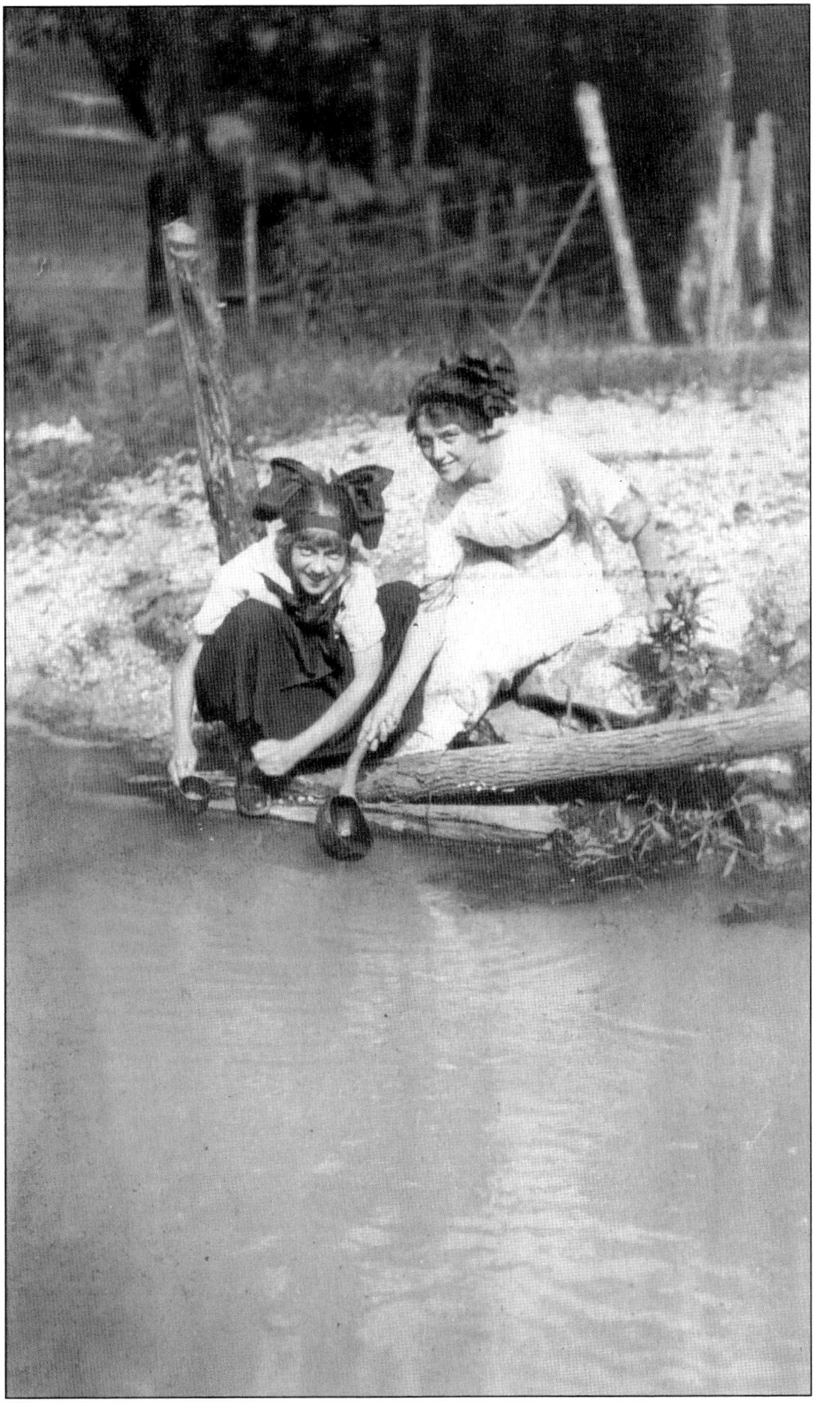

Located near the current site of Alabama Adventure theme park, Prince's Spring was a popular destination for picnics, a day in the country, or overnight camping. The "Bees and Butterflies" column of the *Bessemer Weekly* regularly reported the Prince's spring excursions of children and groups of young couples courting. Here, Katherine Waller and Zelna Lefkovits are photographed visiting the spring in 1912.

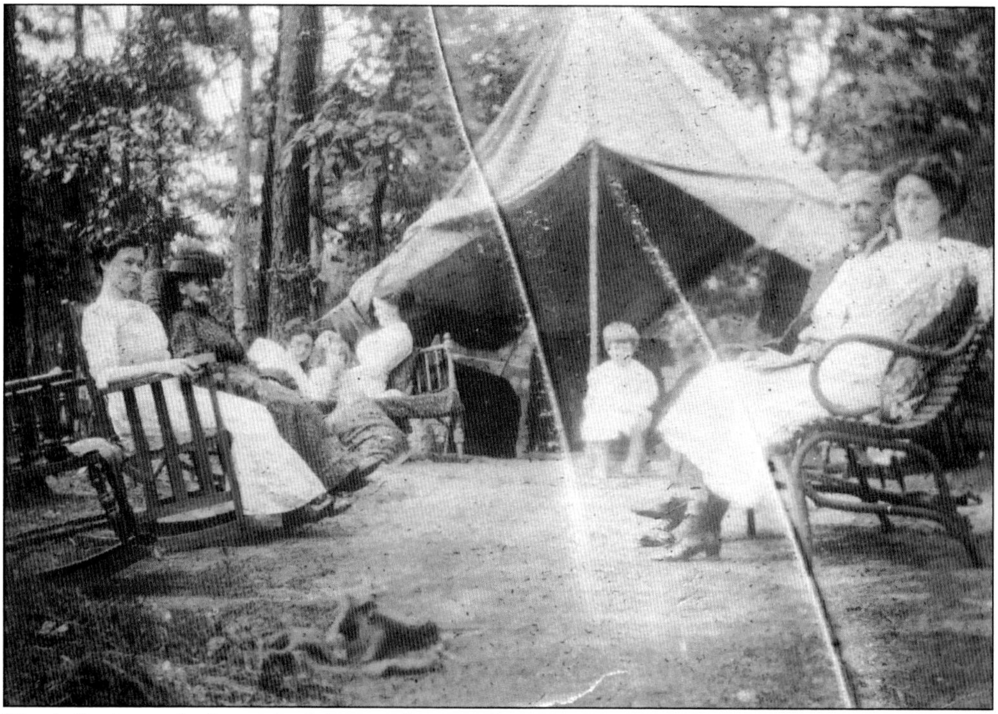

The hillside overlooking the lake at Glenn Hills was another popular destination for camping. Fresh spring water was available at the lake, and the top of the hill captured cool breezes. Now, the Lakewood neighborhood is located at the site of Glenn Hills. In this photograph from about 1910, George William Everette's family has set up a campsite and tent atop the hill.

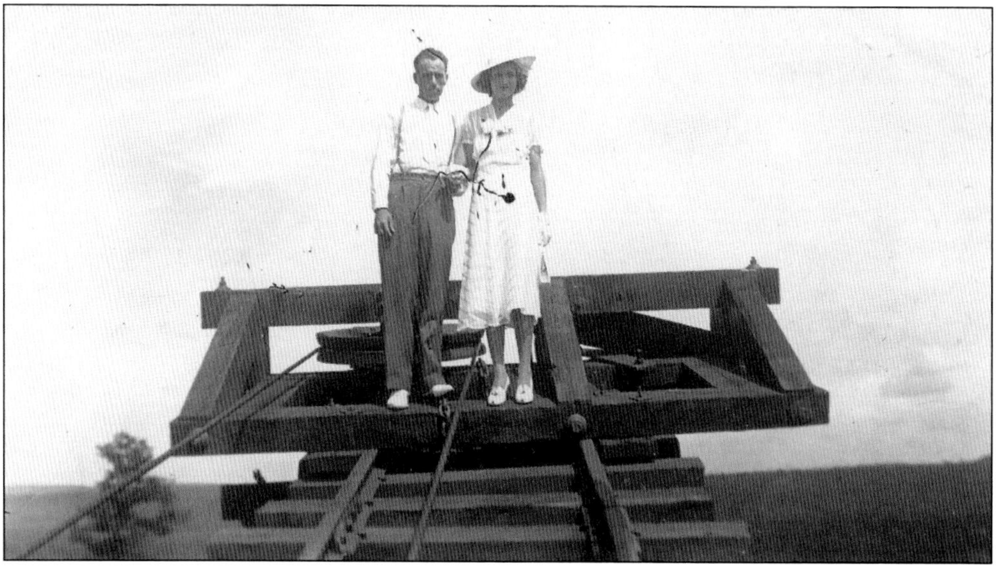

When mines were closed during shutdowns or on holidays, locals would climb the ridges and tipples to enjoy unobstructed views of the city. Carl O'Neal and Bessie Mae Howell pose for this photograph on the Sloss Mine's No. 2 tailings tipple. The ore tipples at Sloss overlooked Bessemer, but just over the crest of Red Mountain, the tailings tipple offered a view of Oxmoor Valley's farms and woodlands.

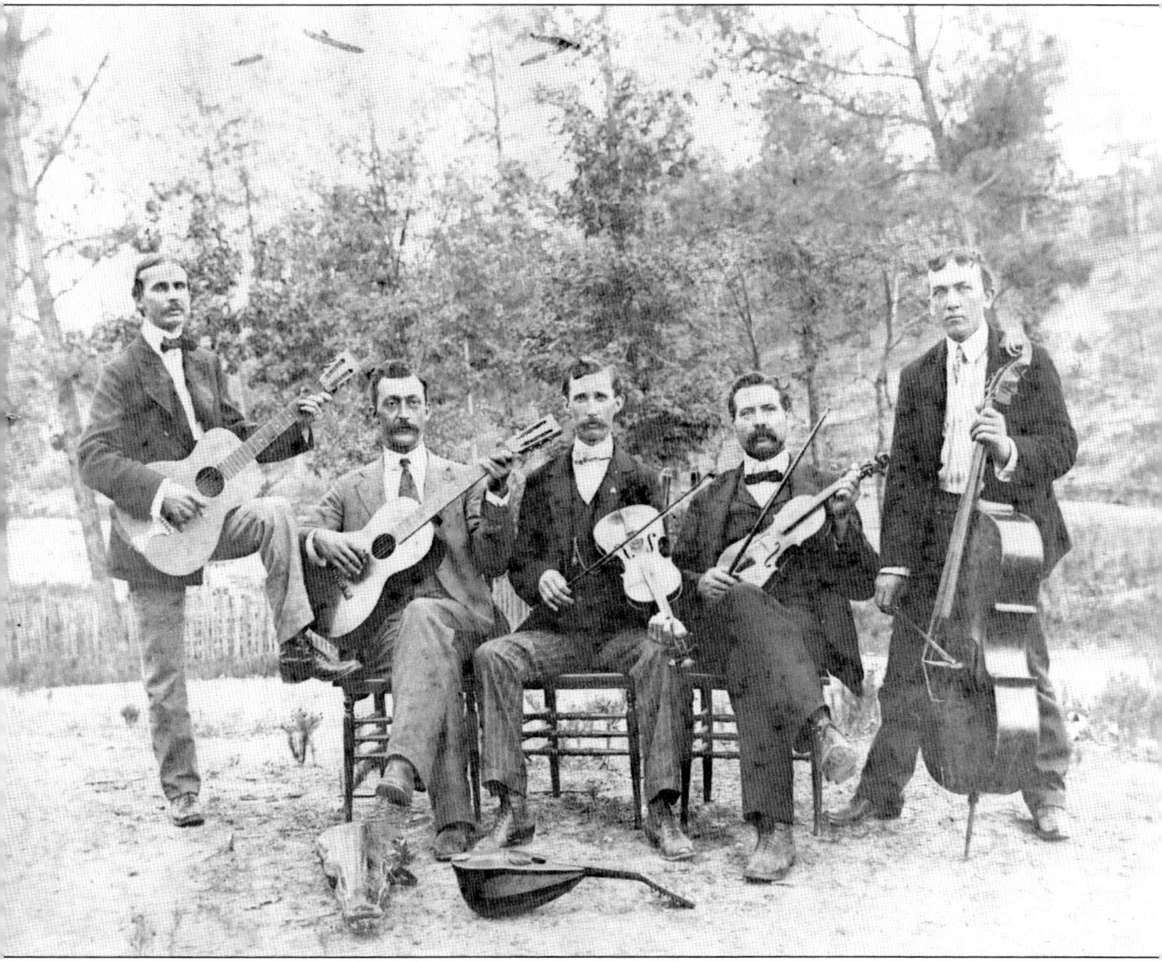

Bessemer has a rich musical history. Local unions, clubs, and societies regularly hosted or even formed bands. This group of musicians from the nearby community of Johns performed in the city. They are, from left to right, unidentified, Porter Miller, Lucian Raney, J.Y. Cargile, and Silas Avery. The city had a brush with musical fame when W.C. Handy worked at Howard-Harrison Iron Company (later US Pipe) in 1892. While working in Bessemer, Handy organized his first brass band and taught music lessons. He also heard eight-bar blues and the song, "Careless Love," the basis for his hit song, "Loveless Love," for the first time during his Bessemer stay.

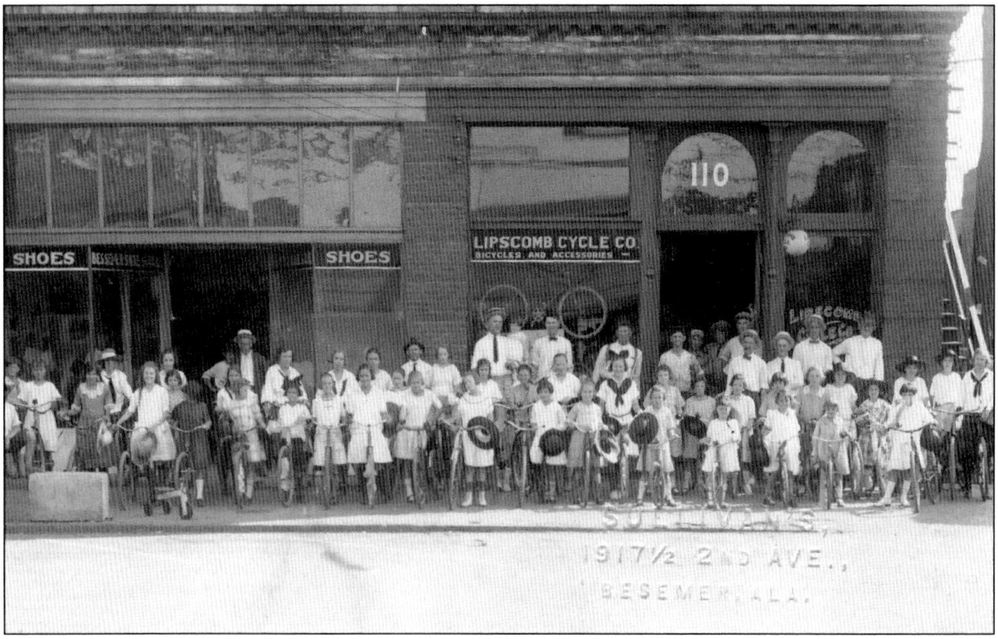

Bessemer's two biggest bicycle companies, Bryant's Bicycle Shop and Lipscomb Cycle Company, hosted an annual bicycle race for boys and a "ride to Westlake" for girls. Above, the girls pose in front of Bessemer Shoe Store and Lipscomb Cycle on Nineteenth Street before pedaling to the lake. Below, the boys wait for the starting gun at the intersection of Nineteenth Street and Second Avenue, in front of Kartus Korner store. L.S. Moorer Jr. (indicated by the arrow, left) won the race and a new bicycle from his father. L.S. Moorer Sr. and W.H. Porter owned Jefferson Real Estate and Loan Company.

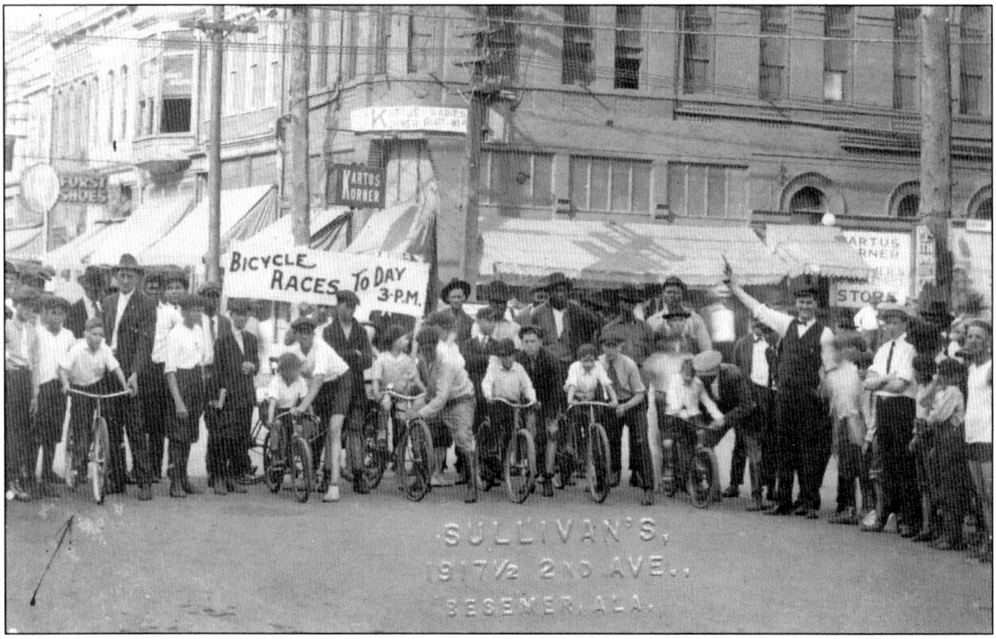

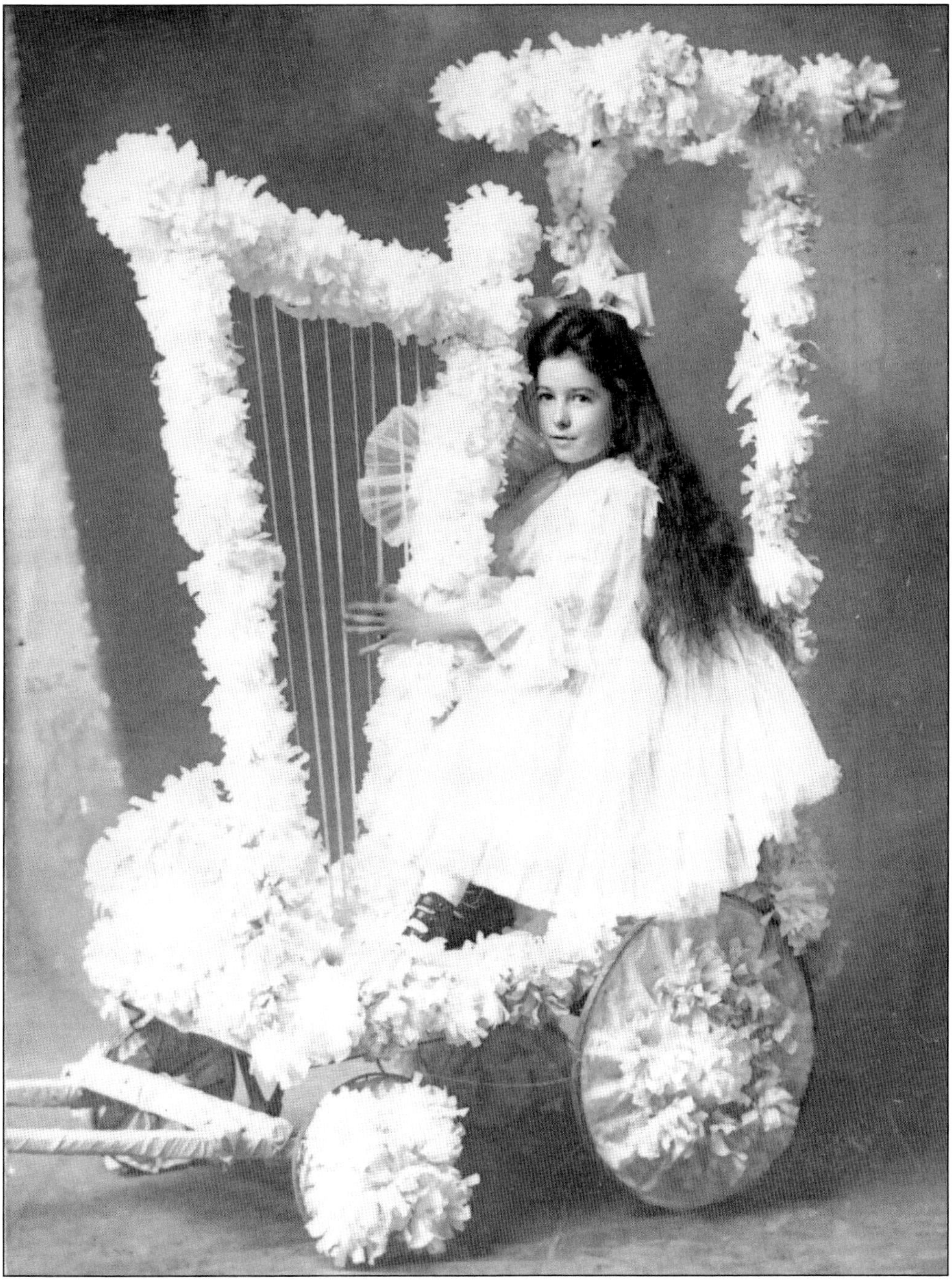

Bessemer held two large annual parades on May Day and on Armistice Day and also saw smaller parades hosted by churches, societies, or schools. Isabel Curry looks like an angel playing her harp on this May Day parade float. Isabel was the daughter of Dr. J.C. Curry, who owned and operated a feed and grain store that remained open on Twentieth Street for nearly a century.

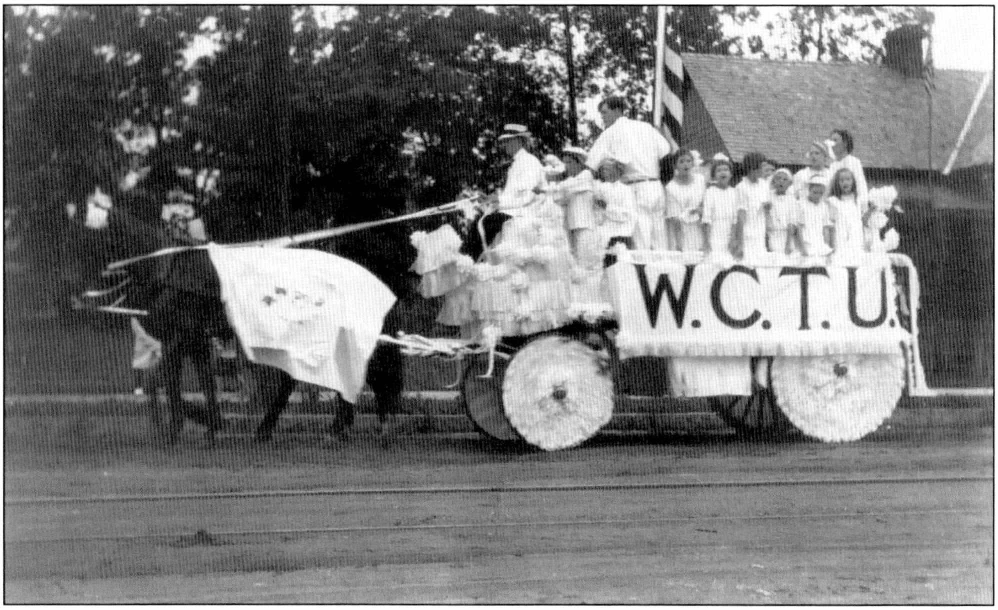

Children sing on the Woman's Christian Temperance Union float. The WCTU spearheaded the drive for prohibition and was very active in the city. This may have been part of a Temperance Day parade. Each year, Bessemer schools were required to observe a Temperance Day when students were taught about the "evils of alcohol."

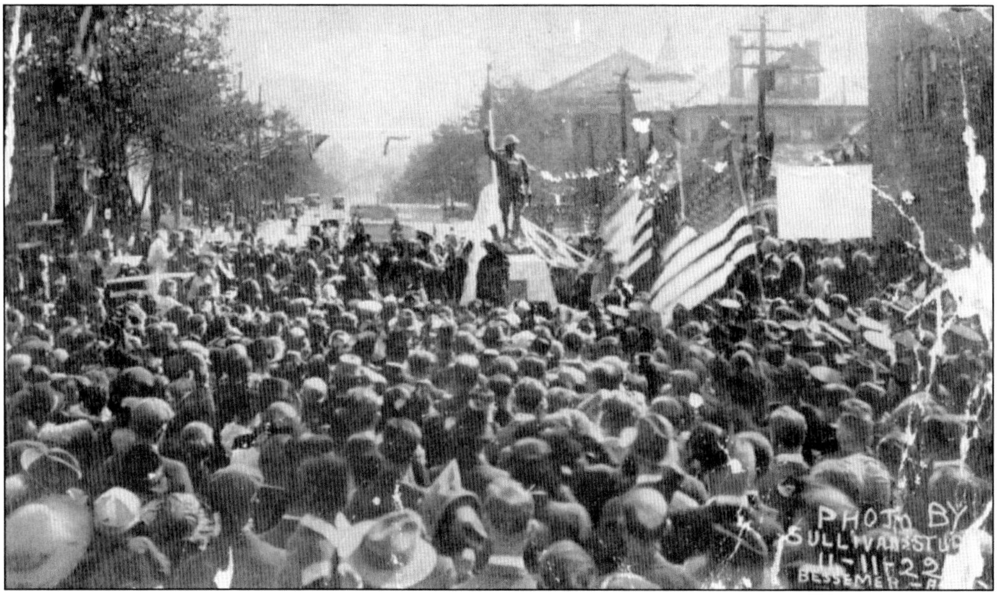

Citizens gathered on Armistice Day 1922 for the dedication of the town's "Doughboy" sculpture honoring veterans and those who were killed in World War I. The statue, "Spirit of the American Doughboy," was designed by E.M. Viquesney and mass-produced through the 1920s and 1930s. The statue's pressed copper construction made it affordable, and as many as 300 towns may have purchased them. Now located in DeBardeleben Park, the statue originally stood in the median of Nineteenth Street, facing Carolina Avenue. Note the pediment of the First Methodist Church and roof of the Sweet House in the background.

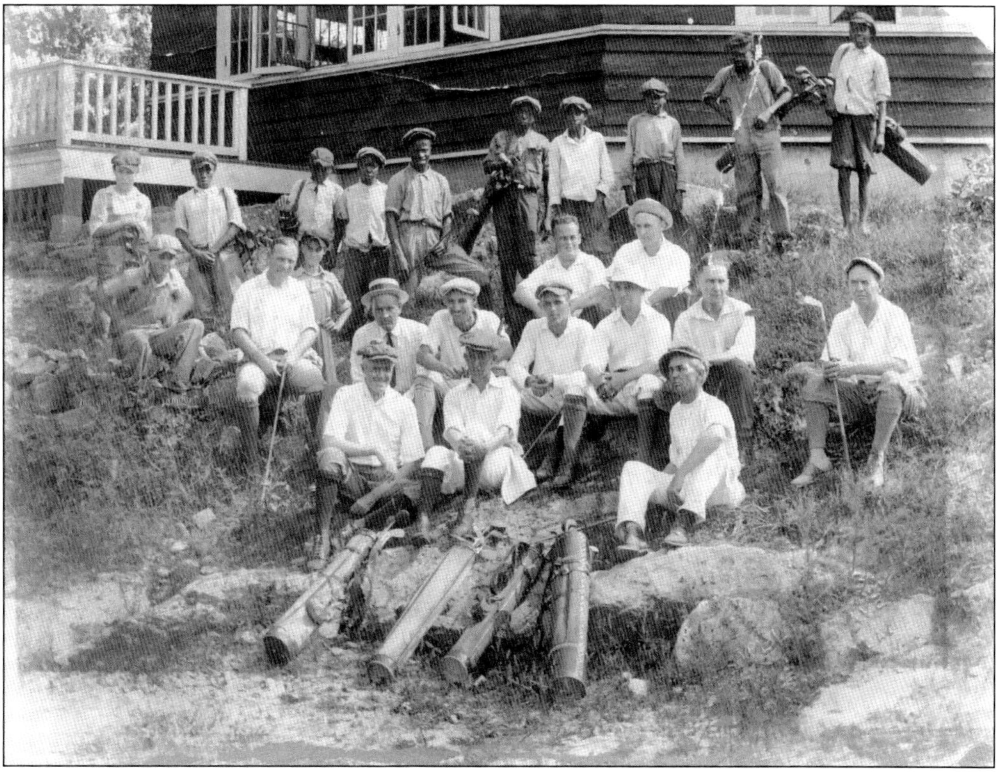

A group of Bessemer businessmen with caddies pose for a snapshot at Woodward Golf & Country Club. Among the group is Fats Snider, whose father owned the first movie theater in Bessemer. Woodward is the oldest golf club at its original location in Jefferson County and one of the oldest in Alabama. The club, near Bessemer, was originally built for Woodward Iron Company employees in 1916 and called the "Employees Club." Rick Woodward, founder of the club, was also the founder of Birmingham's Rickwood Field and owner of the Birmingham Barrons baseball team.

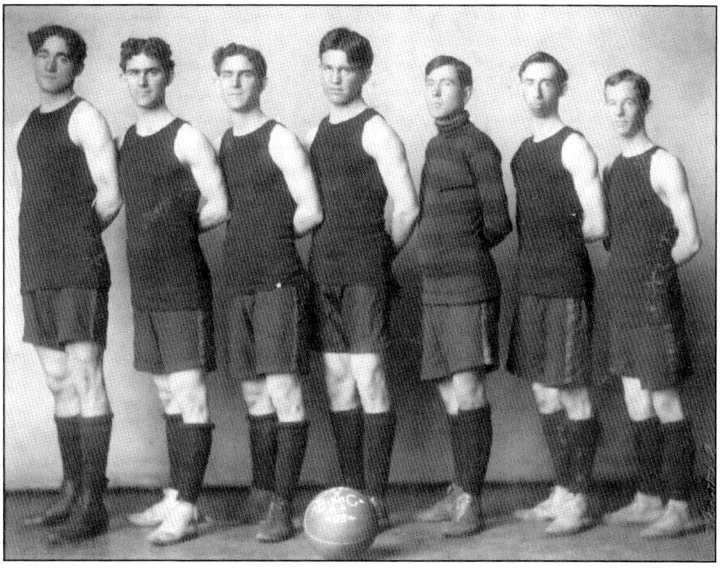

The Bessemer Athletic Club organized the city's first basketball team in 1904. By 1908, they were playing against teams from across the state. The *Bessemer Weekly* noted that Bessemer beat the Scottsboro Institute team in the last game of the season. From left to right, the 1908 team is Ellis Houston, Homer Hurd, Henry Hurd, Will Lacey, unidentified, John McConnell, and Billy Johnson.

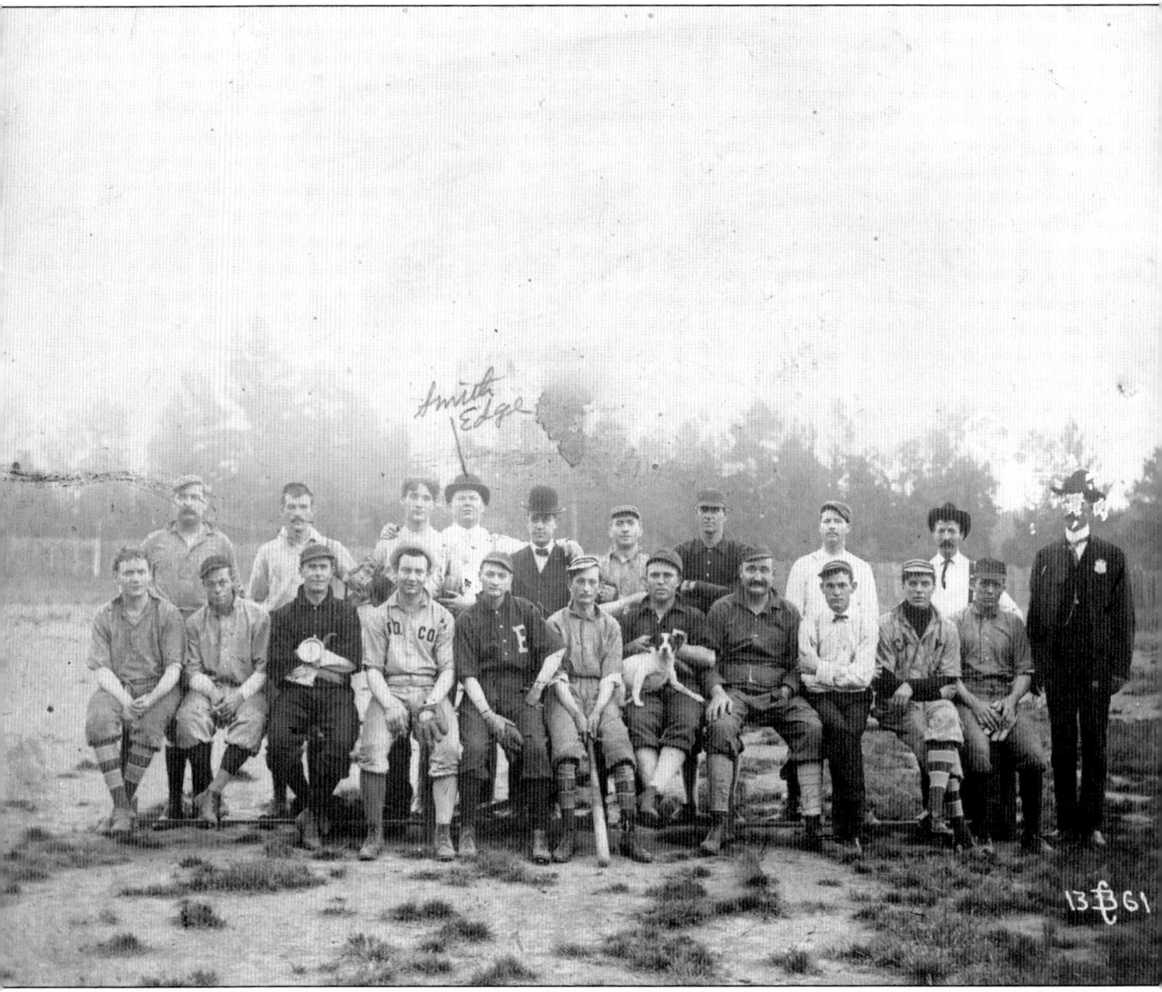

A community baseball team including Smith Edge, Bob Bumgardner, Cleve Earnest, and Ellis Houston poses for a portrait in 1913. Police chief T.B. Wallace stands at the far right. Like many towns early in the 20th century, Bessemer had a case of baseball fever. In addition to community teams like this one, there were school teams, union teams, club teams, and for a few months, Bessemer had a minor league team. Bessemer had organized a baseball association and had been rumbling about a Southeastern League professional team since 1910. F.C. Monasco, who owned the Decatur team and was looking for another, chose Bessemer over Ensley because he felt Ensley was too near the Birmingham Barons. On April 20, 1912, the Bessemer Pipemakers played their first game against Selma and won, 6-4. Attendance at the games was not what Monasco expected, and by June, he cut his losses and abandoned the team. The *Bessemer Weekly* mentioned four players by name over the course of the season—Cochran, Williams, Hickman, and Ramage.

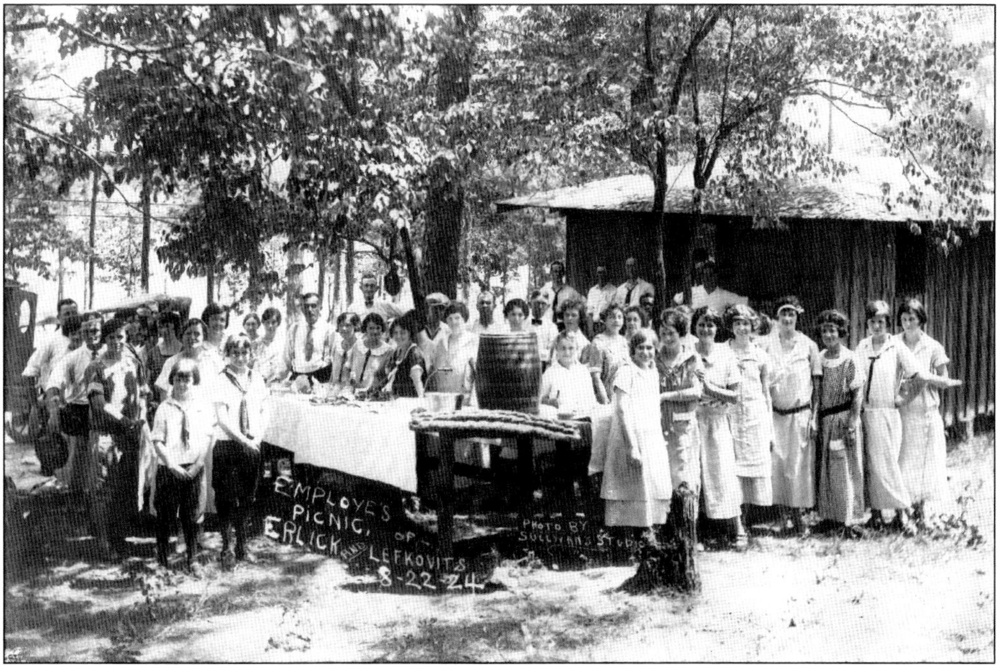

Almost every weekend during the summer, Bessemer companies, unions, and Sunday schools organized their annual picnics at locales around the city. On one Saturday in the summer of 1907, there was a citywide "basket picnic" in City Park, a Knights of Pythias free barbecue picnic in City Park, and the Glee Club's evening hay ride and moonlight picnic. Above, Erlick and Lefkovits, one of the city's oldest and largest department stores, hosts its annual employee picnic at Westlake in August 1924. Below, Local 342 Union of Iron Moulders gathers at Westlake for its annual employee and family picnic in 1913.

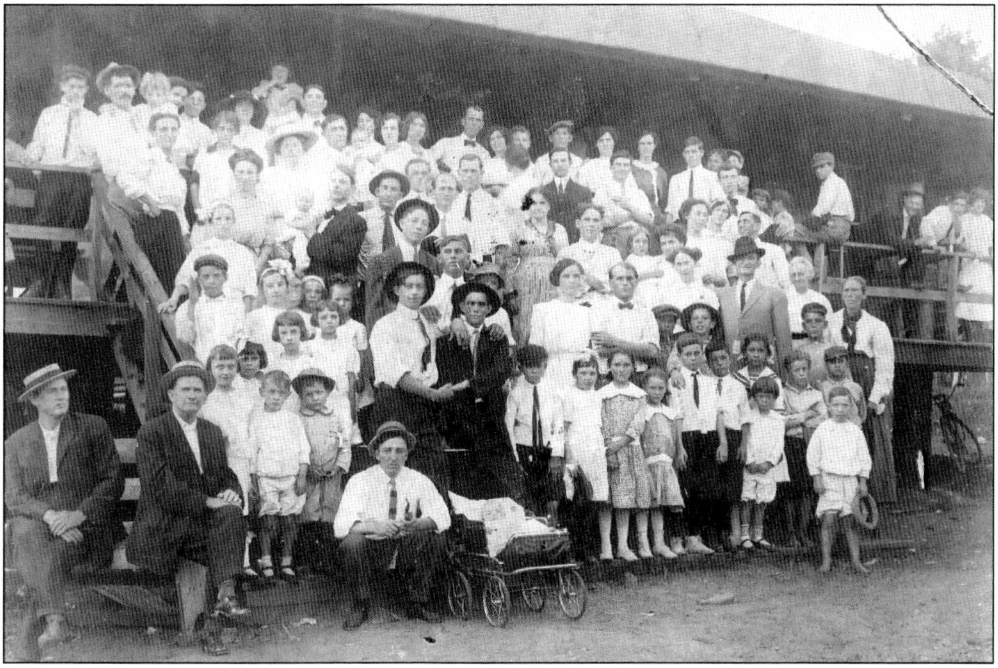

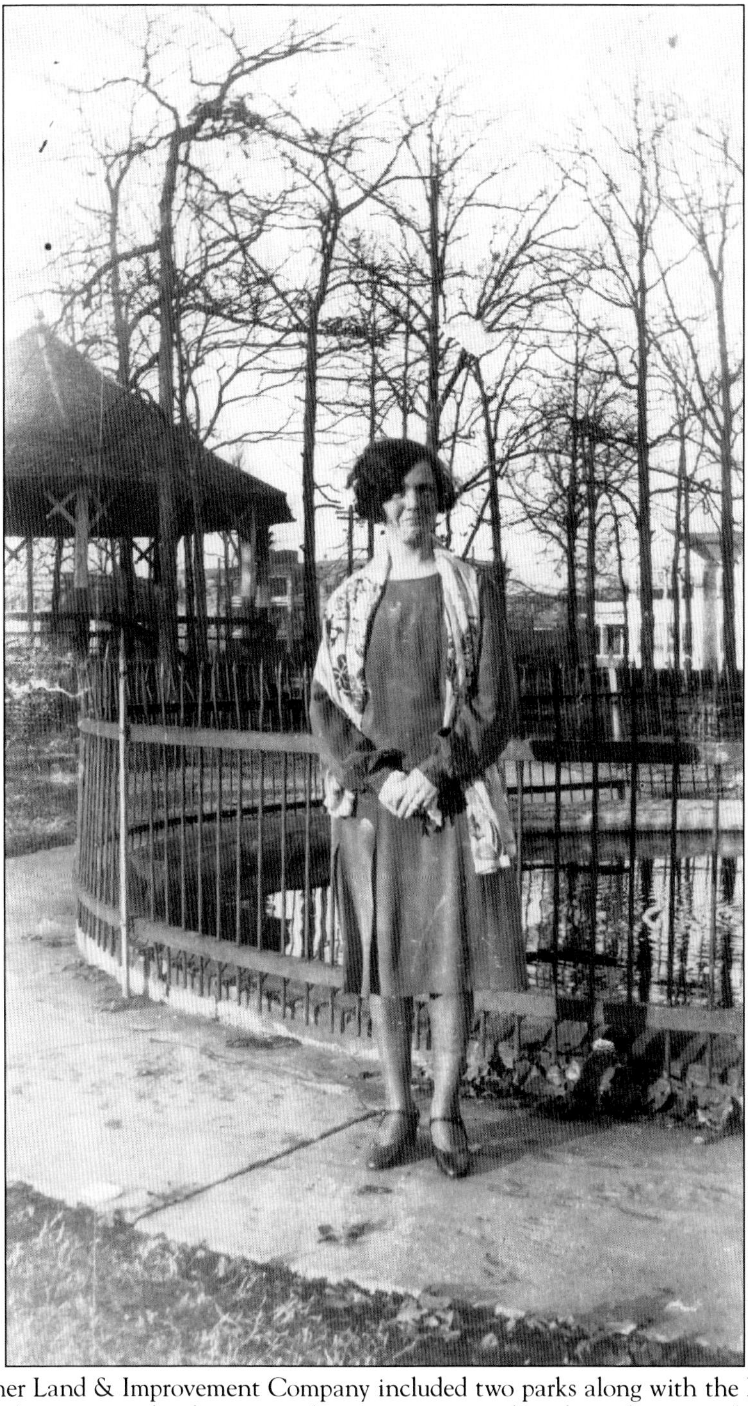

The Bessemer Land & Improvement Company included two parks along with the Montezuma Hotel grounds in its city development. The Montezuma and its dependencies only sat on five acres of its ten-acre site. Five acres of highland grounds that included walkways and open lawns overlooking the city were open to the public. City Park, also called Natural Park, was a 25-acre site with native hardwoods and cedars left untouched other than to open paths. Berney Park, above, now DeBardeleben Park, was a single downtown block with a bandstand and fountain.

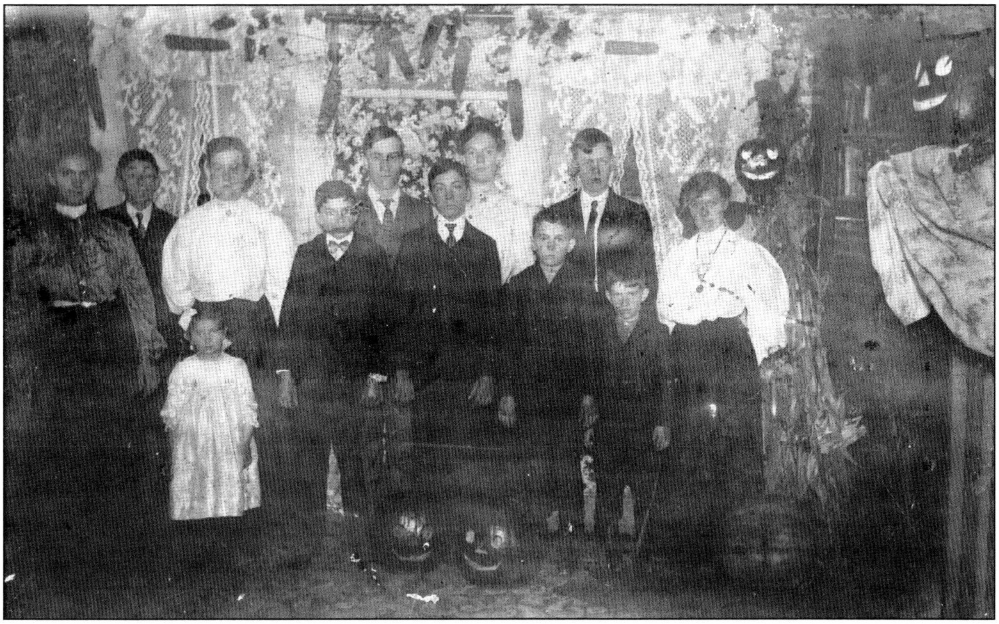

Bessemer families also actively entertained at home, hosting cookouts and parties. The Kintigh family decorated their home with dried corn, cornstalks, and jack-o-lanterns for a Halloween party in 1905. They are (first row) Bertha Kintigh, John Anthony, Anna McCafferty, George Brinton, Naomi Brinton, Roy Brown, and Belle Brown; (second row) Sara Kintigh, Clarence Kintigh, Oscar Anthony, Frank Kintigh, and Roy Kintigh.

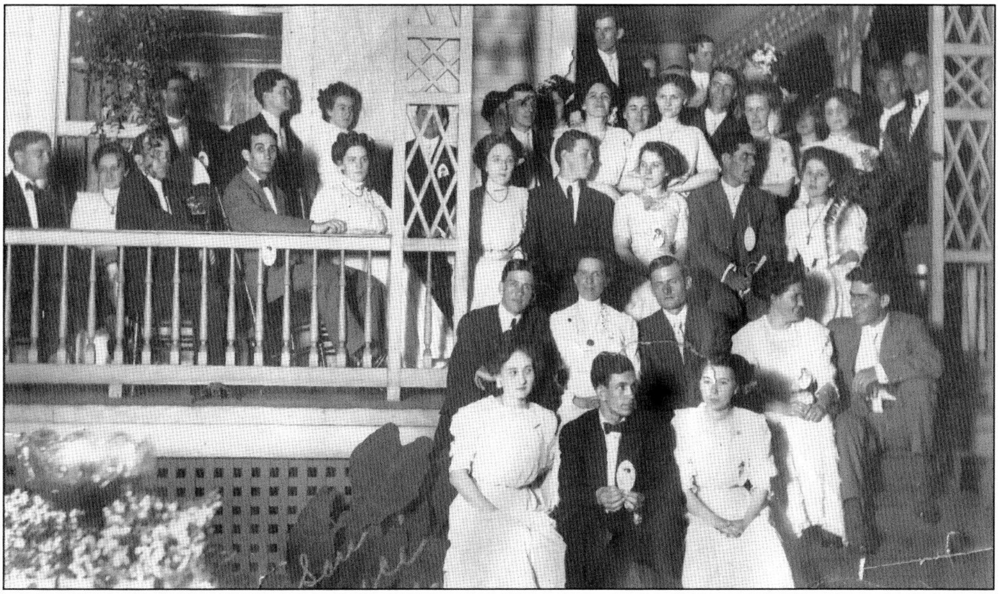

The Sans Souci Club, an early Bessemer social society, meets at the Hollingsworth home in 1908. The club held themed and costume parties. The *Bessemer Weekly* described a Sans Souci George Washington party hosted by Laura Jones. The home was decorated in red, white, and blue, and refreshments included ices frozen in the shape of American flags and cakes in the shape of hatchets. The club officers at the time of this photograph were president Homer Hurd, first vice president Matura Benton, and secretary and treasurer Thomas Carlisle.

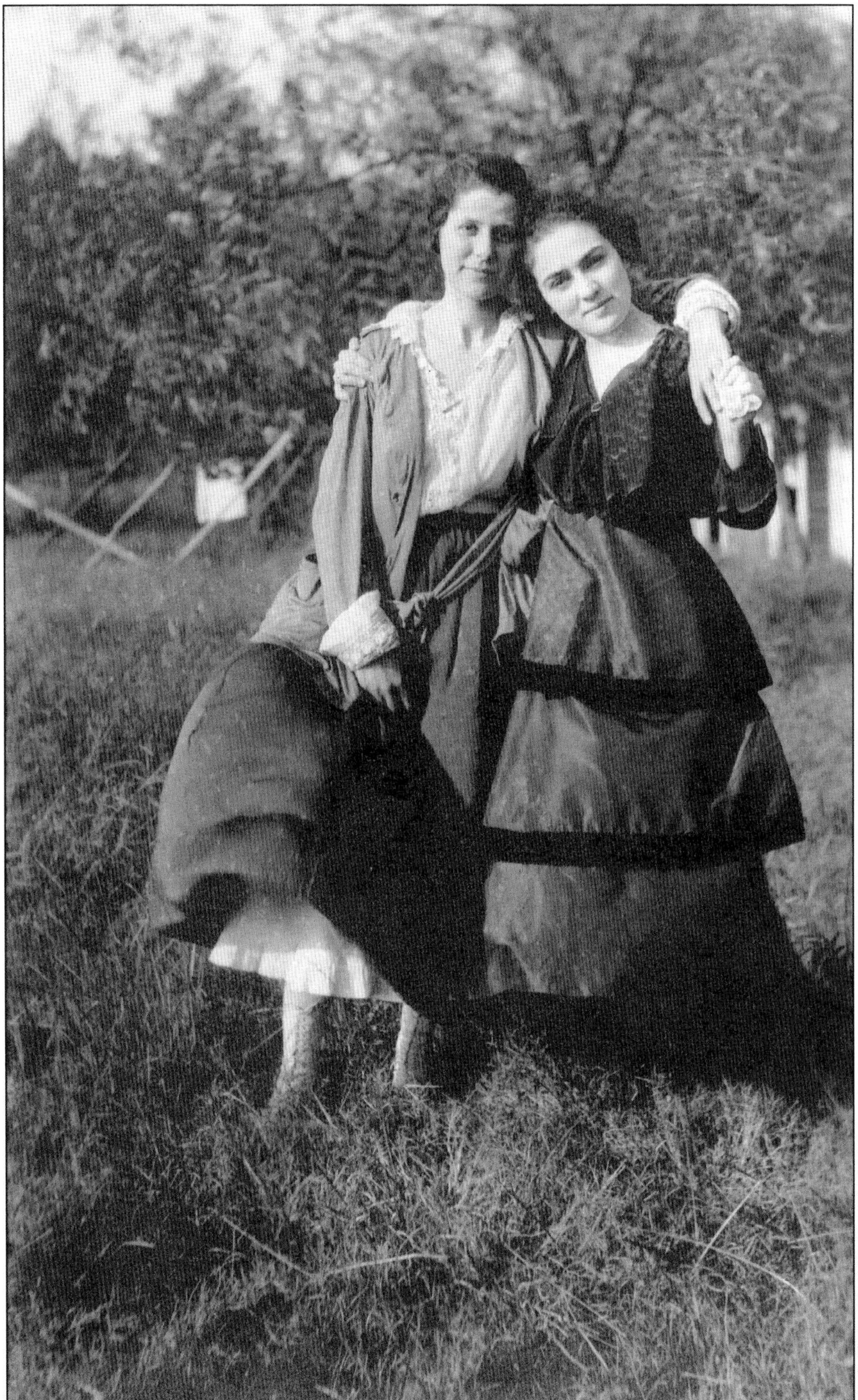

Ida Kartus and Sara Brockman enjoy an autumn outing at Westlake in 1916. Ida's father, Samuel Kartus, opened Kartus Korner, a beloved Bessemer clothing store, in 1902. Her brother, Harry Kartus, took over the family business when his father died in 1919. Harry's home was on Clarendon Avenue.

About the Organization

The Bessemer Hall of History Museum is located in the beautifully preserved Alabama Great Southern Railroad Depot. The museum collection features an extensive photograph archive, early newspapers, clothing, and artifacts illustrating Bessemer's history as a mining, steelmaking, and rail center.

1905 Alabama Avenue
Bessemer, Alabama 35020

www.BessemerHallofHistory.org